The
BARBECUE
COOKBOOK

For Kettle Grills & Other Covered Barbecues

Tess Mallos

WELDON RUSSELL
PUBLISHING

ACKNOWLEDGMENTS

The author and publishers wish to thank the following people and organisations for their invaluable assistance in the preparation of this book: John Ball and staff members of Barbecues Galore, especially Margaret McDonagh, who conducts excellent classes on cooking undercover. Besides providing barbecues and equipment for testing, they advised and answered many queries; Rinnai Australia Pty Ltd for providing a gas grill for testing; George Karafiloff of R. McDonald Co. Pty Ltd, the marketing arm of Weber-Stephen Products, for advice and answering queries on Weber barbecues; the National Office, Meat and Allied Trades Federation of Australia (MATFA), for supplying many of the photographs used in this book; the Australian Meat and Livestock Corporation (AMLC), for supplying photographs; the Fish Marketing Authority (NSW), for supplying photographs, and for answering queries relating to seafoods; photographer Howard Jones and food stylist Carolyn Fienberg, for their excellent work in producing many of the photographs; Carmen Hunter, for her special knowledge of barbecuing American style.

Photography

Cover: Howard Jones, photography; Carolyn Fienberg, food styling; Kathie Baxter Smith, illustrations.

Weldon Trannies: back cover, pp. 4, 19, 22, 30, 31, 32, 33, 34, 35, 36, 37, 39, 40, 41, 42, 43, 45, 53, 58, 64, 66, 72, 73, 74, 78, 79, 80, 81, 84, 86, 88, 89, 90, 91, 92, 93, 94, 95, 96, 97, 102, 103, 104, 105, 106, 107, 108, 109, 112, 115, 116, 117, 119

Howard Jones: title page, pp. 24, 71, 75, 85, 99, 101, 111, 114, 118

MATFA: pp. 21, 44, 46, 47, 48, 50, 54, 56, 57, 59, 62, 63, 65, 67, 69

AMLC: pp. 49, 51, 52, 55, 60, 61

Tess Mallos: pp. 23, 77, 83

Fish Marketing Authority: pp. 82, 87

Published by Weldon Russell Pty Ltd
4/52 Ourimbah Road
Mosman NSW 2088 Australia
A member of the Weldon International Group of companies

First published 1990
Reprinted with corrections 1991

© Copyright Tess Mallos 1990

Publisher: Elaine Russell
Managing editor: Dawn Titmus
Editor: Jo Jarrah
Design and cover illustrations: Kathie Baxter Smith
Illustrations: Jan Smith
Production: Jane Hazell

National Library of Australia
Cataloguing-in-Publication data

Mallos, Tess.
The barbecue cookbook for kettle grills and other covered barbecues.

Includes index.
ISBN 1 875202 34 X.

1. Barbecue cookery. I. Title

641.76

Typeset by Midland Typesetters, Maryborough, Australia
Produced by Mandarin Offset, Hong Kong

A KEVIN WELDON PRODUCTION

CONTENTS

Left: Tacos with chilli con carne; right: Plum-glazed American spareribs

INTRODUCTION

This is not your traditional barbecue cookbook. There are, of course, some of the usual barbecue recipe favourites, but what makes this book different is the emphasis on cooking undercover—in covered barbecues. The three basic types of barbecue are dealt with: the popular charcoal kettle, the gas kettle and the covered gas grill (the 66 cm [26 in] gas grill was used for testing).

These versatile units give you more options in the kinds of food you can cook outdoors than you ever thought possible. So great is the range that all kinds of meals can be cooked and served in the garden or on the terrace. Al fresco eating is much favoured on warm days and balmy evenings—now you can cook and eat in the one place. Working in the garden? Cook up a batch of scones for the tea or coffee break, then add a slow-cooking casserole alongside a dessert, which will be ready to serve while you admire your endeavours. Friends dropping in for brunch? Cook and serve the whole meal from the barbecue. Dinner during the week? Why not cook and eat the usual evening meal outside—there are many alternatives to the traditional barbecue.

There's one advantage to all this cooking outdoors (and don't let your partner read this!) When you are chained to the kitchen, there's little chance of getting a helping hand or two. But cook outdoors, and there is help aplenty. However, you must curb overenthusiasm, as too much lifting of the hood to 'have a look' can put you behind schedule.

Many of the recipes have been specially devised with the busy cook in mind. Preparation is brief in such recipes, so that they can be put together with a minimum of fuss and equipment—just the types of recipes cooks of today like to have on hand.

Real-life situations have also been carefully considered. For example, under normal circumstances you prepare a cake or dessert and it goes straight into the oven. With outdoor cooking, you do a certain amount of kitchen preparation, then move out to the barbecue to complete cooking. You will find guidance in relevant recipes on how long food can be kept aside before being cooked—useful information where baked goods are concerned and the barbecue is not quite ready to receive them. So a few rules are broken! The results, however, are surprisingly good.

Apologies to pasta-lovers for the absence of hot pasta recipes—their exclusion is only because of the need to cook pasta in copious amounts of water, which can be a bit of a bother when there isn't a kitchen sink on hand!

While many people and organisations have offered generous assistance, acknowledged elsewhere in this book, I would like especially to thank John Ball of Barbecues Galore, and Margaret McDonagh, home economist for that organisation, for their invaluable assistance, both in providing barbecues and equipment for testing purposes, and for graciously answering my many queries.

Enjoy your next barbecue-with-a-difference!

Tess Mallos

KNOW YOUR BARBECUE

I f you are going to get the most out of your barbecue kettle or covered gas grill, you have to get to know it as well as your kitchen range or microwave oven. Basically, there are three types of covered barbecue:
- the charcoal kettle
- the gas kettle
- the covered gas grill.

All can be used for direct cooking, but the emphasis is more towards indirect cooking—in other words, cooking in an outside oven. Not only can it cook a wider variety of foods right there in your backyard or terrace, it can be the second oven you have often wished for, to take some of the load off the kitchen oven when catering for a crowd. The following sections will help you to get to know your particular outdoor cooker, so that you can roast, bake, casserole, smoke-cook and steam all kinds of foods—and barbecue as well!

THE CHARCOAL KETTLE

There are many models on the market, but basically they consist of a pressed-steel bowl with a domed hood or cover, the whole usually coated in vitreous or porcelain enamel. The bowl is supported by three legs, two with wheels for mobility.

How the charcoal kettle cooks: The charcoal kettle, when used for direct cooking, cooks by radiant heat similar to the domestic stove burner or griller (broiler) unit. When covered and set up for indirect cooking, it works on the same principle as the domestic oven. Hot air cools as it rises, then falls to be heated again, so setting up a convection current of hot air around the food.

Vent function: The vents (dampers) in the base of the cooking bowl and on the top of the kettle feed a continuous supply of oxygen into the kettle to keep the fire burning. If either or both vents are partly closed, the heat is reduced; if entirely closed, the fire is extinguished. Even closing only the hood vent will extinguish the fire—ensure that this does not occur during cooking. Some kettles have a handy lever so that the base vent may be adjusted easily, while others have lugs on these vents which require a well-gloved hand for adjustment.

Heat intensities: Recipes use three basic heat intensities for the charcoal kettle.
Hot: For direct cooking and lengthy indirect cooking.
Medium: For indirect cooking. When used with direct cooking, food is simply moved to the outer section of the cooking grill where heat is not as intense. 'Medium' is the same as 'Normal' given in some kettle manuals.
Low: Used for smoke-cooking of certain foods.

Heat indicator: Some models are fitted with a heat indicator in the hood. See Guide to Temperatures, page 14, which relates to all covered barbecues.

Fuel for the kettle: The type of fuel and the amount used determine the heat of the kettle, and the length of time cookable heat is produced.

Barbecue briquets: These consist primarily of compressed brown coal (such as 'heat beads' or 'hot shots'), or compressed charcoal, with variations in density and size. Briquets give off excellent heat and burn for a longer period than charcoal.
Do not use briquets for household heating on the barbecue.

Charcoal: This is prepared from various woods; it gives off excellent heat but usually of shorter duration than briquets. Charcoal lights more quickly and gives a wood-smoke flavour to foods. It may be used with coal-based briquets for direct cooking.

How much fuel?: The following quantities apply to a kettle of average size, 57 cm (22½ in) in diameter. Because size and density of fuel vary considerably, amounts are given by weight rather than by number. As a guide to the number of briquets in 500 g (1 lb), there are 12-17 of the dense, long-burning briquets, 18-20 of the lighter types. Weigh out a quantity of your favourite briquets and make a note of the number. In time you will be able to judge the required amount without the need to weigh or calculate.

Hot fire: 3 kg (6½ lb) barbecue briquets = 6 hours of cookable heat, which reduces to Medium fire after 2-2½ hours.

Medium fire: 2.25 kg (5 lb) barbecue briquets = 4-5 hours of cookable heat.

Low fire: 750 g (1½ lb) barbecue briquets = 1-1½ hours of low-temperature heat.

If you wish to boost the heat of the fire during cooking, add 6-10 briquets each side at one-hour intervals, dropping them through the gaps under the grill handles.

Position of charcoal kettle: Select a position at least 60 cm (2 ft) from flammable materials. Place the charcoal kettle with the front facing into the wind to prevent ash blowing onto the cook or the serving table.

Lighting up
Fire starters: Solid fire starters or fire-lighters are the easiest and safest method to use. In some areas liquid starter is available—use it strictly according to the manufacturer's directions. Never use petrol (gasoline), alcohol or other highly inflammable liquids to light the barbecue.

Fire starters are based on a combustible ingredient, usually a petroleum derivative or paraffin. When ignited, they burn with a hot, yellow flame and give off fumes to a greater or lesser degree, depending on the formulation. For these reasons (and for a good supply of oxygen), the cooking grill should not be in place and the kettle should not be covered or used

PARTS OF A CHARCOAL KETTLE

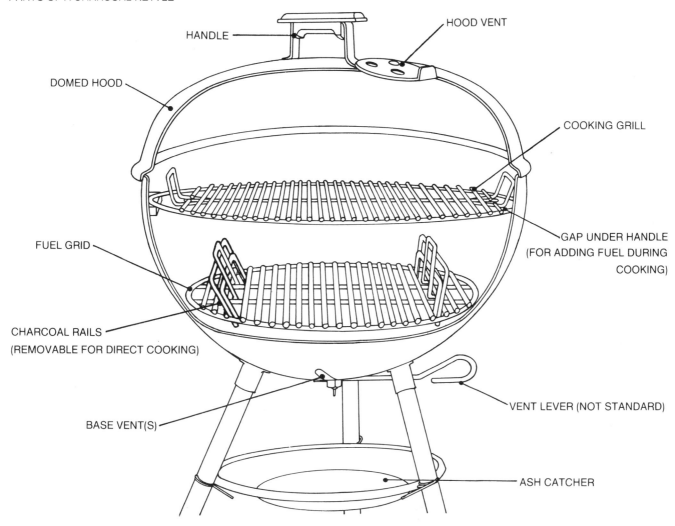

HANDLE

DOMED HOOD

HOOD VENT

COOKING GRILL

GAP UNDER HANDLE
(FOR ADDING FUEL DURING
COOKING)

FUEL GRID

CHARCOAL RAILS
(REMOVABLE FOR DIRECT COOKING)

BASE VENT(S)

VENT LEVER (NOT STANDARD)

ASH CATCHER

for cooking until flaming ceases and the barbecue fuel is ignited.

Do not add fire starters of any type to a warm fire; while it may seem only warm to you, the briquets could be alight. Remove briquets with tongs to a metal tray, add fire starters and a small quantity of cold briquets and light fire again. When these briquets are ignited, return the first lot of briquets to the kettle.

Fire chimney: This is a more environment-friendly means of starting a charcoal fire. There are various designs on the market, but the basic model is a perforated metal cylinder which is placed on the fuel grid. Put wadded newspaper in the base, add a few pieces of charcoal, and fill to the top

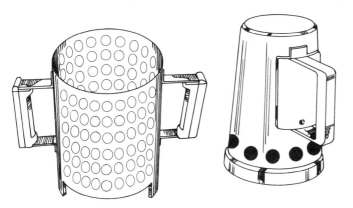

with briquets. Light the paper through the holes at the base; in 30 minutes the coals will be alight. Tip them onto the fuel grid—spread them to each side for indirect cooking and spread out from the centre for direct cooking. More briquets may be added if necessary.

Preheating charcoal kettle: While the fire is ready for immediate cooking once the briquets are ashed over, it is often necessary to build up heat within the kettle so that food, such as a cake, is immediately subject to the desired heat level—this is the same as preheating the oven. See Guide to Temperatures, page 14, and how temperatures relate to the heat indicator if your kettle is fitted with this device.

When recipes give a preheat time, place hood on kettle, top vent open, for that time. When time has elapsed, remove hood and place food onto cooking grill as quickly as possible, then replace hood.

Fire temperature: To judge the heat of a direct-cooking fire, test as follows:

Hot: Spread your hand out close to the grill. If you have to pull your hand away in 2-3 seconds, the fire is hot.

Medium: Hand can he held just above grill level for 4-5 seconds.

Low: Hand can be held just above grill level for 6-7 seconds.

Indirect cooking: To use your charcoal kettle as an oven, the technique called indirect cooking is used. The fire is set in each side of the kettle and the food is placed along the centre section of the cooking grill. (For information on drip pans, see page 15.)

1. *Open base vents. Place charcoal rails in position as described in kettle manual. (Position varies slightly between different makes of kettles.)*
2. *Place two fire starters on fuel grid on each side, positioning them towards charcoal rails so that they may be reached easily for lighting.*

3. *Divide quantity of briquets equally between each side to completely cover the fire starters. Light the fire starters with a match and do not leave barbecue until fire starters are well alight.*
4. *When a fine ash covers all the briquets (about 40-45 minutes), the fire is ready for cooking. Place drip pan(s) on fuel grid (if to be used), and place cooking grill in position, with handles over the fire. Extra fuel may be fed through gaps under the handles if it is necessary to boost fire heat or extend cooking time.*

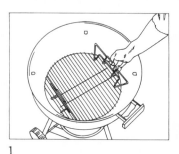
1

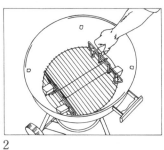
2

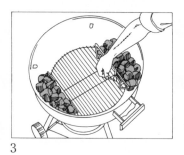
3

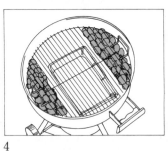
4

Direct cooking: This is the traditional barbecue cooking method. However, fat from steaks, chops and sausages can cause excessive flare-ups and a very greasy barbecue. Use lean cuts of meat, and cook fatty meats and sausages on a hotplate set on the cooking grill. The cooking grill in the kettle cannot be raised or lowered; the distance from top of coals to grill is about 7-8 cm (3-3½ in).

1. *Remove cooking grill and charcoal rails if in position. Spread briquets, or a mixture of briquets and charcoal, to cover the entire fuel grid in a single layer. Spread loosely if using briquets only; make a compact layer for mixture of briquets and charcoal.*

2. *Position 3-4 fire starters about 12 cm (5 in) from centre and heap the fuel from the outer edge on top to form a mound in the centre.*
3. *Light the fire starters. Do not leave the barbecue until you are sure the fire starters remain lit.*
4. *When briquets are covered in ash the fire is ready for cooking. Spread fuel evenly to the area required for cooking. Place cooking grill in position, put hood on, vent open, and let barbecue heat for 2-3 minutes. Remove hood and begin cooking.*

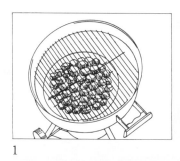
1

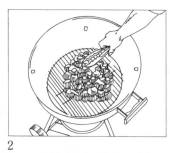
2

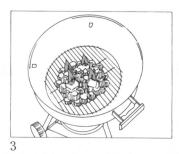
3

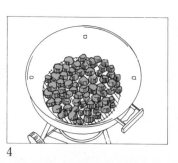
4

Combining indirect and direct cooking: Many recipes instruct you to change from indirect to direct cooking. To do this in the charcoal kettle, food is moved from the centre section of the cooking grill to the sides, placing it directly over the fire. However, the handles and the gaps under the handles limit the grill area. Before moving the food, grip handles with gloved hands and twist grill 90 degrees so that handles face front to back. You will now have more space on the grill over the fire on each side.

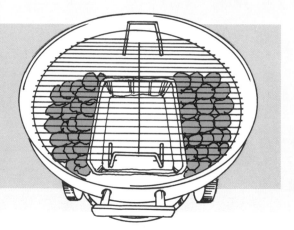

THE GAS KETTLE

Spawned by the popularity of the charcoal kettle, the gas kettle is a viable alternative as it is instantly available for cooking. However, there can be grill-space limitations when cooking indirect, but these are balanced by the gas kettle's ability to allow direct and indirect cooking simultaneously.

How the gas kettle cooks: Your gas kettle must have twin controls if it is to be used for indirect cooking. When used for direct cooking, it cooks by radiant heat similar to the domestic stove burner or griller (broiler) unit. When covered and set up for indirect cooking, it works on the same principle as the domestic oven. Hot air cools as it rises, then falls to be heated again, so setting up a convection current of hot air around the food.

Vent function: Just as a domestic gas oven is vented, so too is the gas kettle. The adjustable vent (damper) at the top of the domed hood and the vent slots around the side allow a continuous supply of oxygen into the kettle to keep the gas burning and to maximise the convection current. The adjustable vent may be partly closed to increase heat in the grill when additional food-browning is required. Leave the vent open when cooking direct with hood on, to allow smoke and steam to escape.

Heat intensities: Recipes use five basic heat intensities for the gas kettle:

Hot:	For direct and indirect cooking.
Medium-hot:	For direct and indirect cooking.
Medium:	For direct and indirect cooking.
Medium-low:	For indirect cooking.
Low:	For smoke-cooking of certain foods.

Note: When the heat direction in a recipe is given as 'Hot/Medium', either the Hot or Medium setting is used, depending on the heat used for the main food item being cooked.

Heat indicator: See the Heat Indicator section, page 14, which relates to all covered barbecues.

Gas fuel: The gas kettle is usually fuelled with liquid petroleum gas (LPG/propane) from a cylinder. When assembling your kettle, follow the instructions in your manual to the letter, paying particular attention to testing the gas connections.

Position of gas kettle: Select a position at least 60 cm (2 ft) from flammable materials. The unit becomes very hot when in use.

PARTS OF A GAS KETTLE

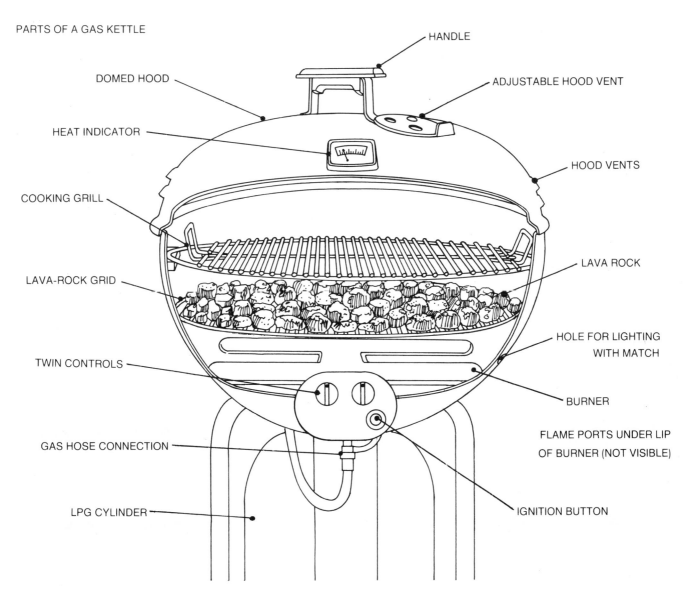

HANDLE

DOMED HOOD

ADJUSTABLE HOOD VENT

HEAT INDICATOR

HOOD VENTS

COOKING GRILL

LAVA ROCK

LAVA-ROCK GRID

HOLE FOR LIGHTING WITH MATCH

TWIN CONTROLS

BURNER

FLAME PORTS UNDER LIP OF BURNER (NOT VISIBLE)

GAS HOSE CONNECTION

IGNITION BUTTON

LPG CYLINDER

Indirect cooking: To use your gas kettle as an oven, the technique called indirect cooking is used. One side of the kettle remains lit, and the food is placed on the cooking grill over the unlit burner. (For more information on drip pans, see page 15.)

1. *Remove hood from kettle. If a drip pan is to be used, remove the cooking grill and move lava rocks from the side to be used for cooking, preferably the side not connected to the ignition button. Put drip pan in position if to be used and replace grill. Check that both burner controls are on OFF position. Turn on the gas at the LPG cylinder valve.*
2. *If unit is fitted with an ignition button, turn control adjacent to button onto HIGH position, then push ignition button several*

times in quick succession until gas ignites. If it does not ignite within five seconds, turn control to OFF and wait five minutes for gas to disperse before trying again.
3. *Alternatively, light the gas with a long taper through the hole provided. If ignition is delayed with either method, always wait a few minutes before trying again. Check manual, and go through the check list provided.*
4. *Once one side is lit, turn second control onto HIGH to ignite the other side. Put hood in position and preheat for time specified in recipe.*
5. *Place food on cooking grill, turn gas off under food, replace hood and adjust the other control onto heat level specified in recipe.*

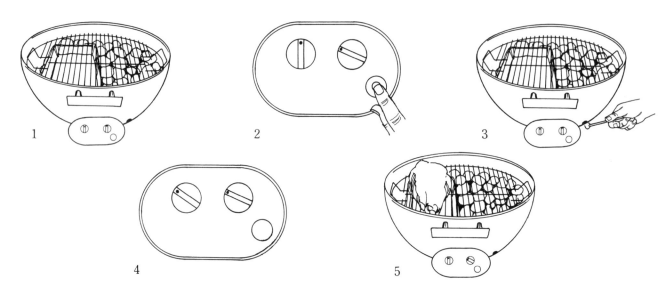

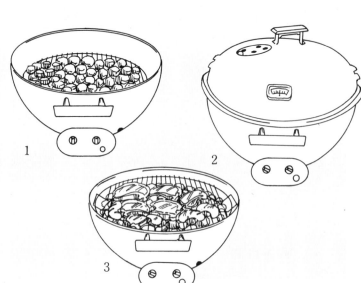

Direct cooking: This is the traditional barbecue cooking method. The cooking grill in the kettle cannot be raised or lowered; the distance from the top of the lava rocks to the grill is about 4 cm (1½ in). If a hotplate is required in the recipes, it is possible to purchase a semicircular plate which fits onto the cooking grill, otherwise use a griddle.

1. *Remove hood and cooking grill and spread lava rock evenly on fuel grid, packing it close together over the burner. Check that both burners are in OFF position.*
2. *Ignite both sides as described for indirect cooking (steps 2 and 3) and replace hood with adjustable vent open. Preheat for about 10 minutes.*
3. *Remove hood, add food and cook, reducing heat to Medium as necessary. For a small amount of food, heat and use only one side. The hood may be replaced for speedier direct cooking.*

When cooking is completed, turn off gas at cylinder valve, then turn off burners. This removes any gas from the hose.

Preheating gas kettle: For indirect cooking, the gas kettle is preheated with hood down and both burners on HIGH for the time specified in recipes. This also heats the lava rocks under food to be cooked without a drip pan (cakes, etc.), and the lava rocks hold sufficient heat to augment heat

circulating around the food from the lit burner. See Guide to Temperatures, page 14, for information on temperatures and their relation to the heat indicator.

Combining indirect and direct cooking: Many recipes instruct you to change from indirect to direct cooking. Simply move food to the lighted side of kettle, or turn on the burner under the food.

THE COVERED GAS GRILL

Only models with two or more burners with separate controls may be used for both indirect and direct cooking. The capacity for indirect cooking depends on the size of your unit. The recipes in this book have been tested on two-burner covered gas grills. **If your grill has three or more burners, heat settings in the recipes might be too high. Use the following information and recipes in conjunction with the user manual accompanying your unit.**

There is a wide range of covered gas grills available, and many components differ. The units used in testing these recipes had burners running from front to back. There are models with burners along the length of the gas grill; these can be used for indirect cooking, but it is recommended that the manual be consulted when using the recipes.

Variations in covered gas grill components

Burners: These should be such that one section of the grill may be lit, with the other section(s) turned off. They can be if stainless steel in one double-U shape or two separate U shapes, with each 'U' connected to its own control; or they can be cast metal or stainless steel, similar in shape to the

gas burner found in domestic griller (broiler) units. Burner design varies according to the manufacturer.

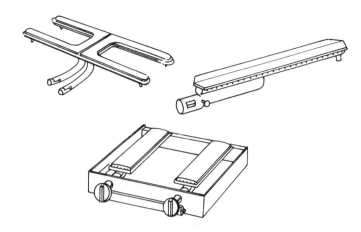

Heat distributors: A grid is fitted over the burners to hold various types of heat distributors. These can be:
Lava rock—medium to large chunks of nature's own lava rock, known as flower rock. It is very porous, holds heat well and is easy to clean. When meat juices and fat drip onto lava

PARTS OF A COVERED GAS GRILL

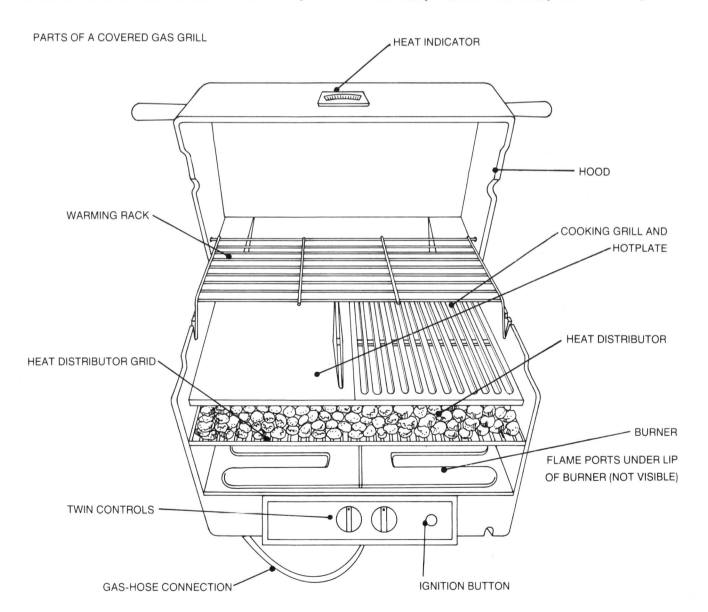

rock, smoke and steam rise and add more flavour to the meat being cooked, giving it the outdoor flavour one expects from a barbecue. Flare-ups can occur, so move the food to another section of the grill when this occurs—**do not spray with water.**

Compressed lava rock—these can be disc- or pyramid-shaped and are made from a compound including lava rock. They are usually creamy white in colour, hold heat well, and are smooth, not porous. They work in the same way as lava rock.

Flavour bars—a gridwork of movable metal bars coated with vitreous (porcelain) enamel, placed on the rack over the burners. They are smooth, vary in shape and nomenclature according to manufacturer, and minimise flare-ups. They might take longer to heat up, so preheat times might have to be extended, but they hold heat well. If fitted in your unit, consult the manual regarding use of drip pans and preheating for indirect cooking.

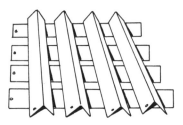

Warming rack: When used as an open grill unit, foods can be kept warm on the warming rack. When unit is closed for direct or indirect cooking, foods can be cooked on the rack. It is also excellent as a means of elevating foods (see page 14).

Indirect cooking: To use your covered gas grill as an oven, indirect cooking is used. Part of the gas grill remains lit, and the food is placed on the cooking grill over the unlit section. (For more information on drip pans, see page 15.)

1. *Raise hood of grill. If using a drip pan, remove cooking grill and place drip pan on top of the heat distributor (lava rock, etc.), or move heat distributor and place drip pan onto fuel grid. Favour the section not connected to the ignition button. Replace grill. If unit is fitted with a hotplate as well as a grill, remove hotplate. Check that all burners are in OFF position before turning gas on at cylinder valve (LPG).*
2. *If unit is fitted with an ignition button, turn control adjacent to button onto HIGH position, then push ignition button several times in quick succession until gas ignites. If it does not ignite*
within five seconds, turn control to OFF and wait five minutes for gas to disperse before trying again.*
3. *Alternatively, light the burner with a long taper through the hole provided. If ignition is delayed with either method, always wait a few minutes before trying again. Check manual, and go through check list provided.*
4. *Once one burner is lit, turn remaining control(s) onto HIGH to ignite the remaining burner(s). Close hood and preheat for time specified in recipe.*
5. *Place food on cooking grill, turn gas off under food, replace hood and adjust control(s) onto heat level specified in recipe.*
When cooking is completed, turn off gas at cylinder valve, then turn off burners. This removes any gas from the hose.

1

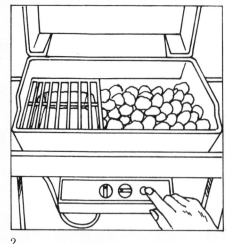

2

5

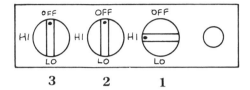

1. *3-burner unit: No. 1 ON, 2 and 3 OFF*

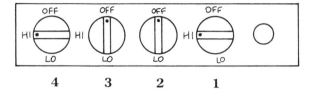

2. *4-burner unit: No. 1 and 4 ON, 2 and 3 OFF*
   OR No. 1 ON and 2,3 and 4 OFF

Configurations of burners that are ON and OFF increase, decrease or divide indirect cooking area as required.

How the covered gas grill cooks: The gas grill cooks similarly to the gas kettle for both indirect and direct cooking (see page 10).

Vent function: The back of the hood, where it hinges onto the firebox, flares out slightly, leaving a gap for air intake. The firebox floor of some models also has apertures for air intake. In other words, venting is usually fixed, and requires no attention on your part.

Heat intensities: See this section for the gas kettle, page 9, as descriptions are similar.

Heat indicator: See Guide to Temperatures, page 14, which concerns all covered barbecues, relating temperature to the heat indicator.

Gas fuel: Gas grills can be connected to the domestic gas supply or fuelled with liquid petroleum gas (LPG/propane) from a cylinder. Units for domestic gas must be connected by a licensed gasfitter in accordance with local gas-installation requirements. For LPG models, follow instructions in your manual to the letter, paying particular attention to testing gas connections. A domestic gas model cannot be connected to LPG and vice versa, unless adaptions are made by a gasfitter.

Preheating covered gas grill: For indirect cooking, the gas grill is preheated with hood down and all burners on HIGH for the time specified in the recipes. This also heats the heat distributor (lava rock, etc.) under food to be cooked without a drip pan (cakes, etc.). The heat distributor holds sufficient heat to augment the heat circulating around the food from the lit burner(s). See Guide to Temperatures, page 14, for information on temperatures and their relation to the heat indicator.

Direct cooking: This is the same as for direct cooking with a gas kettle (see page 10). However, distance from the heat distributor (lava rock, etc.) is usually greater—about 6-8 cm (2½-3 in). The hood acts as an excellent windbreak when cooking direct with the hood raised. Some units are fitted only with cooking grills, others include a hotplate as well as a cooking grill. If a hotplate is not part of your unit, it is possible to purchase one for it. Alternatively, place a griddle on the grill when recipes require cooking on a hotplate.

Combining indirect and direct cooking: Many recipes instruct you to change from indirect to direct cooking. Simply move food to the lighted side of the grill, or turn on the burner under the food.

INFORMATION FOR ALL COVERED BARBECUES

As you and your covered barbecue become acquainted, you will find it necessary at times to resort to those extra touches you probably already use in your domestic oven. Such methods include shielding, raising food so that it browns on top and adjusting temperature because of food load.

Shielding: Large items such as turkey or ham can scorch on the sides because of the long cooking time involved. Rotating food helps to a certain extent, but it is usually necessary to shield the food with foil. Use strips of foil on the sides, and a piece on top if necessary if food is browning too quickly. With a large turkey, shield it from the beginning of cooking, and remove the foil 30-45 minutes before cooking is completed.

Another application is to use a shield as a baffle to deflect heat. In the gas kettle, for example, a tray of muffins set on the cooking grill can overcook because of one side being close to the lit burner, and the other side overcooking from the deflected heat off the kettle itself. Cut two strips of foil to the length of the tray and tuck one side under the tray; then stand the foil up vertically so that it protects the sides.

Elevating: Recipes often refer to elevating food. The upper section of all covered barbecues is hotter than at grill level because of rising heat and the heat absorbed by the hood. Flat foods which require browning, pastries and scones all benefit if they are given a lift.

To elevate food, place tray with food on an upturned layer-cake pan. In some cases, elevating with an item which does not impair heat absorption to the bottom of the food is an advantage. A roasting rack with a basket-like shape works very well. Just place the tray of food across the top.

If your covered gas grill is fitted with a warming rack, this can be used as a higher shelf for browning, or as a second shelf for cooking two trays of pastries or other small baked goods. It can also be used for cooking vegetables and fruit.

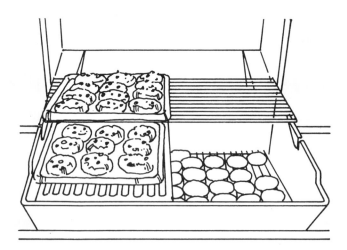

Guide to temperatures: Preheating times given in recipes have the purpose of heating the covered barbecue to a certain level before food is added. For preheating the charcoal kettle, the hood is put on when the fire is alight. For gas barbecues, preheat with the hood down and all controls on Hot. When changing over to indirect cooking, the temperature in the oven reduces to the desired level. Preheating times are higher than the level required in cooking, as heat is lost when the hood is raised for adding the food, and the food itself decreases the internal temperature. Weather can also play a part in temperature fluctuation—if it is a very cool, windy day, expect to use higher control settings than those given.

Temperatures do not have to be exact for successful cooking, and the following tables give a range as a guide. Endeavour to achieve a temperature within this range for each level required. To check the temperature of your particular unit, it is recommended that an oven thermometer be placed on the section of the grill to be used for indirect cooking. Preheat for a given time, check temperature, add food and check temperature again after 15 minutes. Make a note of the setting used and the temperature of the unit. Adjust the recipes accordingly if your unit does not agree with the following temperatures:

Note: Hot gradually reduces to Medium cooking temperature after 2-2½ hours, Medium gradually reduces to Low after 3-3½ hours. (Table 2)

Heat indicator: In some models the heat indicator is just a series of numbers related to heat levels, while others

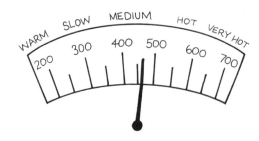

have temperature gauges. Unfortunately some temperature gauges are not accurate, so check against an oven thermometer and note the difference, if any, for future use. However, both are reliable guides to let you know if the heat level of your unit, whether charcoal or gas, is rising or falling, and whether heat control should be adjusted.

Through testing, it was found that 190°C (375°F) inside showed as 475 (MED) on the heat indicator, which is a very

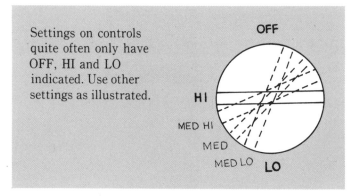

Settings on controls quite often only have OFF, HI and LO indicated. Use other settings as illustrated.

Table 1

Control setting: gas kettle & grill	Approximate pre-heat temperature on HOT	Approximate cooking temperature
Hot	230–260°C (450–500°F)	220–230°C (425–450°F)
Medium-hot	220–230°C (425–450°F)	200–220°C (400–425°F)
Medium	190–200°C (375–400°F)	180–190°C (350–375°F)
Medium-low	180–190°C (350–375°F)	160–180°C (325–350°F)
Low	180–190°C (350–375°F)	150–180°C (300–350°F)

Table 2

Fire: charcoal kettle	Approximate pre-heat temperature —lid on	Approximate cooking temperature
Hot	230–260°C (450–500°F)	200–230°C (400–450°F)
Medium	200–230°C (400–450°F)	180–200°C (350–400°F)
Low	180–190°C (350–375°F)	150–160°C (300–325°F)

good guide to the degree of heat in the unit. Do keep in mind that the more food added, and the more the barbecue is opened, the more heat is lost, lengthening cooking time. As a general rule, add five minutes to the cooking time each time the lid is opened.

Recipe cooking times are the actual times taken to cook foods with normal opening of the barbecue to attend to the foods—turning, basting and adding other foods given in recipe.

Drip pans: These are essential for use in a charcoal kettle when cooking indirect except when food is in a dish or pan. While not considered essential in gas grills, they do keep the unit clean, and have the advantage of catching flavourful meat drippings which can be used for a gravy or sauce. Foil drip pans are disposable for convenience, but baked-enamel drip pans are more economical in the long run. Metal baking dishes, slab-cake pans and other shallow metal pans serve the purpose just as well. Choose drip pans slightly larger than the area of the meat or poultry to be cooked.

Place the drip pan(s) on the fuel grid of the charcoal kettle before placing the cooking grill in position. For gas kettles and grills, put pan(s) on top of the heat distributor (lava rock, etc.), or move this and place the pan(s) on the grid over the burners, then replace the cooking grill. To prevent fat igniting or scorching of meat juices, recipes often recommend adding water to the pan. This should be done before unit is heated.

Grease trays and containers: Gas grills are fitted either with a slide-out grease tray or a container fitted onto a wire holder under the aperture in the base of the grill unit. To clean a grease tray easily, line the base closely with foil with a layer of sand sprinkled over the top. Fat absorbers (soaks) are also available to use in place of sand. When necessary, roll up the foil and dispose of it. Check the grease tray often, as an accumulation of grease could cause a flare-up.

Where grease containers are fitted, it is better to replace the container supplied with an empty food can. When filled, replace with another can.

Flare-ups: While these have been mentioned elsewhere, another warning won't go astray. If flare-ups occur when cooking direct on a gas kettle or grill, **do not spray with water.** Move the food and reduce heat if necessary. Excessive flare-ups indicate that it is time to clean the lava rock (see page 18).

Flare-ups when cooking over charcoal can be minimised if lean meat cuts and poultry are cooked. However, when they occur, move the food to another part of the grill to prevent food burning.

SMOKE-COOKING

Wood smoke adds that extra flavour to foods which lifts them out of the ordinary. Your barbecued meats, poultry and fish take on a whole new flavour when smoke-cooked. Cold-smoking, where food is smoke-cured in a flow of smoke cooled before it envelops the food, is not possible in a covered barbecue. Hot-smoking, on the other hand, with food cooked in an aromatic vapour of wood smoke, is entirely possible. There are smoke-cookers available which do just that. Heated with charcoal, electricity or gas, with a water container and racks stacked above, they cannot be used for any other purpose. By contrast, your covered barbecue, whatever the type, grills, roasts and bakes, and smoke-cooks too.

Foods suitable for smoke-cooking

- Beef roasts, thick beef steaks, beef ribs
- Lamb roasts
- Lean pork roasts (without rind/skin, with thin fat layer), pork ribs, fillets (tenderloins)
- Chicken (whole), chicken pieces, particularly wings and drumsticks
- Turkey (whole), turkey breast, drumsticks, goose
- Duck, quail, pheasant and other game birds
- Whole fish, especially trout, salmon, tailor (bluefish), (fish for smoking should have a good oil content).

Woods suitable for smoking: Hardwoods are preferable, as wood has to smoulder rather than burn with a flame. Wood should not have been treated in any way, and it is better to obtain your wood from an outlet specialising in barbecue supplies, from an orchard or prunings from your own backyard, or direct from nature (fallen branches).

While recipes use hickory or mesquite—both readily available from barbecue suppliers along with chips made from oak barrels in which Jack Daniels whiskey was aged—apple, peach, cherry, oak, she-oak, pecan, walnut, alder and grapevine can also be used. Do not use green wood, or woods such as cedar, pine, eucalyptus, spruce or fir, as these impart a bitter taste to foods.

Herbs such as fresh rosemary sprigs, thyme and dried fennel stalks add a mild smoky flavour coupled with the flavour of the herb. Fennel is particularly good for fish.

Chunks or chips?: For the sake of consistency, chips have been used in recipes. However chunks or small logs may also be used, substituting a 125 g (4 oz) chunk for 2 cups (125 g/4 oz) of woodchips.

Preparing woods for smoke-cooking: Wood should smoulder rather than burn with a flame. When wood has been soaked it begins to give off aromatic steam as the water is driven off, then smoulders slowly to an ash. Simply soak wood in cold water for at least one hour for chips, 1-2 hours for chunks or logs.

To smoke-cook foods direct: As cooking time is usually shorter, simply place a soaked 60 g (2 oz) wood chunk or one foil 'log' containing one cup of soaked chips onto the fire when ready to cook (charcoal kettle), or onto the heat distributor of gas barbecues. Preheat for 10 minutes or so to get wood smouldering, open hood and cook when smoke is evident.

Smoke time: It takes 10-15 minutes before smoking begins, then foil 'logs' will smoulder and smoke for 25-30 minutes; a 125 g (4 oz) wood chunk will smoke for 30-45 minutes. Add more logs or chunks as required.

A number of recipes are for smoke-cooking; use these as a guide for the various foods listed previously. Note that the trout is salted for Smoked Trout, page 85; all fish must be salted before smoking—use this recipe as a guide. Note that suggested barbecued accompaniments are either wrapped in foil or cooked in a covered dish or pan; this prevents the smoke flavouring other foods.

To make woodchip 'logs':

Using woods for smoke-cooking: Soaked chunks or logs should be placed on a double layer of foil or in a small foil food tray. Chips are wrapped in foil to make 'logs'.

1. *Take a strip of foil 30 cm (12 in) wide and 35-40 cm (14-16 in) long. Fold in half across the length (18-20 cm/7-8 in).*
2. *Place one cup (or amount specified in recipe) of soaked woodchips across the centre of the foil.*

3. *Bring up the two sides and double-fold firmly across the top, leaving sides open. Puncture top with a thick skewer in 5-6 places—holes will allow better dispersion of smoke.*
4. *Alternatively, fill a cast-iron grill smoker with soaked wood chips. Place directly onto heat distributor, or on cooking grill over direct heat (charcoal or gas kettle). Chips in the grill smoker give off smoke for a longer period with a smaller quantity of chips.*

To smoke-cook foods indirect:

(Use in conjunction with indirect cooking directions for your particular barbecue.)
1. *For charcoal kettle, when fire is ready for cooking place drip pan containing 4 cups of water on fuel grid. Place one 'log' on each side of fire and put cooking grill in position. Put food on grill, cover with hood and cook.*
2. *For gas kettle or grill, place drip pan containing 4 cups of water on fuel grid or heat distributor on indirect cooking side of barbecue. Place two foil 'logs' on heat distributor on side to*

remain lit during cooking, then preheat with hood down. If cooking time for food is longer than one hour, put 'logs' in position when food is added.
3. *Place food on cooking grill of gas kettle or grill and lower hood. Turn off heat under food and cook. Adjust remaining burner to setting required for food.*
4. *If using grill smoker, put in position when preheating. Place on cooking grill over fire on one side of charcoal kettle. For gas kettle, place on cooking grill on side to be left on; for gas grill, place on heat distributor on side to be left on.*

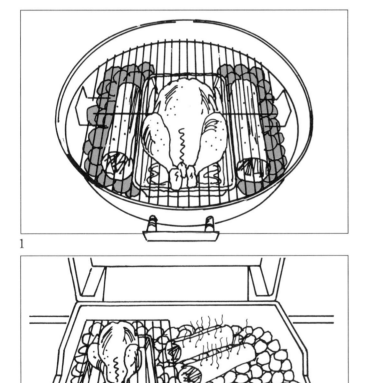

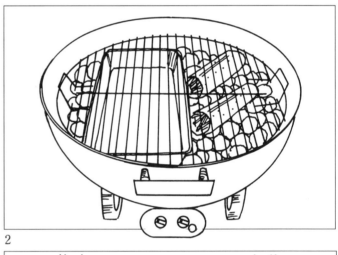

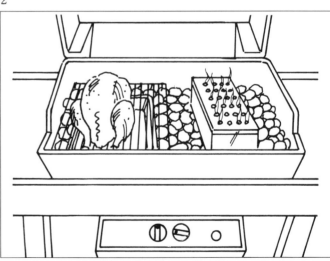

TOOLS OF TRADE

Most of the equipment required for undercover cooking is to be found in a reasonably equipped kitchen. Any roasting pans, ovenproof baking dishes and casserole dishes may be used for indirect cooking. Take care if using heatproof glass at the barbecue, bearing in mind that moving from a hot surface to a cool one could be a shattering experience—place such a dish when hot onto a dry, wooden surface.

Frying pans (skillets) and saucepans: Handles can get in the way, but can usually be accommodated. If not heatproof, wrap the handle in a double layer of foil, shiny side out, to insulate it from the heat. Watch the knobs on lids; if not heatproof, cover them with foil.

Dutch ovens: These have the advantage of having small lugs for lifting. Being flameproof and heatproof, they can be used for direct and indirect cooking with ease.

Woks: For gas grills, a wok burner can be fitted to a gas jet. If you do a lot of wok cooking, see what your barbecue supplier has to offer. A wok can be placed onto the cooking grill, but takes a long time to heat. It is better to place it directly onto the heat distributor, closer to the flame. For charcoal kettles, your manual will guide you regarding wok use. As an alternative to the wok, use a large frying pan or even a Dutch oven—both are good for stir-frying.

Tools: Long and short tongs are essential for moving glowing coals and for turning and removing foods. Long cooking forks are handy for lifting heavy foods from the grill. A long-handled, flat lifter or spatula (such as for lifting eggs) is good for fish fillets, hamburgers, eggs and griddle cakes.

Hand protectors: Long barbecue mitts or gloves are essential. Have them separate, not joined together with a tape. The length over the wrist is necessary for good protection for the arms.

Roasting racks: These are of two types for the barbecue. The basket-shaped rack is excellent for holding a meat joint or poultry as it allows more food to be put onto the grill around it. It can serve double duty as a device to elevate foods. Another type of roasting rack has two prongs on which to impale joints

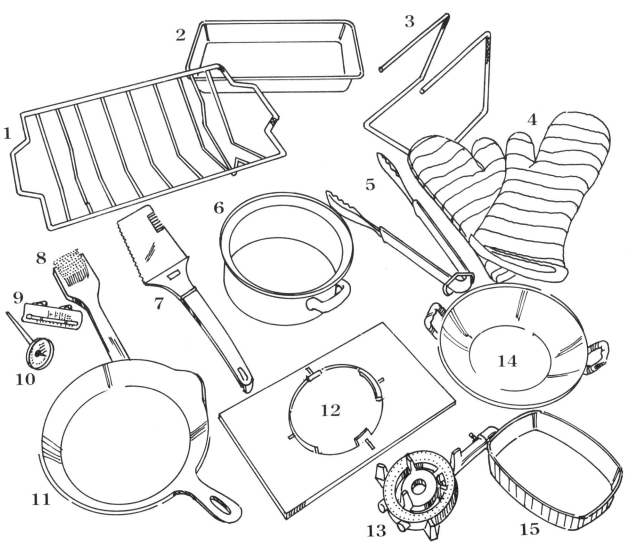

1. Basket-shaped roasting rack. 2. Drip pan. 3. Pronged roasting rack. 4. Long barbecue mitts. 5. Tongs. 6. Dutch oven. 7. Turning spatula. 8. Wire brush (for cleaning grill). 9. Oven thermometer. 10. Meat thermometer. 11. Frying pan (skillet). 12. Wok ring. 13. Wok plate. 14. Wok. 15. Baking dish.

and poultry. This also allows more space on the grill for vegetables, and is an excellent alternative to the rotisserie.

Oven thermometer: This is a handy gadget to have to check the heat of your unit. See page 14 for its application. It is useful for the kitchen oven anyway in order to check that your thermostat is adjusted properly.

Meat thermometer: This certainly takes the guesswork out of cooking meat and poultry. More details on page 19.

Wire grill baskets: These are hinged, can be rectangular in shape, or shaped for large fish. They are not essential, but are useful to have if you like fish simply grilled, or like to turn chops and sausages in one go.

Drip pans: See page 15.

Timer: This is essential to remind you to check the food. Use a clockwork type, or obtain the more expensive electronic timer which can be set for more than one hour.

CLEANING THE BARBECUE

One advantage of indirect cooking is that the barbecue needs cleaning less often, except for cooking grills and hotplates. To clean the interior of a gas kettle or grill properly, which should be done once a year, consult your user manual for directions regarding removal of burners and protection of the connections. Charcoal kettles can be cleaned with oven cleaners when grease build-up inside the unit needs removal— again, your manual covers this.

Cooking grill: When cooking is finished, turn gas burners on High for a few minutes, with hood down. Turn off gas and brush grill with a wire brush to remove charred food remains. Alternatively, brush well with crumpled foil. For the charcoal kettle, put the lid on, close dampers to extinguish fire and clean grill when cool. Occasionally, grills benefit from a good scrub in hot suds; dry well and wipe over lightly with oil if cast iron.

Hotplate or griddle: Heat barbecue as above, then scrape surface with a paint scraper. Wash occasionally in hot suds, dry thoroughly and rub lightly with oil to preserve surface.

Lava rock: When excessive flare-ups occur during cooking, it is time to clean the lava rock—the natural type (flower rock), not the compressed variety. Dissolve a tablespoon of an alkaline-based dishwasher detergent in a bucket of hot water, add lava rocks and soak overnight, giving the bucket a good shake while the water is hot. Drain rocks and spread out onto a rack suspended on bricks (use the rock grid from the barbecue as a rack). Hose well with cold water, turning rocks so that all detergent is removed. Dry for a while in the sun, hose once more, then leave to dry thoroughly in the sun. Shake rack occasionally to turn rocks. Do not use wet or damp rocks in the barbecue.

USING THE RECIPES

Whether you are a cup-and-spoon cook, or one who relies on scales, there is a measure to suit your particular cooking preferences. Recipes have been tested with the Australian 250 ml cup measure, 20 ml tablespoon and 5 ml teaspoon, cross-checking with the US 8 fl oz cup measure, ½ fl oz (15 ml) tablespoon and ⅙ fl oz (5 ml) teaspoon. The UK tablespoon and teaspoon measures are the same as those of the US.

Where spoon measures are crucial, they have been given in teaspoons rather than tablespoons. All dry measures, whether in tablespoons, teaspoons, cups or graduated cups, are levelled.

Rarely are exact conversions given in weight or volume measures; 500 g is not the same as 1 lb, however, it is better to round off weights logically. If using a 250 ml metric cup and metric measures, your yield is about 10 per cent greater than if an 8 fl oz cup and imperial measures are used. If cooking by weights and liquid measures, follow either the metric or imperial measures—do not mix the two.

Just remember cooking is not an exact science, except where baked goods are concerned, and these have been carefully checked so that they work whatever system is used.

Bread and cakes: Preheating is very important for these recipes; refer to the index to locate directions relating to your particular barbecue.

To test if your cake is cooked, either press the top lightly with two fingers—it should spring back when cooked; or insert a fine skewer in the centre—it should come out clean. Shrinkage from side of pan is not always an indication that the cake is cooked in the centre.

Notes on ingredients

Beurre manié: This is the classic French way to thicken sauces and is very handy to use at the barbecue. Place ½ cup (125 g/4 oz) butter at room temperature in a bowl and work in ½ cup (60 g/2 oz) plain (all-purpose) flour with a wooden spoon, until smooth. Place tablespoon portions on foil and freeze until firm. Pack portions into a container, keeping them separate with plastic film (wrap) or foil. Store in the freezer and use as required.

Court bouillon: To make court bouillon, put 4 cups (1 1/32 fl oz) of water in a pan with 1 sliced carrot, 1 sliced stick of celery, 1 sliced onion, 1 sliced lemon, 1 bay leaf and 2 sprigs of parsley. Cover and bring to the boil. Simmer for 10 minutes; strain and use as a poaching liquid for seafood.

Eggs: The 55 g (2 oz) eggs (1 dozen = 660 g/1½ lb) were used in testing. Where large eggs are specified, use the 60 g (2¼ oz) eggs (1 dozen = 720 g/1 lb 11 oz).

Fish stock: Boil 500 g (1 lb) fish heads and bones with 4 cups (1 1/32 fl oz) of water, ½ cup (125 ml/4 fl oz) white wine, ½ sliced lemon, 1 sliced onion, 1 bay leaf and 2 sprigs of parsley. Simmer for 20 minutes and strain.

Molasses: The Australasian and the UK treacle is the same as the standard molasses of North America. Do not use blackstrap molasses ; it does not have the right flavour.

Self-raising flour: Known as self-rising flour in North America, it is preferred for the majority of recipes as it saves time in kitchen preparation. If plain (all-purpose) flour is preferred, add the standard proportion of baking powder (2 teaspoons baking powder to 1 cup [125 g/4 oz] flour). Where baking powder is given in conjunction with self-raising flour, add the extra amount indicated as more raising would be required in that particular recipe. Self-raising flour used in recipe testing did not contain salt.

Shallots: These are small, brown-skinned onions, similar in shape, but larger than garlic cloves. Substitutes have been given in recipes.

Spring onions: 'Scallions' is given as an alternative name; both are the slender green onions with a white section at the base. The bulbous spring onions should not be used.

Sugar: While superfine sugar is given as an alternative to caster sugar, North American cooks can use standard sugar, which is similar to the caster sugar used for baking in Australasia and the UK.

BASIC COOKING GUIDE

When is the meat or poultry cooked? Timing is only part of it; knowing how to judge the degree of cooking is part and parcel of successful barbecue cooking. Don't rely on cooking until the meat is tender—this is relevant for meats only if cooking a casserole or similar dishes cooked in liquid; roast and grilled meats become less tender as they are cooked.

COOKING A BETTER ROAST

Timing: Cooking times vary between barbecues, according to weather conditions (not that you are likely to cook outside during a gale!) and according to other foods, such as vegetables, cooked at the same time. Timing in the tables is based on cooking at an ambient temperature of 20-25°C (70-75°F). Normal opening of hood and addition of basic vegetables have both been factors in determining minutes per 500 g/1 lb.

Using a meat thermometer: This cooking aid takes the guesswork out of judging when your roast is cooked. Open hood and insert thermometer so that tip is in the centre of the thickest part of the meat, not touching bone. When indicator stops, take the reading. When it is about 3–5°C or 5–10°F below the internal temperature required (see tables), remove meat to platter, cover loosely with foil and stand in a warm place for 10–20 minutes, according to size of the roast. Heat continues to penetrate to the centre; the internal temperature increases and juices settle within the meat. It is then easier to carve, and is more succulent and tender.

COOKING A BETTER STEAK OR CHOP

Use tongs to turn steaks and chops; a fork pierces the seared surface, causing loss of juices. To check if cooked, press surface with tongs. The exception to this method of testing is fillet (tenderloin) from any of the meats. Because it has so little connective tissue, even well-done fillet yields to pressure, but less so than when rare.

Rare: Meat is very resilient, yielding readily to pressure. It shows signs of texture change just under the seared surface—the centre is hot, with the appearance of raw meat. This is the stage most beef connoisseurs prefer.

Medium-rare: Meat is less resilient, yielding a little less readily to pressure. It is just set, deep pink in colour with a thin core of 'raw' meat. This is a good stage for quality beef and lamb cuts. The tables do not give timing for this stage—just cook meat a little longer than rare.

Medium: Meat yields slightly to pressure; beads of juice appear on surface; meat is evenly pink. Cook beef and tender cuts of lamb to this stage.

Medium to well done: Meat yields slightly to pressure and is barely pink when cut; for 'well-done' addicts, this stage is better as it is more tender. Cook veal and pork to this stage too.

Well done: Meat is firm, with little or no resilience; it is not recommended, unless you can judge it as cooked immediately it gets to this stage. Cook it any longer and the meat toughens.

BEEF AND VEAL

CK—Charcoal Kettle; GK&G—Gas Kettle and Covered Gas Grill; MT—meat thermometer; (R) Rare; (M-R) Medium-rare; (M) Medium; (M-WD) Medium to well done; (WD) Well done.

Meat cut	Weight or thickness	Cooking method & heat level or setting	MT temp. & cooking time (minutes per 500 g/lb; minutes per steak/chop)
Large beef roasts, bone-in (standing or prime rib, sirloin)	2.5-4 kg (5-9 lb)	Indirect: CK—Medium; GK&G—Hot, reduce to Medium if necessary	MT: 60°C/140°F (R); 65°C/150°F (M); 70°C/160°F (M-WD) 22-27 mins/500 g; 20-25 mins/lb
Large beef roasts, boneless (rolled roasts and roasting pieces)	2-3 kg (4-6 lb)	Indirect: CK—Medium; GK&G—Hot, reduce to Medium if necessary	MT: 60°C/140°F (R); 65°C/150°F (M); 70°C/160°F (M-WD) 27-32 mins/500 g; 25-30 mins/lb
Small beef roasts, boneless (fillet/tenderloin, rib eye, long, slender roasts)	1-1.5 kg (2-3 lb)	Indirect: CK—Medium; GK&G—Hot, reduce to Medium if necessary	MT: 60°C/140°F (R); 65°C/150°F (M); 70°C/160°F (M-WD) 22-27 mins/500 g; 20-25 mins/lb
Beef steaks, bone-in or boneless (sirloin, T-bone, New York cut, rump/top sirloin, fillet/tenderloin)	2 cm (¾ in) 2.5 cm (1 in) 34 cm (1½ in) 5 cm (2 in)	Direct (all thicknesses): CK, GK&G—Hot, then Medium for M & M-WD, hood down for thick steaks	5-6 mins (R); 7-9 mins (M); 10-12 mins (M-WD), turn during cooking 6-8 mins (R); 9-12 mins (M); 14-16 mins (M-WD), turn during cooking 10-12 mins (R): 14-16 mins (M); 18-20 mins (M-WD), turn during cooking 12-15 mins (R); 18-20 mins (M); 22-25 mins (M-WD), turn during cooking
Veal roasts, bone-in whole leg (small veal), half leg/round or rump roast	2-3 kg (4-6 lb)	Indirect: CK—Medium; GK&G—Medium	MT:75-77°C/165-170°F (M-WD); 33-35 mins/500 g; 30-32 mins/lb
Other bone-in veal roasts (loin, rib loin, rack, shoulder)	1.5-2.5 kg (3-5 lb)	Indirect: CK—Medium; GK&G—Hot/Medium	MT: 75-77°C/165-170°F (M-WD); 30-33 mins/500 g; 28-30 mins/lb
Boneless veal roasts (round/nut of veal/rump, rolled loin, rolled shoulder)	1.5-2.5 kg (3-5 lb)	Indirect: CK—Medium; GK&G—Hot/Medium	MT: 75-77°C/165-170°F (M-WD); 33-35 mins/500 g; 30-32 mins/lb
Veal loin chops	2-2.5 cm (¾-1 in)	Direct: CK, GK&G—Hot, then Medium after searing	9-12 mins (M-WD), turn during cooking, do not overcook, baste often

LAMB

CK—Charcoal Kettle; GK&G—Gas Kettle and Covered Gas Grill; MT—meat thermometer; (M-WD) Medium to well done; (WD) Well done.

Meat cut	Weight or thickness	Cooking method & heat level or setting	MT temp. & cooking time (minutes per 500 g/lb; minutes per steak/chop)
Leg, bone-in, boned and tied or boned and butterflied	2–3 kg (4–6 lb)	Indirect: CK, GK&G—Medium on grill, Hot if placed in dish	MT: 65°C/150°F (M); 70°C/160°F (M-WD); 75°C/170°F (WD); 30–35 mins/500 g; 26–30 mins/lb
Loin, bone-in, boned and tied; rib loin/rack/best end of neck, bone-in	1–2 kg (2–4 lb)	Indirect: CK—Medium; GK&G—Hot	MT: 65°C/150°F (M); 70°C/160°F (M-WD); 75°C/170°F (WD); 25–30 mins/500 g; 24–28 mins/lb
Forequarter/shoulder/neck end, bone-in or boned and tied	1.5–2.5 kg (3–5 lb)	Indirect: CK—Medium; GK&G—Medium	MT: 70°C/160°F (M-WD); 75°C/170°F (WD); 35–40 mins/500 g; 33–36 mins/lb
Forequarter/shoulder chops	2–2.5 cm (¾–1 in)	Direct: CK, GK&G—Medium	12–16 mins (M-WD), turn during cooking
Chops, cutlets (leg, chump/rump, loin, rib loin/best end of neck)	2–2.5 cm (¾–1 in) 4 cm (1½ in)	Direct: CK, GK&G—Hot, reduce to Medium after searing	8–10 mins (M); 12–14 mins (M-WD), turn during cooking 14–16 mins (M); 18–20 mins (M-WD), turn during cooking

Butterflied lamb with rosemary

PORK AND HAM

CK—Charcoal Kettle; GK&G—Gas Kettle and Covered Gas Grill; MT—meat thermometer; (M-WD) Medium to well done.

Meat cut	Weight or thickness	Cooking method & heat level or setting	MT temp. & cooking time (minutes per 500 g/lb; minutes per steak/chop)
Pork leg/fresh ham bone-in (whole leg, half leg—shank end or butt/rump)	3–5 kg (6–11 lb)	Indirect: CK—Hot; GK&G—Hot, reduce to Medium after 30–45 mins	MT: 75–77°C/165–170°F (M-WD); 33–35 mins/500 g; 30–32 mins/lb
Pork loin, bone-in or boneless (loin roast, crown roast)	2–3 kg (4–6 lb)	Indirect : CK—Medium; GK&G—Hot, reduce to Medium after 30 mins	MT: 75–77°C/165–170°F (M-WD); 28–30 mins/500 g; 25–28 mins/lb

Meat cut	Weight or thickness	Cooking method & heat level or setting	MT temp. & cooking time (minutes per 500 g/lb; minutes per steak/chop)
Pork forequarter, bone-in or boneless (forequarter/shoulder/neck end)	1.5-3 kg (3-6 lb)	Indirect: CK—Medium; GK&G—Hot, reduce to Medium after 30 mins	MT: 75-77°C/165-170°F (M-WD); 33-35 mins/500 g; 30-32 mins/lb
Pork chops and steaks	2-2.5 cm (¾-1 in)	Direct: CK, GK&G—Hot, then Medium after searing	10-15 mins (M-WD), turn during cooking, do not overcook
Ham, fully cooked, bone-in or boneless (whole or half leg, shoulder/picnic)	3-6 kg (6-13 lb)	Indirect: CK—Medium; GK&G—Hot, reduce to Medium if necessary	MT: 55°C/135°F 15 mins/500 g; 12 mins/lb
Ham steaks, all cuts	1-2 cm (½-¾ in)	Direct: CK, GK&G—Hot	6-8 mins, turn once

POULTRY

It is very important to cook poultry to the well-done stage. Besides checking with a meat thermometer (page 19), there are other ways in which to check if poultry is cooked as it is not always easy to insert a thermometer deeply enough into small poultry such as chicken and duck. Try the following methods for perfectly cooked poultry.

- For roast chicken or duck, pierce the thigh at the thickest part near the body with a skewer—it is cooked if juices run clear.
- Push chicken leg towards the breast—if its joints move easily, chicken is cooked.
- Place meat thermometer into the thickest part of the breast of roast turkey—the reading is more reliable, and the turkey will be better too. Relying on the thigh temperature can cause the breast to overcook. Cover the bird with foil and leave it for 30 minutes—the thigh completes cooking in this time.
- Poultry cooked by direct heat should be checked by cutting into it to the bone—it should not be pink, and the meat should have a cooked texture. However, the haemoglobin in the thigh bone does give a pink tinge to thigh meat, even when fully cooked.

Roast chicken with currant rice stuffing

POULTRY

CK—Charcoal Kettle; GK&G—Gas Kettle and Covered Gas Grill; MT—meat thermometer; (WD) Well done.

Type of poultry	Weight and/ or portion	Cooking method & heat level or setting	MT temp. & cooking time (minutes per 500 g/lb; minutes per portion)
Whole chicken	1.5-2 kg (3-4 lb)	Indirect: CK—Medium; GK&G—Hot	MT: 85°C/185°F; 30-35 mins/500 g; 28-33 mins/lb (WD), turn if needed
Chicken pieces, halved, quartered Maryland/leg with thigh	1.5-2 kg (3-4 lb) total	Indirect: CK—Medium; GK&G—Hot Direct: CK, GK&G—Medium	1½-2 hours (WD), turn often 40-50 mins (WD), turn often
Chicken breast (bone-in), drumsticks, wings	1 kg (2 lb), half breasts, drumsticks; 1.5 kg (3 lb) wings	Indirect: CK—Medium; GK&G—Hot; Medium (wings) Direct: CK, GK&G—Medium	1½ hours (WD), turn often 25-35 mins (WD), turn often
Whole turkey, small, no stuffing	3-4 kg (6-9 lb)	Indirect: CK, GK&G—Medium	MT: 85°C/185°F; 25 mins/500 g, 23 mins/lb (WD), shield with foil

Type of poultry	Weight and/ or portion	Cooking method & heat level or setting	MT temp. & cooking time (minutes per 500 g/lb; minutes per portion)
Whole turkey, large, no stuffing (add 30 mins to total cooking time with stuffing)	5-7 kg (11-15 lb)	Indirect: CK—Hot; GK&G—Medium, reduce to Low halfway if necessary	MT: 85°C/185°F; 18-20 mins/500 g; 16-18 mins/lb, shield with foil
Turkey breast, whole, bone-in	4-6 kg (9-13 lb)	Indirect: CK—Hot; GK&G—Medium, reduce to Low halfway if necessary	MT: 80°C/180°F; 18-20 mins/500 g; 16-18 mins/lb (WD), shield with foil
Turkey breast, halved, bone-in or boneless; rolled breast	1-2 kg (2-4 lb)	Indirect: CK—Medium; GK&G—Hot	MT: 80°C/180°F; 1½-2 hours, turn during cooking
Turkey leg and thigh, bone-in (hindquarter)	1-2 kg (2-4 lb)	Indirect: CK—Medium; GK&G—Hot	MT: 85°C/185°F; 35 mins/500 g; 31 mins/lb (WD), turn during cooking
Whole duck	2 kg (4 lb)	Indirect: CK—Medium; GK&G—Hot	MT: 85°C/185°F; 30 mins/500 g; 26 mins/lb (WD)
Whole quail	1 kg (2 lb), 8 quails	Indirect: CK—Medium; GK&G—Hot	35-45 mins, turn during cooking. Cut breast—slightly pink near bone
Butterflied quail		Direct: CK & GK&G—Hot	10-12 mins, turn during cooking

SEAFOOD

If you cook a lot of fish on the barbecue, it is worth investing in a wire fish-shaped basket, or a square, hinged basket at least. Turning whole fish, when cooked direct on the cooking grill, can be a problem. Fish steaks, cutlets and fillets also need care, and hotplate or griddle cooking is recommended for skinless fillets in particular. Wrapping in foil is a tried and true method, but does not give a 'barbecued' flavour. However, with indirect cooking, you can use methods employed in the kitchen oven.

Mediterranean fish casserole

Timing: Because of the variables involved in barbecue cooking, use times given in table as a guide only. To check if fish is cooked, probe the thickest part of the fish or portion (fillet or steak) with the point of a knife—the flesh should flake and be opaque in appearance. Crustaceans (lobster, prawns, shrimp etc.) firm up and flesh turns white, yellow tonings become orange-pink, shells turn red or bright pink. No seafood should be overcooked.

Legend for preparation and basic cooking:

BD   Cook in a greased baking dish, brushing seafood with oil or butter. Add flavouring ingredients, wine, sauce according to recipe, as desired.

CG   Cook on oiled cooking grill, baste with butter, oil, marinade or sauce.

CGB Cook in oiled fish or wire basket on cooking grill, baste with butter, oil, marinade or sauce.

CH   Cook on oiled hotplate or griddle, baste with butter, oil, marinade or sauce.

FP   Cook in a frying pan in oil or butter, or a combination of these, and fry. Fish may be coated with seasoned flour if desired.

FW   Foil-wrap in heavy-duty oiled foil with flavouring ingredients.

P   Poach in aromatic fish stock or court bouillon in a covered oven dish or fish kettle.

SC   Score skin each side in 2-3 places with a sharp knife, to allow baste of butter, oil or marinade to flavour flesh.

SEAFOOD

CK—Charcoal Kettle; GK&G—Gas Kettle and Covered Gas Grill

Type of seafood & basic preparation	Weight and/or portion	Cooking method & heat level or setting	Means of cooking & approx. total cooking time
Whole round fish, small SC (e.g. trout, snapper, bream, whiting)	4-6 x 375 g (12 oz) each	Indirect: CK—Medium GK&G—Hot Direct: CK & GK&G—Hot	BD, FW, P 25-30 mins CG, CGB, FP 10-12 mins
Whole round fish, large, SC (e.g. snapper, whitefish)	2-3 kg (4-6 lb)	Indirect: CK—Medium GK&G—Hot Direct: CK & GK&G—Hot	BD, FW, P 45-60 mins CGB, FW 30-45 mins
Whole flat fish, SC (e.g. sole, flounder)	3-4 x 375 g (12 oz) each 1 x 2 kg (4 lb)	Indirect: CK—Medium GK&G—Hot Direct: CK & GK&G—Hot Indirect: CK—Medium GK&G—Hot Direct: CK & GK&G—Hot	BD, FW 20-25 mins CG, CH 12-15 mins BD, FW 25-30 mins CG, CH 20-25 mins

Vegetables and fruit on barbecue

Type of seafood & basic preparation	Weight and/or portion	Cooking method & heat level or setting	Means of cooking & approx. total cooking time
Fish Fillets	750 g–1 kg (1½–2 lb) 1–2 cm (½–¾ in) thick	Indirect: CK—Medium GK&G—Hot Direct: CK & GK&G—Hot	BD, FW, P 20–25 mins CG, CH, FP 4–8 mins
Fish steaks and cutlets	4–6 (1.5–2 kg/3–4 lb total) 2.5–3 cm (1–1¼ in) thick	Indirect: CK—Medium GK&G—Hot Direct: CK & GK&G—Hot	BD, FW, P 45–60 mins CG, CH 8–10 mins
Smoked kippers, soak in boiling water 3 mins, drain	4–6 x 310 g (10 oz) each	Indirect: CK—Medium GK&G—Medium Direct: CK & GK&G—Medium	BD, FW (dot with butter) 20–25 mins CG, CH 8–10 mins
Prawns/shrimp, scampi, raw	25–30 (1 kg/2 lb total), in shell	Direct: CK & GK&G—Hot	CG, CH 3–6 mins, cook in shell or peeled
Scallops, shelled	45–50 (1 kg/2 lb total)	Direct: CK & GK&G—Hot	CG, CH 2–3 mins, skewer if cooking on grill
Mussels in shell, scrubbed and bearded	20–25 (1 kg/2 lb total)	Direct: CK & GK&G—Hot	CG, CH 2–3 mins until open, add flavoured butter
Lobster (see recipe, page 81)			
Oysters, in half shell	24–30	Indirect: CK—Medium GK&G—Hot	BD, flavoured butter on each, 8–10 mins

VEGETABLES AND FRUIT

The table below gives details for popular barbecued vegetables and fruit. While many are cooked whole or sliced, without any wrapping or covering, there are alternatives for covered barbecue cooking. Refer to the basic details below in conjunction with the table.

Basic methods of cooking: The chapter on Vegetables, Rice and Salads covers the basic cooking of many vegetables such as roast vegetables and barbecue-steamed vegetables. When using the barbecue for indirect cooking, cook vegetables as follows:

All barbecues: Indirect—Hot/Medium; Direct— Hot: Preheating is not necessary as the barbecue would already be heated. Heat is the same as that used for the main food being cooked.

Timing is given for indirect and direct cooking. Take heat for indirect as Medium—this is the heat level you will be cooking at, even if the recipe directions give Hot as the setting; where the covered barbecue has to be Hot, this is stated in

the table. As more food is added to the covered barbecue, the heat level decreases, particularly for gas units.

For direct cooking, take heat level as Hot, as the barbecue would be at that setting.

Preparation and cooking: Vegetables can be prepared and cooked in a number of ways, identified by the following legend:

A Wash, peel or trim, place on a sheet of heavy-duty foil or in foil food tray, add 1–2 tablespoons water, salt to taste and 1–2 teaspoons butter; wrap or cover tray with foil.
B Wash or scrub with vegetable brush, do not cut, peel, prick or wrap unless stated. Rub vegetable or fruit with oil and salt if appropriate.
C Wipe only, brush with oil.
D No preparation required, spread onto a baking tray.
E Cut in half or cut in wedges or slices, brush with oil or butter.
F Cook on grill, oiled for uncovered vegetables and fruit.
G Cook on oiled hotplate or griddle.

VEGETABLES AND FRUIT

Vegetable & preparation	Amount or size	Cooking method & time	
		Indirect—Hot/Medium	Direct—Hot
Carrots, whole small: A	500 g/1 lb	25–35 mins: F	15–20 mins: F/G (turn)
Carrots, slices, strips: A	500 g/1 lb	20–30 mins: F	10–15 mins: F/G (turn)
Corn in husks (see page 94) Corn cobs, no husks: A, no salt	4 fresh/6–8 frozen	25–35 mins: F	12–15 mins: F (turn)
Eggplant (aubergine): B	250 g/8 oz		30–40 mins: F (turn)
Mushrooms, whole: C	6–8 large	10–15 mins: F	3–5 mins: F/G (turn)

Vegetable & preparation	Amount or size	Cooking method & time Indirect—Hot/Medium	Direct—Hot
Onions, whole: B	6-8 medium-sized	45-55 mins: F	
Onions, 1 cm (½ in) slices: E	6-8 slices		8-10 mins: F/G (turn)
Peppers (bell), whole (see page 94)			
Potato chips, frozen oven-fries	750 g/1½ lb	20-25 mins: D, Hot	
Potatoes, new (see page 90)			
Potatoes, old: B, unwrapped or in foil	6-8 medium-sized	60-75 mins: F	45-60 mins: F (turn)
Potatoes, sweet: B, prick	1 x 500 g/1 lb	45-60 mins: F	
Pumpkin/squash, butternut (see page 93)			
Pumpkin/squash, golden nugget: B	2-3 x 500 g/1 lb	50-60 mins: F	
Squash, acorn: E, halved, unpeeled	3 medium-sized	35-45 mins: F	
Squash, summer—patty pan, zucchini/courgettes: E, halved	250 g/8 oz	15-20 mins: F	6-8 mins: F/G (turn)
Fruit & preparation	Amount or size	Cooking method & time Indirect—Hot/Medium	Direct—Hot
Apples, whole: B	3-4 medium-sized	40-50 mins: F	
Apples, 1 cm (½ in) slices: E	6-8 slices		6-8 mins: F/G (turn)
Bananas, firm, unpeeled	6-8 medium-sized	12-15 mins: F	10-12 mins: F (turn)
Grapefruit: E, halved, 1 tsp brown sugar on each	6-8 halves	6-8 mins: F	
Melon—canteloupe, musk, honeydew: E, thick wedges	6-8 wedges		4-6 mins: F/G (turn)
Papaya/pawpaw: E, thick wedges	6-8 wedges		4-6 mins: F/G (turn)
Peaches: E, halved, fresh or canned	6-8 halves	10-12 mins: F	6-8 mins: F/G (turn)
Pears: E, 1 cm (½ in) slices	6-8 slices		4-5 mins: F/G (turn)
Pineapple: E, slices, wedges	6-8 pieces	10-12 mins: F	6-8 mins: F/G (turn)

BAKED GOODS AND SUNDRIES

The following table is a guide for many standard foods cooked or heated in the kitchen. Convenience foods are very much a part of today's lifestyle; using one or two such foods, as well as those you prepare from scratch, can reduce food-preparation time. For all foods cooked indirect, see the section on Preheating for your particular unit, and heat or cook at the level given in the table. While heat level for the covered gas grill is given as Hot, if your unit has more than two burners check the recommended heat level in your user manual.

BAKED GOODS AND SUNDRIES

CK—Charcoal Kettle; GK&G—Gas Kettle and Covered Gas Grill; BT—food on baking tray.

Type of food	Weight or amount	Cooking method & heat level or setting	Approx. total cooking time
Bagels, baked—fresh, frozen	6-8	Indirect: CK—Medium GK&G—Hot	BT 10-12 mins
Brioche, baked—fresh, frozen	6-8	Indirect: CK—Medium GK&G—Hot	BT 10-12 mins

Cheese and onion damper

Scones

Type of food	Weight or amount	Cooking method & heat level or setting	Approx. total cooking time
Bread, unbaked	approx. 750 g (1½ lb) dough in loaf pan	Indirect: CK—Medium GK&G—Medium-Hot	40-55 mins, bread sounds hollow when tapped on base
Bread, baked—French bread, garlic bread in foil	2-3	Indirect: CK & GK&G—Medium	8-10 mins
Bread rolls, unbaked	12 x 5 cm (2 in) before proving	Indirect: CK—Medium GK&G—Medium-Hot	BT 20-25 mins, elevate if necessary to brown
Bread rolls, baked	6 large, 12 dinner rolls	Indirect: CK & GK&G--Medium	BT 8-10 mins
Cake mixes, packaged	1 cake	Indirect: CK & GK&G—Medium	5-10 mins longer than time on package, on average
Croissants, baked—fresh, frozen	8-12	Indirect: CK—Medium GK&G—Hot	BT 10-12 mins, elevate to crisp tops
Crumpets	6-8	Direct: CK & GK&G—Hot	2-3 mins each side
Custard, baked	3-cup mix (750 ml/ 24 fl oz)	Indirect: CK & GK&G—Medium	30-40 mins in water bath
English muffins, split	6-8 halves	Direct: CK & GK&G—Hot	1½-2 mins each side
French toast	6-8 slices	Direct: CK & GK&G—Hot	2-3 mins each side on greased hotplate or griddle
Hotcakes, pancakes, flapjacks—package mix or own recipe	1-3 tbsp batter each hotcake, according to size required	Direct: CK & GK&G—Hot	2-3 mins each side on greased hotplate or griddle
Melba toast—crustless white bread, thinly sliced	triangles from 6 slices	Indirect: CK & GK&G—Medium	BT 10-15 mins
Pies, baked meat or fruit— frozen	6-8 individual pies or 1 large	Indirect: CK—Medium GK&G—Hot	35-45 mins, individual; 50-60 mins, large
Pizza, baked—frozen	1 large	Indirect: CK—Medium GK&G—Hot	BT 14-18 mins, elevate to cook top properly
Quiche, baked—frozen	6 individual or 1 large	Indirect: CK & GK&G—Medium	30-40 mins, individual; 50-60 mins, large
Scones/baking powder biscuits	12-14 x 5 cm (2 in)	Indirect: CK—Medium GK&G—Hot	BT 12-15 mins, elevate to brown tops
Sliced bread and split hamburger buns can be toasted on cooking grill over direct heat.			

27

MENUS

The recipes marked with an asterisk are included in the book— see index. Other heated or cooked accompaniments can be found in the various preceding tables for basic barbecued foods, or are self-explanatory.

Menu for direct cooking

TRADITIONAL BARBECUE

Crudités with Two Sauces*

Barbecued Onion Steak* • Devilled Tomato Butter*

Barbecued Whole Mushrooms • Potatoes in Foil • Tossed Salad

Bananas in Rum Syrup*

Coffee

Menu for indirect cooking, changing to direct cooking

DINNER PARTY ON THE TERRACE

Smoked Trout Pâté* • Melba Toast

Mustard Cream Rack of Veal* • Steamed Broccoli* • Ginger Orange Pumpkin*

Hot Dinner Rolls • Butter

Peppered Pineapple with Orange Sauce*

Cheese Platter

Coffee

Menu for indirect cooking

COME FOR A BARBECUE!

Guacamole* with Crudités and Corn Chips

Butterflied Lamb with Rosemary* • Roast Potatoes* • Green Pasta Salad*

Date and Banana Slice* • Fruit and Cheese Platter

Coffee

Menu for direct cooking

WEEKEND BRUNCH

Mangoes in Champagne*

Scrambled Eggs with Smoked Salmon* • Hot Buckwheat Griddle Cakes*

Toasted English Muffins • Butter • Honey • Fruit Conserves

Fresh Fruit Platter

Coffee

Menu for indirect cooking

FAMILY SUNDAY LUNCH

Chicken Liver and Mushroom Pâté* • Savoury Crackers

Roast Chicken with Sage Potatoes* • Tossed Salad • Warmed French Bread

Chocolate Self-saucing Pudding*

Coffee

STARTERS AND SNACKS

Planning is the key to a successful barbecue meal. There's no point in putting too much pressure on the cook— or the barbecue! After all, a barbecue is a relaxed meal that everyone should enjoy. If you have chosen to cook a joint of meat or some poultry indirect, then prepare a starter ahead of time. Chilled soup is excellent on a hot day; dips and spreads with crisp vegetables, crusty bread or crackers keep guests busy and happy while the barbecue gets on with its job. If steak, satays or similar foods are to be cooked by direct heat, then use the barbecue for indirect cooking first, and serve up nachos, crisp fillo pastries, pizza or pissaladière hot from the barbecue.

CRUDITÉS WITH TWO SAUCES

Serves: 6-8

250 g (8 oz) broccoli

3 sticks celery

12-16 spring onions (scallions)

2 medium-sized carrots

1 bunch small radishes

125 g (4 oz) button mushrooms

Herb Mayonnaise

1 cup (250 ml/8 fl oz) quality mayonnaise

2 tbsp sour cream

1 tsp Dijon mustard

2 tsp each finely chopped parsley and watercress

Bagna Cauda

1 cup (250 g/8 oz) butter

¼ cup (60 ml/2 fl oz) olive oil

3 cloves garlic, crushed

2 tbsp mashed anchovy fillets

Cut broccoli into small florets and blanch in boiling water for 1 minute. Drain in a colander, run cold water through to arrest cooking, then drain well. Cut celery sticks into 8 cm (3 in) lengths; cut short slits close together at each end and put into iced water to curl. Trim spring onions and shred ends, place ends down into iced water with celery. Peel carrot and cut into strips. Wash radishes, trim tops and roots, drain. Trim mushrooms and wipe with a damp cloth.

Arrange vegetables in groups on a large platter or in a basket. Place bowl of Herb Mayonnaise in centre. Serve the Bagna Cauda separately in its pan. Vegetables are dipped in either sauce and accompanied with warm, crusty bread.

Crudités with herb mayonnaise

Herb Mayonnaise: Mix ingredients together and spoon into a bowl. Cover with plastic wrap and refrigerate until needed.

Bagna Cauda: Heat butter and oil in a small pan or flameproof dish over direct heat on the barbecue. Add garlic and cook gently for 2-3 minutes without browning, add mashed anchovies and cook gently until anchovies almost dissolve into butter mixture. The sauce is used hot as a dip for the vegetables.

NEAPOLITAN PIZZA

> *Charcoal kettle: Indirect—Medium—Preheat 8-10 minutes*
> *Gas kettle: Indirect—Medium—Preheat 8-10 minutes*
> *Covered gas grill: Indirect—Medium—Preheat 8-10 minutes*
> *Cooking time: 30-35 minutes*
> *Serves: 4-6*

Pizza Base

1½ cups (185 g/6 oz) plain (all-purpose) flour

2 tsp baking powder

1 egg

½ cup (125 ml/4 fl oz) milk

¼ cup (60 g/2 oz) butter or margarine, melted

olive oil

Topping

¾ cup (185 ml/6 fl oz) bottled tomato pasta sauce

½ green (bell) pepper, chopped

3 spring onions (scallions), chopped

6 small mushrooms, chopped

125 g (4 oz) ham or peperoni sausage, chopped

½ cup (60 g/2 oz) shredded natural Cheddar cheese

½ cup (60 g/2 oz) shredded mozzarella cheese

1 tbsp chopped parsley

Sift flour and baking powder into a mixing bowl and make a well in the centre. Beat egg into milk and pour into flour with the melted butter. Mix to a soft dough and turn onto a lightly floured board. Knead lightly until smooth and roll out to fit an oiled 25

Top: Pissaladière; bottom: Neapolitan pizza

cm (10 in) pizza pan. Brush top with olive oil.

Mix topping ingredients together, except for the cheeses and parsley, and spread over the pizza base. Mix cheeses and parsley together and sprinkle on top of the pizza. If necessary, pizza may be set aside for up to 1 hour before baking.

Place pizza on barbecue grill and cook indirect, hood down, for 30-35 minutes until cheese is bubbling and base is cooked. Serve hot or warm.

PISSALADIÈRE

> *Charcoal kettle: Indirect—Medium—Preheat 8-10 minutes*
> *Gas kettle: Indirect—Hot—Preheat 8-10 minutes*
> *Covered gas grill: Indirect—Hot—Preheat 8-10 minutes*
> *Cooking time: 50-55 minutes*
> *Serves: 8-10*

1 quantity Rich Shortcrust Pastry (page 38)

2 tbsp olive oil

3 medium-sized onions, thinly sliced

2 cloves garlic, crushed

freshly ground black pepper

425 g (15 oz) can tomatoes

1 tbsp tomato paste

12 anchovy fillets

6-8 Greek-style black olives

Make pastry according to directions, roll out and line a 30 cm (12 in) pizza plate or ovenproof platter. Fold edge under to make a rim. Cover and refrigerate for 20 minutes or so.

Heat oil in a large frying pan, add onions and cook on low heat for about 20 minutes, add garlic and cook gently for further 5 minutes. Onions should be very soft and golden, but not browned. Remove to a bowl, add pepper to taste and leave aside to cool. Add tomatoes and their liquid to frying pan, mash in pan with a fork and stir in tomato paste. Cook on high heat until most of liquid is evaporated and tomato is reduced to a coarse purée. Keep aside. Halve anchovy fillets lengthwise and halve olives, removing seeds.

Spread onions onto pastry base. Top with tomato mixture. Make a lattice pattern on top with anchovy fillets and position olive halves in each diamond. Pissaladière may be set aside in refrigerator for up to 1 hour before baking if necessary.

Place the Pissaladière on barbecue grill and bake indirect, hood down, for 15-20 minutes until pastry is cooked. Rotate during cooking if necessary to brown edge evenly. Cut in wedges to serve as a first course with salad.

ICED SOUP OF SUMMER FRUITS

Cooking time: 25-30 minutes *Serves: 6-8*

2 ripe peaches
4 dark table plums
4 ripe apricots
1 punnet (250 g/8 oz) strawberries
1 punnet (250 g/8 oz) raspberries
3 cups (750 ml/24 fl oz) water
1 cup (250 ml/8 fl oz) rosé wine
5 cm (2 in) cinnamon stick
½ cup (125 g/4 oz) sugar, or to taste
light sour cream or yoghurt for serving

Wash fruits, halve stone fruits and remove seeds. Hull strawberries, reserving 6-8 whole fruit. Pick over raspberries and wash only if necessary. Place all fruits in a large stainless steel or enamelled saucepan, add water, wine and cinnamon stick and bring to the boil. Simmer for 20-25 minutes until fruits are tender. Stir in sugar to taste—amount will depend on tartness of fruit. Remove cinnamon stick and discard, also remove any loose fruit skins. Cool a little, then purée in food processor or blender in 2-3 batches, transferring puréed soup to a serving bowl. Cool completely, then cover and chill for several hours or overnight. Just before serving, halve reserved strawberries and float in the centre of the soup. Serve soup into glass bowls with light sour cream or yoghurt served separately.

Iced soup of summer fruits

CHEESE FILLO TRIANGLES

Fillo pastry is a popular alternative for traditional pastry. Besides being less temperamental in the cooking, it is more suited to serving in the backyard than the living room when prepared as an appetiser. Delicious as it is, the pastry tends to shatter easily when eaten as finger food. Better crumbs on the lawn than on the carpet!

Charcoal kettle: Indirect—Medium— *Preheat 8-10 minutes* *Gas kettle: Indirect—Hot—Preheat 8-10* *minutes* *Covered gas grill: Indirect—Hot—* *Preheat 8-10 minutes* *Cooking time: 15-18 minutes* *Makes: about 30*

½ cup (90 g/ 3 oz) crumbled feta   cheese
½ cup (125 g/4 oz) cottage cheese
2 tbsp finely chopped parsley
1 tsp finely chopped mint
1 egg, beaten
freshly ground black pepper
8-10 sheets fillo pastry
½ cup (125 g/4 oz) butter, melted

Mix the cheese in a bowl with the herbs. Add egg and pepper to taste; mix well. Grease 2 baking trays with butter.

Cut fillo sheets into strips about 12 cm (5 in) wide and 30 cm (12 in) long. Stack and cover with heavy plastic to prevent drying. Place a strip of fillo on a board, brush lightly with melted butter and fold in half across its width. Brush again with butter. Place a heaped teaspoonful of cheese filling near base of strip, fold corner of pastry over filling so that bottom edge lines up with side. Fold once straight up, then across at an angle to other side (folding action is the same as folding a flag). Fold in this fashion to end of strip and place seam side down on greased baking tray. Repeat with remaining ingredients. Brush finished triangles with melted butter. At this stage, triangles may be covered with plastic and set aside in refrigerator for up to 2 hours.

Place a tray of triangles on barbecue grill, elevated if necessary (page 14), and bake indirect, hood down, for 15-18 minutes or until puffed and golden. Cook second lot after first is baked, or bake the two together, depending on capacity of your barbecue. Place on a serving platter and serve immediately.

GUACAMOLE

Serves: 6-8

1 small white onion, finely chopped

juice of 1 lime

1-2 red chillies

2 large ripe avocados

salt to taste

The onion should be very finely chopped, preferably with a knife. Place in a bowl with the lime juice and leave to stand for 2 hours. Seed the chillies and chop very finely.

Halve avocados, remove seeds (reserve one seed) and place flesh in a bowl. Mash well with a fork—do not use food processor. Add chopped onion, reserving some of the lime liquid. Add chopped chilli and salt to taste. Adjust flavour, adding more of the lime liquid if necessary. Place reserved avocado seed into the Guacamole, cover bowl and chill. (The seed helps prevent the avocado flesh from discolouring.) When ready to serve, remove seed and pile Guacamole in a serving bowl. Serve with corn chips for dipping. Guacamole may also be served as a sauce for Crudités (page 30).

CHILLED YOGHURT AND CUCUMBER SOUP

Serves: 6-8

2 small cucumbers

3 cups (750 ml/24 fl oz) natural yoghurt

3 spring onions (scallions), finely sliced

1 tbsp finely chopped mint

1 tbsp olive oil

about 1 cup (250 ml/8 fl oz) iced water

salt and white pepper to taste

thin cucumber slices and mint sprigs to garnish

Cucumbers should be small and firm, with underdeveloped seeds. Peel thinly and cut into very small dice. Place in a large bowl. Add yoghurt, spring

Chilled yoghurt and cucumber soup

onions, mint and olive oil and stir well. Add iced water until soup is a thin cream consistency—amount depends on thickness of the yoghurt. Season to taste with salt and pepper. Set bowl in another bowl of ice for serving, and float cucumber slices and mint sprigs on top.

EGGPLANT AND TAHINI PURÉE

All barbecues: Direct—Hot reducing to Medium
Cooking time: 30-40 minutes
Serves: 6-8

2 medium-sized eggplants (aubergines), each about 250 g/ 8 oz

¼ cup (60 ml/2 fl oz) lemon juice

1/3 cup (90 ml/3 fl oz) tahini (sesame seed paste)

2 cloves garlic, chopped

1 tbsp olive oil

2 tsp salt or to taste

freshly ground black pepper

3 tbsp chopped flat-leaf parsley

finely chopped parsley for serving

Place eggplants on barbecue grill over a hot fire and grill until skins are well-charred, turning often. Reduce heat to medium or move eggplants to cooler section of charcoal fire and continue to cook, hood down, for 15-20 minutes longer until eggplants are soft. Turn once during this stage of cooking. Have a baking tray at hand and place cooked eggplants onto this for easier handling. To make the process easier, complete the purée in the kitchen.

Halve eggplants lengthwise, scoop out pulp into a colander and leave for a minute or so for juices to drain off. Place pulp in bowl of food processor or blender jar. Discard skins and stems. Process until puréed, gradually add most of the lemon juice, then add the tahini, garlic, oil, salt and pepper to taste. Purée until smooth, taste, and add more lemon juice if necessary. Lastly, add parsley and process just long enough to chop the parsley finely—it should still be visible. Turn out into a serving dish or bowl and sprinkle with additional chopped parsley. Serve with flat breads, cut into pieces, for scooping up the purée. It is also good spread onto savoury crackers or crusty slices of French bread.

NACHOS

> **Charcoal kettle**: *Indirect—Medium—Preheat 6-8 minutes*
> **Gas kettle**: *Indirect—Medium—Preheat 6-8 minutes*
> **Covered gas grill**: *Indirect—Medium—Preheat 6-8 minutes*
> **Cooking time**: *10-12 minutes*
> **Serves**: *6-8*

125 g (4 oz) corn chips

1½ cups (185 g/6 oz) shredded natural Cheddar cheese

3 tbsp finely chopped red (bell) pepper

3 spring onions (scallions), finely chopped

3 tsp chilli sauce

extra chilli sauce for serving

Place a layer of corn chips on a lightly greased flat ovenproof platter, large flan dish or pizza plate. Mix remaining ingredients together, except for extra chilli sauce, and sprinkle some of the mixture over the corn chips. Top with more corn chips and cheese mixture and repeat until ingredients are used, finishing with a cheese layer.

Place on barbecue grill and cook indirect, hood down, for 10-12 minutes until cheese is melted and bubbly. Serve immediately. The Nachos are eaten directly from the dish.

REFRIED BEANS

> **All barbecues**: *Direct—Medium*
> **Cooking time**: *15-18 minutes*
> **Serves**: *8-10*

2 x 440 g (1 lb) cans pinto or red kidney beans

¼ cup (60 ml/2 fl oz) corn oil

1 medium-sized onion, finely chopped

1 tbsp finely chopped coriander leaves (cilantro)

1 cup (125 g/4 oz) shredded natural Cheddar cheese

2 spring onions (scallions), finely chopped

corn chips for serving

Drain beans, reserving about ½ cup of the bean liquid. Tip beans into a bowl and mash well with potato masher.

Refried beans

Take out to barbecue with reserved bean liquid and remaining ingredients.

Place a large frying pan on the barbecue, add oil and onion and cook onion gently on medium heat until soft—about 10 minutes. Add beans and stir over heat until combined and well heated, adding a little bean liquid if too dry. Consistency should be that of creamy mashed potatoes. Stir in coriander, cheese and spring onions and add pepper to taste. Transfer to a bowl, place on a platter and surround with corn chips for dipping. Serve hot or warm.

BUCKWHEAT GRIDDLE CAKES

> **All barbecues**: *Direct—Hot*
> **Cooking time**: *10-12 minutes*
> **Makes**: *20-24*

½ cup (90 g/3 oz) buckwheat flour

1 cup (125 g/4 oz) plain (all-purpose) flour

3 tsp baking powder

¼ tsp salt

2 tsp caster (superfine) sugar

2 eggs

1 cup (250 ml/8 fl oz) milk

2 tbsp melted butter or margarine

additional melted butter for cooking

Sift flours, baking powder and salt into a bowl, returning any coarse flakes from sieve to flours. Stir in sugar and make a well in the centre. Beat eggs lightly and beat in milk. Add to flour with melted butter and stir quickly to a smooth batter. Do not stir longer than necessary. Cover and stand batter in refrigerator for at least 2 hours. Heat hotplate or griddle on barbecue and grease with melted butter. Drop batter in generous tablespoonfuls onto hotplate and cook until bubbles appear on the surface, brush a little butter on top then turn and cook second side. Remove to a napkin-lined plate as they cook. Serve hot with butter and fruit conserves, honey or maple syrup. As these are an easy version of the Russian Blini (normally made with yeast), they are very good served with smoked salmon or caviar and sour cream.

GLAZED PEPPER-PORK BITES

Charcoal kettle: Indirect—Medium—Preheat 8-10 minutes
Gas kettle: Indirect—Hot—Preheat 8-10 minutes
Covered gas grill: Indirect—Hot—Preheat 8-10 minutes
Cooking time: 20-25 minutes
Serves: 6-8

2 medium-sized red (bell) peppers

2 medium-sized green (bell) peppers

125 g (4 oz) lean ham

4 spring onions (scallions), roughly chopped

1 clove garlic, chopped

1 tsp chopped fresh ginger

500 g (1 lb) ground pork

¼ cup (30 g/1 oz) dry breadcrumbs

1 egg

1 tsp salt

freshly ground black pepper

Glaze

1 clove garlic, crushed

1 tbsp oil

2 tbsp dry sherry

¼ cup (60 ml/2 fl oz) soya sauce

2 tsp hoisin sauce

2 tsp sugar

1 tsp cornflour (cornstarch)

¼ cup (60 ml/2 fl oz) water

Glazed pepper-pork bites

Choose peppers with a pronounced bell shape. Wash well, halve lengthwise and cut around stem to remove. Cut out white ribs and remove seeds. Halve lengthwise again, then halve the strips to give small, curved pieces of pepper. Keep aside.

Put ham, spring onions, garlic and ginger in bowl of food processor. Process until finely ground. Add pork, crumbs, egg, salt and pepper to taste and process until combined. Mould heaped teaspoons of the mixture into each pepper piece and place them in an oiled metal roasting pan. Brush with glaze.

Place pan of pepper pieces on barbecue grill and cook indirect, hood down, for 20-25 minutes, brushing twice with glaze. Lift out carefully onto serving platter and spoon on any remaining glaze. Serve hot, providing cocktail picks for convenience.

Glaze: In a small pan gently cook garlic in oil for 2 minutes, and add sherry, sauces and sugar. Bring to a simmer. Mix cornflour with water and stir into simmering sauce to thicken. Place pan of glaze at side of grill with the peppers so that it simmers gently.

CHICKEN LIVER AND MUSHROOM PÂTÉ

Cooking time: 20-25 minutes
Serves: 8-10

500 g (1 lb) chicken livers

125 g (4 oz) bacon, roughly chopped

1 large onion, chopped

1 bay leaf

1 clove garlic, chopped

185 g (6 oz) mushrooms, chopped

½ tsp dried thyme leaves

½ cup (125 g/4 oz) butter

125 g (4 oz) ricotta cheese

½ tsp ground nutmeg

2 tbsp brandy or Cognac

salt and freshly ground black pepper

Clean chicken livers, removing any threads and gall, and chop roughly. Heat a large frying pan, add bacon and cook until fat renders and bacon is cooked but not browned. Add onion and bay leaf and cook gently for about 10 minutes until onion is soft. Stir in garlic, mushrooms and thyme and cook for further 5 minutes or until mushroom liquid evaporates, stirring often. Remove bay leaf and discard. Tip pan contents into food processor bowl and leave until cool.

Melt butter in pan, add chicken livers and cook on medium heat, stirring often, until livers change colour but are still slightly pink inside. Cool and add to food processor bowl. Add ricotta cheese and process until smooth. Add nutmeg, brandy and salt and pepper to taste, process briefly, then transfer pâté to an earthenware or china pot. Smooth top, cover with plastic film (wrap) and chill for several hours or overnight. Serve with sliced crusty French bread, savoury crackers or Melba toast.

CHICKEN AND PORK IN LETTUCE

All barbecues: Direct—Hot
Cooking time: 6-8 minutes
Serves: 6-8

lettuce cups (allow 2-3 per person)

250 g (8 oz) ground chicken

500 g (1 lb) ground pork

1 egg

4 spring onions (scallions), finely chopped

1 tsp grated fresh ginger

10 canned water chestnuts, chopped

8 small mushrooms, chopped

1 tsp cornflour (cornstarch)

freshly ground black pepper

2 tbsp oil

2 tbsp soya sauce

1 tbsp hoisin sauce

about ¼ cup (60 ml/2 fl oz) chicken stock (broth)

Prepare lettuce cups from 2 heads of lettuce, rinse, drain and wrap in a tea-towel. Put into refrigerator and leave until crisp—about 2 hours.

Place ground chicken and pork in a bowl and add egg, spring onions, ginger, water chestnuts, mushrooms and cornflour, adding pepper to taste. Mix with a fork until combined. Take out to barbecue with remaining ingredients.

Heat a wok or large frying pan over hot barbecue, add oil and the meat mixture. Stir-fry until crumbly and lightly browned, add soya and hoisin sauces and stock. Toss well, adding a little water if too dry. Transfer to a deep bowl. Arrange lettuce cups on a platter. Guests can roll up portions of filling in lettuce cups to eat as finger food.

Chicken and pork in lettuce

GLAZED CHIPOLATAS IN A BASKET

All barbecues: Direct—Medium
Cooking time: about 15 minutes
Serves: 6-8

1 kg (2 lb) chipolata sausages

oil

1 quantity Plum Barbecue Sauce (page 101)

Bread Basket (page 112)

Leave sausages in links and place in a pan with water to just cover. Bring slowly to a simmer, remove from heat and leave aside until sausages are firm. Drain, separate sausages and refrigerate them in a sealed container until needed.

Heat barbecue hotplate or griddle and brush with oil. Place Plum Barbecue Sauce in a pan on the grill to heat. Cook sausages on hotplate, basting them frequently with sauce. Transfer the sausages to hot Bread Basket and place on a platter with remaining sauce served separately in a bowl. Provide cocktail picks for convenience.

To heat Bread Basket: Directions are given for heating indirect. While this may be done before cooking the sausages, it is possible to heat the bread direct. Wrap bread in foil with lid in place and place on grill. Heat for 10 minutes, turning once. Remove from foil and place base and lid separately on side of grill for 2-3 minutes to crisp the crust.

SEEFOOD PLATTER

If a fish main course is planned, begin with a cold seafood platter to set the tone of the meal. The amount of individual ingredients used depends on the number of guests.

oysters in the shell

cooked large prawns (jumbo shrimp)

cooked yabbies (crayfish/crawfish)

boiled crab

steamed mussels

mayonnaise

For each person, allow 2-3 oysters, 3-4 prawns, 2-3 yabbies and 1 crab per 2-4 serves, according to size. See Mussels Marinière (page 81) for preparing steamed mussels, allowing 2-4 mussels per serve, according to size. After steaming, remove mussels and their liquid to a dish, cover and chill. Arrange seafood on a bed of ice so that it stays fresh and cool for serving. Garnish with lemon slices and parsley. Serve mayonnaise in a bowl.

Seafood platter

SMOKED SALMON AND RICOTTA PUFFS

Charcoal kettle: Indirect—Medium—Preheat 6-8 minutes
Gas kettle: Indirect—Hot—Preheat 8-10 minutes
Covered gas grill: Indirect—Hot—Preheat 8-10 minutes
Cooking time: 15-18 minutes
Makes: about 30

125 g (4 oz) smoked salmon

1 cup (250 g/8 oz) ricotta cheese

3 spring onions (scallions), finely chopped

¼-½ tsp dried dill tips

10-12 sheets fillo pastry

½ cup (125 g/4 oz) butter melted

Chop the smoked salmon and mix with the ricotta cheese and spring onions, adding dill tips and pepper to taste. Grease 2 baking trays with butter.
  Cut fillo into strips 12 cm (5 in) wide and 30 cm (12 in) long. Butter, fold, fill and fold into triangles as described for Cheese Fillo Triangles, page 32. Place on greased baking trays and brush tops with melted butter. Finished puffs may be covered with plastic film (wrap) and set aside in the refrigerator for up to 2 hours if necessary.
  Place a tray of puffs on barbecue grill, elevated if necessary (page 14), and cook indirect, hood down, for 15-18 minutes until puffed and golden. Cook second batch after first is baked, or bake the two together, depending on capacity of your barbecue. Remove to a platter and serve hot as a finger food.

SMOKED TROUT PÂTÉ

Serves: 6-8

2 small smoked trout, each about 250 g (8 oz)

1 tbsp chopped spring onions (scallions)

125 g (4 oz) packaged cream cheese

¼ cup (60 ml/2 fl oz) sour cream

2 tsp tomato paste

freshly ground white pepper

2 tbsp lime or lemon juice

toast fingers or Melba toast for serving

If preparing your own smoked trout, see page 85 for details. However, smoked trout is readily available from fishmongers and specialty food stores.
  Remove skin from trout and lift flesh from the bones. Place in food processor bowl. Use white and pale green parts only when preparing spring onions, and add to trout with cream cheese. Process until puréed. Add sour cream, tomato paste and white pepper to taste and process briefly. Add half the lime or lemon juice, process until pâté is smooth and taste it. Add more juice if necessary and process once more. Transfer to individual pots for single serves, or to a bowl to be passed around. Serve with dry toast fingers or Melba toast.

LIGHT MEALS

Breakfast, brunch, lunch—all are occasions when something light is the order of the day. Savoury flans have wide appeal, so why not cook and serve them hot from the covered barbecue? While a recipe has been given for rich shortcrust pastry, there are excellent prepared pastries and dry packaged mixes which can be used instead.

Many of the following recipes are also ideal for barbecue meals when there could well be a guest (or three) who does not eat meat or fish.

RICH SHORTCRUST PASTRY

Makes: 1 x 20-23 cm (8-9 in) two-crust pie; 2 x 20-23 cm (8-9 in) flan cases or pie crusts; 1 x 18 cm (7 in) and 1 x 25 cm (10 in) flan case or pie crust

2 cups (250 g/8 oz) plain (all-purpose) flour

2 tsp caster (superfine) sugar* (optional)

2/3 cup (150 g/5 oz) butter or margarine

1 egg yolk

2 tsp lemon juice

2-4 tbsp cold water

Put flour, and sugar if used, in food-processor bowl. Add firm butter or margarine cut into small pieces. Process until mixture resembles breadcrumbs. Add egg yolk and lemon juice and sufficient water gradually until dough leaves sides of bowl cleanly. Stop as soon as dough is formed. Turn out onto a lightly floured board and knead lightly to smooth. If only one flan case or pie crust is required, divide dough in two and place one portion in a freezer bag, seal and freeze for later use.

To prepare flan case or pie crust: Roll out required amount of pastry on a lightly floured board. Lift into ungreased flan dish or pie plate, press gently into shape. For flan case, trim top level with dish. For pie crust, fold excess pastry under to build up rim, press lightly, then crimp with fingers or press with fork tines. Chill for 20-30 minutes.

* Note: Use sugar only if making pastry for sweet pies, although pastry without sugar is suitable for such pies.

ASPARAGUS FLAN

Charcoal kettle: Indirect—Medium—Preheat 10-12 minutes
Gas kettle: Indirect—Medium—Preheat 10-12 minutes
Covered gas grill: Indirect—Medium—Preheat 10-12 minutes
Cooking time: 40-45 minutes
Serves: 4-6

1 unbaked 23 cm (9 in) Rich Shortcrust Pastry flan case

3 large eggs

1 cup (250 ml/8 fl oz) cream

1/2 cup (125 ml/4 fl oz) milk

1 tsp French mustard

1/8 tsp nutmeg

salt and freshly ground black pepper

4 spring onions (scallions), finely chopped

1 cup (125 g/4 oz) shredded natural Cheddar cheese

340 g (12 oz) can asparagus spears, drained

Prepare flan case as directed in Rich Shortcrust Pastry recipe, lining a 23 cm (9 in) flan dish with half the pastry. Chill flan case in refrigerator until filling is ready.

Beat eggs in a large bowl, beat in cream, milk, mustard, nutmeg and salt and pepper to taste. Stir in spring onions and cheese. Pour into chilled flan case and arrange drained asparagus spears on top.

Place flan dish on barbecue grill and bake indirect, hood down, for 40-45 minutes, rotating if necessary during cooking to brown evenly. When filling is nearly set (after 35 minutes), turn burner on to low under flan so that base of pastry browns; for charcoal kettle, move flan over direct heat. Test to see if cooked by inserting a knife in the centre—it should come out clean. Let stand for 5 minutes before slicing in wedges to serve. Serve with a tossed salad.

FLAN OF ROOT VEGETABLES

Charcoal kettle: Indirect—Medium—Preheat 10-12 minutes
Gas kettle: Indirect—Medium—Preheat 10-12 minutes
Covered gas grill: Indirect—Medium—Preheat 10-12 minutes
Cooking time: 60-65 minutes
Serves: 4-6

1 unbaked 23 cm (9 in) Rich Shortcrust Pastry flan case

1 medium-sized leek

2 tbsp butter or margarine

1 tsp grated fresh ginger

1½ cups (185 g/6 oz) shredded parsnip

1½ cups (185 g/6 oz) shredded carrot

1 cup (150 g/5 oz) shredded potato

½ tsp nutmeg

1 tsp grated orange rind

salt and freshly ground black pepper

½ cup (125 ml/4 fl oz) sour cream

2 eggs, beaten

Crumb Topping

2 tbsp melted butter or margarine

Left: Asparagus flan; top: Flan of root vegetables; right: Seafood flan (see p. 87)

1 cup (60 g/2 oz) soft wholemeal (whole wheat) breadcrumbs

1 tbsp chopped coriander leaves (cilantro)

2 tbsp snipped chives

Prepare flan case as directed in Rich Shortcrust Pastry recipe, lining a 23 cm (9 in) flan dish with half the pastry. Chill flan case in refrigerator until filling is ready.

Trim leek, slit lengthwise and wash well to remove soil. Slice thinly, including some of the tender green top. Melt butter in a large frying pan, add leek and ginger and cook gently until soft. Add shredded vegetables, stir well, cover and simmer for 6-8 minutes until vegetables are just softened. Leave aside until cool. Stir in nutmeg, orange rind, salt and pepper to taste, sour cream and eggs. Turn into chilled flan case. Sprinkle Crumb Topping evenly over filling (see below).

Place flan dish on barbecue grill and cook indirect, hood down, for 45-50 minutes until golden brown. When filling is nearly set (after 40 minutes), turn burner on to low under flan so that base of pastry browns; for charcoal kettle, move flan over direct heat. Let stand for 5 minutes and cut into wedges to serve. If desired, serve with Sour Cream and Orange Sauce.

Crumb Topping: Toss ingredients together to mix thoroughly.

Sour Cream and Orange Sauce: Into 1 cup (250 ml/8 fl oz) sour cream, mix grated rind and juice of 1 orange, 1 teaspoon ground ginger and 2 teaspoons brown sugar.

SCRAMBLED EGGS WITH SMOKED SALMON

All barbecues: *Direct—Hot/Medium*
Cooking time: *4-6 minutes*
Serves: *6*

10 eggs

½ cup (125 ml/4 fl oz) cream

1 tsp salt

freshly ground black pepper

¼ cup (60 g/2 oz) butter or margarine

125 g (4 oz) smoked salmon, flaked

2 tsp chopped fresh dill

2 tbsp sour cream

1 tbsp salmon roe (optional)

additional sour cream for serving

Beat eggs with cream and add salt and pepper to taste. Heat a heavy saucepan on barbecue grill, add butter, and when melted, add eggs. Cook, stirring occasionally, until eggs are creamy, fold in flaked salmon and continue to cook and stir until eggs are just set but still creamy. Turn into a hot dish, sprinkle with chopped dill and top with sour cream and salmon roe if used. Serve for breakfast or brunch with hot croissants or Buckwheat Griddle Cakes (page 34), and additional sour cream.

SPINACH AND CHEESE PIE

Charcoal kettle: Indirect—Medium—Preheat 8-10 minutes	
Gas kettle: Indirect—Medium—Preheat 8-10 minutes	
Covered gas grill: Indirect—Medium—Preheat 8-10 minutes	
Cooking time: 1¼ hours	
Serves: 8-10	

250 g (8 oz) packet frozen leaf spinach

2 small leeks

8-10 spring onions (scallions)

⅓ cup (90 ml/3 fl oz) olive oil

3 tbsp chopped parsley

2 tsp chopped fresh dill

¾ cup (150 g/5 oz) crumbled feta cheese

½ cup (125 g/4 oz) cottage or ricotta cheese

1 cup (125 g/4 oz) shredded natural Cheddar cheese

¼ tsp nutmeg

4 eggs, beaten

salt and freshly ground black pepper

12 sheets fillo pastry

½ cup (125 g/4 oz) melted butter

Use whole or coarsely chopped frozen leaf spinach if possible, not the very finely chopped frozen spinach. Thaw spinach and drain well in a sieve, pressing with the back of a spoon to extract excess moisture. Turn onto a board and chop if necessary. Place in a large mixing bowl.

Trim leeks, halve lengthwise and rinse well to remove soil. Chop finely, including tender green section. Trim spring onions and slice thinly, including some of the green. Heat oil in a frying pan, add leek and spring onions and cook gently for 5-6 minutes until softened. Add pan contents to spinach and add herbs, cheeses and nutmeg. Toss well to mix, stir in beaten eggs and add salt and pepper to taste.

Grease a 25 x 30 cm (10 x 12 in) metal baking dish with butter and line with 6 sheets of pastry, brushing each sheet with melted butter. Spread spinach filling. Top with remaining pastry, brushing each sheet with butter. Trim pastry about 1 cm (½ in) above level of pie and brush top with butter. Score top layers of pastry with a sharp knife into diamonds, that is, make 4 evenly spaced straight cuts along length of pie, then cut across diagonally. Pie may be set aside in refrigerator for up to 2 hours before baking if necessary.

Just before cooking, sprinkle top of pie with cold water to prevent pastry curling during cooking. Place on barbecue grill and bake indirect, hood down, for 1 hour or until puffed and golden. Let stand for 10 minutes, then cut into diamonds. Serve hot or warm.

TOMATO AND PEPPER QUICHE

Charcoal kettle: Indirect—Medium—Preheat 10-12 minutes	
Gas kettle: Indirect—Medium—Preheat 10-12 minutes	
Covered gas grill: Indirect—Medium—Preheat 10-12 minutes	
Cooking time: 55-65 minutes	
Serves: 6	

1 unbaked 23 cm (9 in) Rich Shortcrust Pastry flan case (page 38)

2 tbsp butter or margarine

1 medium-sized onion, thinly sliced

2 tsp plain (all-purpose) flour

1 small green (bell) pepper, seeded and sliced

1 small red (bell) pepper, seeded and sliced

2 medium-sized tomatoes, chopped

½ tsp dried basil

salt and freshly ground black pepper

1 cup (125 g/4 oz) shredded natural Cheddar cheese

3 large eggs

½ cup (125 ml/4 fl oz) milk

½ cup (125 ml/4 fl oz) cream

1 medium-sized tomato, extra

4-5 black olives, pitted and halved

Prepare a flan case as directed in Rich Shortcrust Pastry recipe (page 38),

Spinach and cheese pie

Tomato and pepper quiche

lining a 23 cm (9 in) flan dish with half the pastry. Chill.

Melt half the butter in a frying pan, add onion and cook gently until soft. Turn into a bowl, cool and mix in the flour. Spread over base of flan case. Add remaining butter to pan with sliced peppers and cook 2-3 minutes. Remove 2 rings each of green and red pepper and reserve for garnish. Add chopped tomatoes to peppers and cook until juices evaporate. Stir in basil and salt and pepper to taste. Spread over onions and top with the cheese. Beat eggs with milk and cream and pour into flan. Cut the extra tomato into 8 wedges and remove seeds. Arrange on top of flan with reserved pepper rings and olives.

Place flan dish on barbecue grill and bake indirect, hood down, for 45-50 minutes, rotating if necessary during cooking to brown evenly. Test to see if cooked by inserting a knife in the centre—it should come out clean when flan is set. Let stand for 5 minutes and serve with a tossed salad.

CHEESE AND CHIVE STRATA

> **Charcoal kettle**: Indirect—Medium—Preheat not necessary
> **Gas kettle**: Indirect—Medium-Hot—Preheat 6-8 minutes
> **Covered gas grill**: Indirect—Medium-Hot—Preheat 6-8 minutes
> **Cooking time**: 40-45 minutes
> **Serves**: 4-6

6 eggs

2 tsp Dijon mustard

1 tsp salt

freshly ground black pepper

pinch cayenne pepper

1/8 tsp nutmeg

1½ cups (375 ml/12 fl oz) milk

2 cups (125 g/4 oz) soft white breadcrumbs

3-4 tbsp snipped chives

1 cup (125 g/4 oz) shredded natural Cheddar cheese

2 tbsp grated Parmesan cheese

In a large bowl beat eggs with mustard, salt, pepper to taste, cayenne pepper and nutmeg. Stir in milk, crumbs, chives and cheeses, reserving half the Parmesan cheese. Pour into a greased oval ovenproof dish about 28 x 23 cm

Ratatouille

(11 x 9 in) and 5 cm (2 in) deep. Sprinkle remaining Parmesan over the top, cover with plastic film (wrap) and refrigerate for at least 4 hours or overnight. Leave at room temperature for 1 hour before cooking.

Place strata on barbecue grill and cook indirect, hood down, for 40-45 minutes until set. Serve hot, cut in squares, with a tossed salad. It is also good when served cold.

RATATOUILLE

> **Charcoal kettle**: Indirect—Medium—Preheat not necessary
> **Gas kettle**: Indirect—Hot—Preheat 8-10 minutes
> **Covered gas grill**: Indirect—Hot—Preheat 8-10 minutes
> **Cooking time**: 55-60 minutes
> **Serves**: 6-8

2 medium-sized eggplants (aubergines)

1 red (bell) pepper

2 green (bell) peppers

6 zucchini (courgettes)

425 g (15 oz) can peeled tomatoes, chopped

½ tsp dried basil

½ tsp dried marjoram

2 tbsp chopped parsley

1 tsp sugar

1 tsp salt

freshly ground black pepper

½ cup (125 ml/4 fl oz) olive oil

3 medium-sized onions, sliced

2 cloves garlic, crushed

Trim eggplants and cut in 1 cm (½ in) slices. Sprinkle with salt and leave for 20 minutes, rinse and drain. Seed peppers, cut out ribs and slice. Trim zucchini and cut in 2 cm (¾ in) slices. Put all these vegetables together in a bowl. Chop tomatoes and add to bowl with their liquid; add herbs, sugar, salt and a good grinding of pepper. Place oil, onion and garlic in a large oven dish. Take out to barbecue.

Place oven dish containing oil, onion and garlic on barbecue grill and cook indirect, hood down, for 10 minutes. Add contents of bowl and toss well to distribute flavourings. Cover dish with lid or foil and cook indirect, hood down, for 30 minutes, remove lid and cook for further 15-20 minutes, hood down, until vegetables are tender. Serve from dish as a light meal with warm, crusty bread, or as an accompaniment to main meals.

TACOS WITH REFRIED BEANS

Cooking time: *15-18 minutes*
Serves: *6-8*

185 g (6 oz) natural Cheddar cheese

8 spring onions (scallions)

2 firm, ripe tomatoes

1 small head lettuce

1 cup (250 ml/8 fl oz) bottled taco sauce

12–16 taco shells

1 quantity Refried Beans (page 34)

Shred the cheese; trim and chop spring onions, including part of the green tops; peel tomatoes, halve and remove seeds, then dice; shred the lettuce. Arrange in groups on a platter. Put taco sauce in a bowl. Have taco shells in a cloth-lined basket.

Prepare Refried Beans on the barbecue, omitting cheese and spring onions. When hot, transfer to a bowl. Guests place a spoonful of beans in a taco, top it with salad ingredients and cheese and add taco sauce to taste.

Tacos with Chilli Con Carne: Replace Refried Beans with Chilli Con Carne (page 48) and serve as above.

GADO GADO

Cooking time: *20-30 minutes*
Serves: *4 as a meal, 6-8 as an accompaniment*

4-6 eggs

500 g (1 lb) small new potatoes

125 g (4 oz) young green beans

2 medium-sized carrots, julienned

1 cup (150 g/5 oz) bean sprouts

½ small head Chinese cabbage

1 small cucumber

1 medium-sized white onion

watercress sprigs

1 quantity Satay Sauce (page 98)

Place eggs in boiling water and simmer for 12 minutes until hard-boiled. Drain and run cold water into pan for a minute or so, then leave in cold water until cool. Shell immediately they are cooled so that eggs retain a good colour.

Gado gado

Boil potatoes in their skins for 15 minutes until tender, drain, rinse in cold water and peel when cold. Halve if necessary. Trim beans and leave whole or cut into 8 cm (3 in) lengths. Parboil beans and carrots separately in boiling, salted water until barely tender, drain in colander and run cold water over each vegetable to arrest cooking. Drain well. Rinse bean sprouts and nip off any dark ends. Shred cabbage finely. Peel cucumber if desired and slice thinly. Halve onion and slice thinly in semicircles. Prepare enough watercress sprigs to cover serving platter and soak cress in cold water to become crisp.

Drain watercress and spread onto serving platter. Pile shredded cabbage in centre and group other vegetables around cabbage. Quarter the eggs and arrange on vegetables. If not required immediately, cover platter with plastic film (wrap) and leave in refrigerator for up to 3 hours.

Make Satay Sauce and when cool, check consistency. If necessary thin down to a thick cream consistency with additional coconut milk. Place in a bowl. Serve the Gado Gado with warm or cool Satay Sauce.

PIPERADE

All barbecues: *Direct—Hot/Medium*
Cooking time: *20-25 minutes*
Serves: *6*

2 large green (bell) peppers

1 large onion

425 g (15 oz) can peeled tomatoes

3 tbsp olive oil

1 clove garlic, crushed

90 g (3 oz) sliced ham, cut in strips

salt and freshly ground black pepper

10 eggs

2 tbsp grated Gruyère cheese

1 tbsp chopped parsley

Seed the peppers and cut out ribs. Slice in strips and place in a bowl. Halve onion lengthwise and slice in semicircles, add to pepper strips. Chop the canned tomatoes and place in a bowl with liquid from can. Assemble other ingredients and take all out to barbecue.

Heat a large frying pan on the barbecue grill and add olive oil, onion and pepper strips. Cook gently on cooler section of grill until onion is transparent and pepper strips partly cooked. Move pan to hot section of grill or increase heat, add garlic, tomatoes, ham and salt and pepper to taste. Bring to the boil and cook until most of liquid has evaporated. Whisk eggs, add to vegetables and cook, stirring occasionally, until it is the consistency of moist scrambled eggs. Sprinkle on cheese and stir in lightly. Sprinkle with chopped parsley, and serve on warm plates with warm, crusty bread and a tossed green salad.

VEGETARIAN FRIED RICE

> **All barbecues:** *Direct—Hot*
> **Cooking time:** *7-9 minutes*
> **Serves:** *4-6*

1½ cups (315 g/10½ oz) short-grain rice

2 cups (250 g/8 oz) diced mixed vegetables

4 tbsp oil

1 clove garlic, crushed

1 tsp grated fresh ginger

250 g (8 oz) firm tofu (beancurd), diced

4 spring onions (scallions), chopped

2 tbsp soya sauce

1 tbsp dry sherry

salt and freshly ground black pepper

Boil rice beforehand using plenty of water, drain in colander and spread in a flat dish. Cover and chill for several hours. For the mixed vegetables, select from the following—diced young carrot, zucchini (courgettes), celery; small florets of broccoli or cauliflower and their stems, finely sliced; frozen green peas, green beans cut in short pieces. Prepare and assemble remaining ingredients and take all out to barbecue.

Place a wok, large frying pan or metal roasting pan on barbecue and add the oil. When fairly hot, add garlic and ginger and cook a few seconds, then add diced tofu and stir-fry over a hot fire for 1 minute. Add prepared vegetables and stir-fry for 2–3 minutes until crisp-tender, sprinkling in a little water to create steam to soften them. Add spring onions and rice and stir and toss over a hot fire until heated through. Sprinkle on soya sauce and sherry, season to taste with salt and pepper and toss well to distribute the flavours. Serve fried rice immediately as a light meal, or as an accompaniment to Chinese-style dishes.

Note: Purchase firm tofu from natural-food stores; soft tofu is not suitable as it breaks up.

EGGPLANT PILAF

> **Charcoal kettle:** *Indirect—Medium—Preheat 6-8 minutes*
> **Gas kettle:** *Indirect—Medium—Preheat 6-8 minutes*
> **Covered gas grill:** *Indirect—Medium—Preheat 6-8 minutes*
> **Cooking time:** *40-45 minutes*
> **Serves:** *6*

2 medium-sized eggplants (aubergines)

salt

1/3 cup (90 ml/3 fl oz) olive oil

1 large onion, chopped

1 clove garlic, crushed

425 g (15 oz) can peeled tomatoes, chopped

1 tbsp tomato paste

2 tbsp chopped flat-leaf parsley

2 tsp chopped fresh mint

1 tsp sugar

salt and freshly ground black pepper

2 cups (420 g/14 oz) long-grain rice

2½ cups (625 ml/20 fl oz) boiling water

natural yoghurt for serving

Cut eggplants into 2 cm (¾ in) cubes with skin on. Place in a colander, sprinkle with salt, and leave for 20–30 minutes. Rinse well and dry by pressing between layers of kitchen paper.

Heat oil in a Dutch oven or flameproof casserole dish, add eggplant cubes and fry on high heat until lightly browned, stirring often. Reduce heat, add onion and garlic and cook on low heat for 8–10 minutes until onion is soft. Add tomatoes and their liquid, tomato paste, herbs, sugar and salt and pepper to taste. Bring to the boil, simmer for 5 minutes and remove from heat. Recipe may be prepared in advance to this stage.

Rinse rice until water runs clear. Add to eggplant mixture. Stir in boiling water and cover tightly with lid. Place pilaf on barbecue grill and cook indirect, hood down, for 20 minutes until rice is just tender. Stand, covered, for 10 minutes, fluff up with fork and serve as a light meal with natural yoghurt and warm pita breads. Pilaf may also be served as an accompaniment to meats and poultry.

Vegetarian fried rice

BEEF AND VEAL

Meat is the traditional star of a barbecue meal, and beef is preferred to other meats. The recipes show clearly that there are many options to the traditional steak, options which were not possible until covered barbecue grilling. Your covered grill is virtually an outdoor oven, so use it to its full potential—cook a magnificent roast, simmer a casserole, increase your meal choices with veal, a meat not recommended for traditional barbecue cooking because it is so lean and ends up dry and unappetising. But not with the covered grill!

For roasts, refer to page 19 for further details about cooking times and checking internal temperature with a meat thermometer.

Steak and kidney pie

STEAK AND KIDNEY PIE

The first stage of the recipe is cooked in a conventional oven, although directions give the barbecue alternative. Directions for the various barbecues relate to final cooking with pastry.

> *Charcoal kettle: Indirect—Medium—Preheat 10-12 minutes*
> *Gas kettle: Indirect—Hot/Medium—Preheat 10-12 minutes*
> *Covered gas grill: Indirect—Hot/Medium—Preheat 10-12 minutes*
> *Cooking time: 3-3½ hours*
> *Serves: 6-8*

1.25 kg (2½ lb) chuck steak

125 g (4 oz) beef kidney or 2-3 lamb kidneys

½ cup (60 g/2 oz) plain (all-purpose) flour

1½ tsp salt

freshly ground black pepper

1 small onion, chopped

1 cup (250 ml/8 fl oz) dry red wine

2 tbsp port

½ cup (125 ml/4 fl oz) strong beef stock (broth)

375 g (12 oz) prepared puff or shortcrust pastry

beaten egg to glaze

Trim and cube the steak. Skin kidney, cut out fatty cores and dice. Mix flour with salt and plenty of pepper in a plastic bag, add meats and shake well to coat. Tip into a 6-cup deep pie dish. Add onion, wine, port and stock. Cover with foil and cook in conventional oven at 150-160°C (300-325°F/Gas 2) for 2-2½ hours. Alternatively, cook in a covered barbecue; preheat on high for 5-6 minutes then cook indirect, hood down, on low heat or medium fire for charcoal kettle. When meat is tender, allow to cool. Filling can be prepared a day or two ahead and stored in refrigerator.

Place a pie funnel in the centre of the pie filling. Roll out pastry and cut generously to fit dish top. Brush rim of dish with water and place pastry on top. Press onto dish, trim off excess and glaze top with beaten egg—do not glaze cut edge of puff pastry. Cut a vent in the centre and decorate with shapes cut from trimmings.

Place on grill in hot gas barbecue and cook indirect, hood down, for 15 minutes or until puff pastry is risen and golden brown, reduce to medium and cook for further 30-35 minutes; check during cooking and reduce further if necessary. For charcoal kettle, temperature is hot at beginning of cooking and reduces as coals burn down. Serve with vegetables of choice.

BARBECUED ONION STEAK

All barbecues: *Direct—Hot reducing to Medium*
Cooking time: *18-24 minutes*
Serves: *5-6*

1 slice rump (boneless top sirloin) steak cut 4 cm (1½ in) thick

1 quantity Red Wine Marinade (page 100)

3 spring onions (scallions), thinly sliced

Devilled Tomato Butter (page 101), optional

Trim fat if necessary and nick selvedge on steak in 3-4 places to keep it flat during cooking. Place in a shallow dish, pour on Red Wine Marinade and marinate at room temperature for up to 2 hours, turning occasionally. Steak may be marinated in refrigerator, covered, overnight.

Heat barbecue until hot, with hotplate in position if using instead of grill. Drain marinade into a small pan and place on side of grill to heat. Place steak on grill or hotplate and sear for 2-3 minutes each side. Reduce heat or move steak to cooler part of barbecue and cook, hood down, for further 7-9 minutes each side, basting occasionally with marinade. Remove to a warm platter and sprinkle spring onions on top. Stand for 5 minutes, then carve in thick slices and serve with Devilled Tomato Butter (if desired), a salad and other accompaniments of choice.

Suggested BBQ accompaniment: Whole mushrooms cooked alongside the steak halfway through cooking time, basted with marinade.

Barbecued onion steak

BEEF AND BLUE CHEESE IN FILLO

Charcoal kettle: *Indirect—Medium—Preheat 8-10 minutes*
Gas kettle: *Indirect—Hot—Preheat 8-10 minutes*
Covered gas grill: *Indirect—Hot—Preheat 8-10 minutes*
Cooking time: *12-15 minutes*
Serves: *6*

6 fillet (tenderloin) steaks, 4 cm (1½ in) thick

freshly ground black pepper

2 tbsp butter

3 spring onions (scallions), chopped

1 cup (125 g/4 oz) chopped small mushrooms

½ cup (30 g/1 oz) soft white breadcrumbs

1 tbsp port

125 g (4 oz) blue vein cheese

12 sheets fillo pastry

⅓ cup (90 ml/3 fl oz) melted ghee (clarified butter)

Trim any fat and visible silver skin from sides of steaks. Season beef with pepper. Heat butter in a frying pan and sear steaks on both sides. Remove to a plate. Add spring onions and mushrooms to pan and cook gently until softened. Cool, mix in crumbs, port and crumbled cheese.

Butter 2 sheets fillo pastry together, brush top with butter and fold in half across the length. Place a steak in the centre, top with a portion of cheese mixture. Bring pastry up over filling, double-fold, fold in sides as if wrapping a package and tuck sides under. Place on a greased baking tray. Repeat with remaining ingredients. Brush parcels with remaining butter. Parcels may be covered with plastic and refrigerated overnight; bring to room temperature 2 hours before cooking.

Place tray of parcels on barbecue grill and cook indirect, hood down, for 12 minutes for rare beef, 15 minutes for medium. Serve immediately with steamed yellow button squash and steamed julienne carrots tossed with butter and chives.

Suggested BBQ accompaniments: Cook squash and carrots by direct heat before heating barbecue for beef parcels (see Barbecue-steamed Vegetables, page 89). Reheat quickly over direct heat just before serving—both vegetables can be reheated. Timing is important for the beef; parcels should cook without other foods.

FESTIVE ROAST BEEF

> **Charcoal kettle**: *Indirect—Medium—Preheat not necessary*
> **Gas kettle**: *Indirect—Hot—Preheat 8-10 minutes*
> **Covered gas grill**: *Indirect—Hot—Preheat 8-10 minutes*
> **Cooking time**: *2-2½ hours*
> **Serves**: *8-10*

1 beef rib roast, about 3 kg (6 lb)

2 tbsp butter

1 small onion, finely chopped

1 cup (125 g/4 oz) finely chopped mushrooms

½ cup (60 g/2 oz) finely chopped walnuts

125 g (4 oz) pâté de foie gras

salt and freshly ground black pepper

Stand roast upright on a board. With a pointed knife, cut deep pockets into the meat from the top of the roast, just in front of each rib bone. Heat butter in a pan, add onion and cook gently until soft, add mushrooms and cook until limp, increase heat and evaporate liquid. Cool mixture, then stir in walnuts and pâté, and season with salt and pepper. Spoon mixture into pockets with a teaspoon, pressing it down with the spoon. Rub meat surfaces with pepper, fat surface with salt and pepper.

Place roast upright on barbecue grill, directly over drip pan containing 2 cups water. Cook indirect, hood down, for 2-2½ hours or until cooked to taste (see page 20 for more details). Remove roast to platter, cover loosely with foil and let it stand for 20 minutes before carving. Carve and serve with skimmed juices from drip pan and vegetables of choice.

Suggested BBQ accompaniments: Barbecue-steamed New Potatoes (page 90) or Roast Vegetables (page 88), depending on space available in barbecue. A green vegetable may be cooked by direct heat while roast is standing; see Barbecue-steamed Vegetables (page 89) for details.

BEEF BURGUNDY

> **Charcoal kettle**: *Indirect—Medium—Preheat not necessary*
> **Gas kettle**: *Indirect—Medium/Low—Preheat 6-8 minutes*
> **Covered gas grill**: *Indirect—Medium/Low—Preheat 6-8 minutes*
> **Cooking time**: *2-2½ hours*
> **Serves**: *6*

1.25 kg (2½ lb) chuck steak, cubed

¼ cup (30 g/1 oz) seasoned flour

3 slices bacon, chopped

12 pickling onions

125 g (4 oz) button mushrooms, trimmed

bouquet garni (leafy celery sprig, 3 parsley sprigs, 1 bay leaf)

½ tsp dried thyme leaves

1 tsp sugar

2 tbsp tomato paste

1¼ cups (310 ml/10 fl oz) dry red wine

Trim steak before cubing. Put seasoned flour into a plastic bag, add meat cubes and shake well. Tip into a casserole dish and add the bacon. Peel onions and cut a cross in the root ends to prevent centres popping. Add to casserole dish with the mushrooms and push the bouquet garni into the centre. Mix thyme and sugar into tomato paste and wine, pour over casserole contents and cover with lid.

Place on barbecue grill and cook indirect, hood down, for 2-2½ hours, stirring once or twice during cooking. If casserole boils rather than simmers, reduce heat to low. When beef is tender, remove bouquet garni and discard. Serve the beef from the dish, with barbecue-cooked potatoes, warm crusty French bread and a green vegetable.

Suggested BBQ accompaniments: Prepare Potatoes Boulangère (page 91) and place alongside casserole after it has been cooking for 45 minutes. Select a green vegetable for indirect cooking (see Barbecue-steamed Vegetables, page 89), and add to barbecue during latter part of cooking. Heat French bread on barbecue during last 10 minutes.

CARBONNADE OF BEEF

Barbecue cooking is appropriate for this dish, as 'carbonnade' is a French term meaning 'cooked over hot coals'.

> **Charcoal kettle**: *Indirect—Medium—Preheat not necessary*
> **Gas kettle**: *Indirect—Medium—Preheat 6-8 minutes*
> **Covered gas grill**: *Indirect—Medium—Preheat 6-8 minutes*
> **Cooking time**: *1-1½ hours*
> **Serves**: *6*

1 kg (2 lb) chuck steak

1 packet French Onion soup mix

1 tbsp brown sugar

Festive roast beef

Place rib racks on barbecue grill directly over drip pan. Cook indirect, hood down, for 30 minutes. Brush again with butter during cooking and turn over once. Place pan of sauce on grill and baste racks with sauce. Continue to cook indirect for further hour, baste racks and turn them every 10-15 minutes. Meat should be crusty on the outside, tender and succulent within. Cut between the bones and pile ribs on a platter, spoon over more of the sauce and serve remaining sauce separately. Serve as a finger food.

BARBECUED MEAT LOAF

Charcoal kettle: *Indirect—Medium—Preheat not necessary*
Gas kettle: *Indirect—Hot—Preheat 6-8 minutes*
Covered gas grill: *Indirect—Hot—Preheat 6-8 minutes*
Cooking time: *1-1¼ hours*
Serves: *6-8*

1 cup (60 g/2 oz) soft breadcrumbs

1 cup (250 ml/8 fl oz) Barbecue Sauce (page 98)

1 small onion, grated

2 eggs

1 tbsp chopped parsley

salt and freshly ground pepper

1 kg (2 lb) finely ground beef

1 tbsp oil

Put breadcrumbs in a large bowl and add ⅓ cup (90 ml/3 fl oz) of the prepared Barbecue Sauce. Add onion, eggs, parsley, about 1 teaspoon salt and pepper to taste. Mix thoroughly and stand 5 minutes. Add ground beef and mix lightly and thoroughly until combined. Turn onto a board and shape into a loaf with moistened hands. Brush a roasting pan with oil, lift in meat loaf using 2 wide spatulas and pat back into shape. Brush with oil and score top into diamonds with the back of a knife. Take out to barbecue with remaining Barbecue Sauce in a small pan.

Place pan with loaf on barbecue grill and cook indirect, hood down, for 1 hour. After 15 minutes, brush loaf with sauce and brush again each 10 minutes until loaf is well glazed and cooked through. Remove to a warm platter and stand 10 minutes. Place remaining sauce over direct heat, add pan juices and bring

Carbonnade of beef

1 tsp mustard powder

1 bay leaf

1 cup (250 ml/8 fl oz) beer

Cheese Bread

1 French bread stick

butter

French mustard

shredded Gruyère cheese

Trim the steak and cut into 2.5 cm (1 in) cubes. Put dry soup mix in a plastic bag, add beef and shake to coat. Tip into casserole dish. Mix brown sugar and mustard to break up lumps and add to meat with bay leaf. Pour beer over beef, cover tightly with lid or foil.

Place casserole on barbecue grill and cook, indirect, for 1½-2 hours, until beef is tender. Stir once during cooking. Serve with Cheese Bread and Green Pasta Salad (page 96), omitting the olives.

Cheese Bread: Slice bread stick diagonally 2 cm (¾ in) thick and place on small baking tray. Spread slices with butter and a little French mustard, and sprinkle thickly with cheese. Place tray of bread on warming rack over casserole in gas grill, or elevated on an upturned layer-cake pan in gas or charcoal kettle, 15 minutes before casserole is cooked. Cook until cheese is bubbly and lightly browned.

DEVILLED BEEF RIBS

Charcoal kettle: *Indirect—Medium—Preheat 8-10 minutes*
Gas kettle: *Indirect—Hot—Preheat 8-10 minutes*
Covered gas grill: *Indirect—Hot—Preheat 8-10 minutes*
Cooking time: *1½ hours*
Serves: *6*

3 racks beef ribs, about 1.5 kg (3 lb)

1 tsp salt

1 tsp freshly ground black pepper

1 tsp mustard powder

1 tsp ground ginger

¼ cup (60 g/2 oz) butter or margarine, melted

1 quantity Barbecue Sauce (page 98)

The racks of rib bones are those removed from the prime rib when it is boned. The chine bone (backbone) is removed, leaving long rib bones with succulent meat between the bones. As bones are long, ask butcher to prepare racks with rib bones about 12-15 cm (6-7 in) long. Mix salt, pepper, mustard and ginger and rub onto ribs. Brush with melted butter. Put Barbecue Sauce in a saucepan. Take all out to barbecue.

to the boil. Serve loaf sliced with the sauce, a potato dish and a green vegetable or a tossed salad.

Suggested BBQ accompaniments: Jacket-baked potatoes may be put on to cook 15 minutes before adding meat loaf. Prepare Cauliflower with Creamed Corn Sauce (page 91) and place beside meat loaf halfway through cooking the loaf.

CHILLI CON CARNE

All barbecues: *Direct—Hot reducing to Medium*
Cooking time: *45-50 minutes*
Serves: *6-8*

2 tbsp oil

1 large onion, chopped

2 cloves garlic, crushed

1 kg (2 lb) ground beef

440 g (1 lb) can peeled tomatoes, chopped

2 tbsp tomato paste

1 tsp ground coriander

½ tsp ground cumin

1 tsp dried oregano

½ tsp chilli powder

1 tsp sugar

salt and freshly ground black pepper

1 small green (bell) pepper, chopped

1 small red (bell) pepper, chopped

2 x 440 g (1 lb) cans red kidney beans

Place a large Dutch oven on side of barbecue grill where heat is medium and add oil, onion and garlic. Fry gently until onion is soft. Move to hot part of grill, add beef and cook, stirring often, until lumps are broken up and meat loses red colour. Add tomatoes and their liquid and remaining ingredients except for chopped peppers and beans, seasoning to taste with salt and pepper. Bring to a simmer, cover and move to side of charcoal grill, or reduce flame on gas barbecue to medium. Cook gently, hood down, for 15 minutes. Add peppers, drained beans and a little bean liquid if needed. Cover and simmer for further 30 minutes, reducing to medium-low if Chilli boils too rapidly. Serve hot with corn muffins or corn bread and a green salad.

Chilli con carne

Suggested BBQ accompaniment: Prepare Corn and Bacon Muffins (page 118) and bake indirect before cooking the Chilli. Leave in muffin pan and reheat on grill next to Chilli during last 5 minutes of cooking. Alternatively, omit bacon from muffin mixture, spread batter in a greased 20 cm (8 in) square cake pan and bake for 30–35 minutes; cut into squares to serve.

BEEFBURGERS WITH TOMATO-CHILLI SAUCE

All barbecues: *Direct—Hot*
Cooking time: *12-16 minutes*
Serves: *6*

750 g (1½ lb) finely ground beef

1 small onion, finely chopped

½ small green (bell) pepper, shredded

1 tsp dried oregano

1 tsp salt

freshly ground black pepper

oil

1 quantity Tomato-chilli Sauce (page 99)

6 slices natural Cheddar cheese

6 hamburger buns or round bread rolls

shredded lettuce, tomato and avocado slices, green (bell) pepper rings for serving

Ground beef should be very fresh and stored in refrigerator for no more than 1 day before using; frozen ground beef should be thawed in refrigerator for 24 hours. Put ground beef in a bowl with onion, green pepper, oregano, salt and pepper. Mix lightly and thoroughly until combined, and shape into 6 thick, round patties. Place on a tray, cover with plastic film and chill for 1 hour or longer. Take out to barbecue with remaining ingredients.

Place sauce in a pan and heat at side of barbecue. Brush burgers each side with oil and cook on grill or hotplate of well-heated barbecue. Cook for about 6-8 minutes each side until cooked to taste—preferably underdone. Meanwhile, split the buns or bread rolls and toast cut side on side of grill. Top each burger with a slice of cheese, put hood down for about 30 seconds until cheese melts. Place base of buns on 6 plates, top each with a burger and spoon sauce on top. Lean top of bun on the side of the burger. Add garnish of lettuce, tomato, avocado and green pepper and serve remainder of sauce separately. These should be eaten with a knife and fork.

ROAST BEEF WITH HORSERADISH-MUSTARD BUTTER

> *Charcoal kettle:* *Indirect—Medium—Preheat 8-10 minutes*
> *Gas kettle:* *Indirect—Hot—Preheat 8-10 minutes*
> *Covered gas grill:* *Indirect—Hot—Preheat 8-10 minutes*
> *Cooking time:* *1½ hours*
> *Serves:* *6-8*

1 beef rib eye or boneless sirloin roast, about 1.5 kg (3 lb)

freshly ground black pepper

oil

Horseradish-mustard Butter

1 cup (250 g/8 oz) butter at room temperature

2 tbsp prepared horseradish

3 tsp Dijon mustard

1 tbsp finely chopped parsley

Using a sharp knife, remove any fine membrane on the rib eye roast as this causes the roast to gather up during cooking, making meat thicker and lengthening cooking time. Tie roast at intervals with white string to keep shape. If using boneless sirloin, trim off some of the fat, leaving a thin layer (no need to tie it). Season beef with pepper and brush with oil.

Place roast on barbecue grill directly over drip pan and cook indirect, hood down, for 1-1½ hours or until beef is cooked to taste. Check degree of cooking with meat thermometer (see page 19). Transfer to carving platter, cover loosely with foil and leave to stand 10 minutes before carving. Serve carved in thick slices with barbecued vegetables and Horseradish-mustard Butter served separately.

Horseradish-mustard Butter: Put softened butter in a bowl and cream lightly with a wooden spoon. Add remaining ingredients and mix only until well-combined. Pack into a butter crock, cover and chill until required. Leftover butter is excellent as a spread for cold roast beef sandwiches.

Suggested BBQ accompaniments: Butternut Nutmeg Pumpkin (page 93) and jacket potatoes placed on grill with the beef. Add Corn in Husks (page 94) halfway through cooking. Sliced mushrooms, cooked in butter, can also be added if space permits.

Roast beef with horseradish-mustard butter

SMOKED BEEF FILLET WITH BLACKBERRIES

> *Charcoal kettle:* *Indirect—Medium—Preheat 10-12 minutes*
> *Gas kettle:* *Indirect—Hot—Preheat 10-12 minutes*
> *Covered gas grill:* *Indirect—Hot—Preheat 10-12 minutes*
> *Cooking time:* *40-50 minutes*
> *Serves:* *6-8*

1 beef fillet (tenderloin), about 1.25 kg (2½ lb)

freshly ground black pepper

2 tbsp melted butter

1 cup (250 ml/8 fl oz) canned beef consommé

½ cup (125 ml/4 fl oz) port

1 cup (125 g/4 oz) fresh or frozen blackberries

¼ cup (60 ml/2 fl oz) cream

2 tbsp Beurre Manie (page 18)

2 cups (125 g/4 oz) hickory chips, soaked (see page 15)

Trim silver skin from fillet and tie with string into a neat shape. Season with pepper and brush with melted butter. Mix consomme and port in a jug, put blackberries in a bowl, cream in another jug and beurre manie in a dish. Wrap hickory chips in foil to make 2 'logs'. Take all out to barbecue.

While barbecue is heating, place hickory 'logs' on lava rocks or put one log each side of charcoal fire in kettle. When barbecue is heated, place fillet on grill directly over drip pan. Cook indirect, hood down, for 40 minutes for medium rare, 45-50 minutes for medium. Remove fillet to a platter, cover loosely with foil and keep warm at side of barbecue.

Place a frying pan over direct heat, add consomme–port mixture and bring to the boil. Boil for 3-4 minutes to reduce a little, add blackberries and return to boil. Stir in Beurre Manie, a little at a time, until sauce is lightly thickened, stir in cream and heat through. Serve beef sliced with blackberry sauce served separately.

Suggested BBQ accompaniment: Cook asparagus spears or snow peas (mange-tout) by direct heat when making the sauce. Follow directions for Barbecue-steamed Vegetables, page 89.

BEEF SATAYS

All barbecues: Direct—Hot reducing to Medium
Cooking time: 8-10 minutes
Serves: 5-6

1 kg (2 lb) rump or boneless sirloin steak

1 quantity Satay Sauce (page 98)

½ cup (125 ml/4 fl oz) water

grated rind and juice of ½ lemon

½ tsp ground coriander

½ tsp ground cumin

1 tbsp soya sauce

sliced cucumber

raw onion rings

Trim steak and cut into 2 cm (¾ inch) cubes. In a large bowl, mix ½ cup (125 ml/4 fl oz) of the Satay Sauce with the water, lemon rind and juice, coriander, cumin and soya sauce. Add beef cubes and stir well to coat. Cover and leave at room temperature 1 hour, or refrigerate for several hours until required. Soak 18 bamboo satay sticks in hot water for 1-2 hours.

When required for cooking, thread 5-6 beef cubes close together towards one end of satay sticks, leaving a section of stick free of meat. Place over direct heat and barbecue for 8-10 minutes, searing first on high heat. Complete cooking over medium heat, basting occasionally with marinade. Serve immediately on a bed of sliced cucumber and onion rings with remainder of Satay Sauce and a bowl of boiled rice served separately if desired.

Suggested BBQ accompaniment: Before cooking the satays, cook Barbecue-steamed Rice (page 95), using direct cooking method. Keep warm on side of barbecue while cooking satays.

KOREAN BEEF SHORT RIBS

All barbecues: Direct—Hot reducing to Medium
Cooking time: 12-15 minutes
Serves: 6

2 kg (4 lb) beef short ribs

1 tbsp sugar

1 tbsp sesame oil

2 cloves garlic, finely chopped

2 tbsp dark soya sauce

freshly ground black pepper

oil

The short ribs used for this traditional Korean dish are from the mid rib section of the carcase, just below the prime ribs. Some of the short ribs contain two or three layers of meat separated with fat; for Korean ribs, only one layer of meat with a fine covering of fat should be on each bone. Trim off the excess meat and fat layers, and use for a casserole. Ribs should be about 5 cm (2 in) square.

Score halfway through meat layer in criss-cross fashion. Rub sugar thoroughly into slashes, then rub in sesame oil. Place in a dish, cover and refrigerate for at least 8 hours. Mix garlic with soya sauce and pepper and rub into slashes. Cover and leave for 1-2 hours at least, or refrigerate overnight if necessary.

Oil barbecue grill and place ribs bone side down to begin with. Cook until browned and crisp on all sides, turning frequently. Reduce heat to medium, or move ribs to cooler section of the barbecue so they can finish cooking more slowly. Meat should be cooked to medium; if well-done, meat will toughen. Pile ribs in a large dish and serve as finger food.

CHINESE SIZZLING STEAK

All barbecues: Direct—Hot
Cooking time: about 12 minutes
Serves: 4-5

500 g (1 lb) point of fillet (tenderloin tip) in 1-2 pieces

3 small onions

1 clove garlic, crushed

1 tsp grated fresh ginger

1/3 cup (90 ml/3 oz) bottled plum sauce

1 tbsp Worcestershire sauce

2 tbsp tomato ketchup

1 tbsp soya sauce

1 tbsp dry sherry

3-4 tbsp oil

Point of fillet (tenderloin tip) is the tapered section of a whole fillet, and is the right diameter for preparing this dish. Purchase in one piece or pieces, depending on size. Slice thinly with a sharp knife, and flatten slices with side of cleaver. Quarter onions and separate into leaves. Mix garlic and ginger in a small bowl, sauces, ketchup and sherry in a jug. Assemble all ingredients on a tray and take out to barbecue.

Beef satays

Place 2 cast iron sizzle plates on one side of barbecue grill to heat. Heat a wok or large frying pan over high heat, placing directly onto lava rock, or use a wok ring for gas barbecues. Add 2 tablespoons oil and when hot, add steak slices, spreading them out. Stir-fry rapidly until browned and remove to a bowl. Add remaining oil with onion leaves, garlic and ginger and stir-fry until onion is tinged with brown but still crisp. Stir in sauce mixture, bring to the boil, return steak to wok and toss over heat for 1-2 minutes. Dish out immediately onto hot sizzle plates and lift plates, by special handle for such plates, onto wooden bases. Serve immediately with boiled rice.

Suggested BBQ accompaniment: Boil the rice by direct heat before cooking the steak. Use 1½-cup quantity and follow Chinese Steamed Rice directions on page 95.

STEAK ROLLS TERIYAKI

Charcoal kettle: Indirect—Medium—Preheat 8-10 minutes
Gas kettle: Indirect—Hot—Preheat 8-10 minutes
Covered gas grill: Indirect—Hot—Preheat 8-10 minutes
Cooking time: 45-60 minutes
Serves: 6-8

2 flank skirt steaks, each about 500 g (1 lb), or 1 large steak, about 1 kg (2 lb)

1 medium-sized carrot

12 green beans

4 spring onions (scallions)

10 spinach leaves

freshly ground black pepper

1 quantity Teriyaki Marinade (page 100)

½ cup (125 ml/4 fl oz) beef stock (broth)

Size of flank skirt steak depends on size of beef carcase. If using a 1 kg (2 lb) steak, slit it in half through the centre to give 2 pieces of similar shape and thickness. Score steaks on one side in a diamond pattern, place in a shallow dish and pour on marinade. Cover and marinate 1 hour, turning occasionally.

Scrape carrot and cut into julienne strips the length of the carrot. Trim beans and leave whole. Trim spring onions to same length as steaks. Parboil carrots and beans in lightly salted water for 4 minutes. Wash spinach leaves, place in a colander and pour boiling water over leaves; drain well.

Drain steaks and place scored side down on a board. Put spinach leaves on steaks, and arrange carrots, beans and spring onions lengthways on top of spinach. Roll up from longer side into 2 rolls and secure with string. Put marinade and stock into a small pan.

Place rolls on oiled grill directly over drip pan and cook indirect, hood down, for 45-60 minutes; baste occasionally with marinade placed at side of grill. Add a little water to marinade if it reduces. Place rolls on a warm platter, remove strings, cover with foil and stand 10 minutes. Pour hot marinade into a bowl. Slice rolls and serve with the marinade and boiled rice.

Suggested BBQ accompaniment: Cook Barbecue-steamed Rice (page 95), using 2-cup quantity of short-grain rice. Place next to rolls 20 minutes before end of cooking.

VEAL BIRDS

Charcoal kettle: Indirect—Medium—Preheat not necessary
Gas kettle: Indirect—Medium—Preheat 6-8 minutes
Covered gas grill: Indirect—Medium—Preheat 6-8 minutes
Cooking time: 1-1¼ hours
Serves: 6

750 g (1½ lb) thin veal leg steaks (cutlets)

2 tbsp seasoned flour

2 tbsp butter or oil

1 small onion, chopped

1 medium-sized carrot, chopped

1 stalk celery, finely chopped

¼ cup (60 ml/2 fl oz) dry red wine

½ cup (125 ml/4 fl oz) chicken stock (broth)

salt and freshly ground black pepper

bouquet garni

Herb Stuffing

3 spring onions (scallions), chopped

2 tbsp butter or margarine

1½ cups (90 g/3 oz) soft white breadcrumbs

Veal birds

1 tbsp chopped parsley

1 tsp chopped fresh thyme

pinch dried sage

1 small egg, beaten

Halve veal steaks if large. Prepare herb stuffing and spread on each steak. Roll up and tie securely with wet white string. Dust rolls with seasoned flour.

Heat butter in a frying pan with lid to fit, or in flameproof casserole dish. Add rolls and brown on all sides. Remove to a plate. Reduce heat and add vegetables to pan. Cook gently 5-6 minutes. Stir in wine and stock, season with salt and pepper and add bouquet garni. Place rolls on top of vegetables. Cover and refrigerate at this stage if not to be cooked immediately; may be kept overnight.

To complete cooking, place covered pan or casserole on barbecue grill and cook indirect, hood down, for 50-60 minutes until tender. Remove bouquet garni and strings from rolls. Serve with the vegetables and juices, cooked potato slices and a green salad.

Herb Stuffing: Gently cook spring onion in butter until soft and add to crumbs with herbs. Lightly mix in enough egg to bind, season to taste.

Suggested BBQ accompaniment: Cut 3 large potatoes in 2 cm (¾ in) slices with skin on, brush with oil and place on grill around pan at start of cooking. Turn occasionally.

SWISS VEAL ROAST

Charcoal kettle: Indirect—Medium—Preheat not necessary
Gas kettle: Indirect—Hot—Preheat 8-10 minutes
Covered gas grill: Indirect—Hot—Preheat 8-10 minutes
Cooking time: 1½-2 hours
Serves: 6-8

1 veal loin, boned, about 1.5 kg (3 lb)

salt and freshly ground black pepper

1 tbsp butter or margarine

2 tsp Dijon mustard

1 tbsp finely chopped parsley

1 tbsp finely chopped spring onions (scallions)

2 slices bread, crusts removed

2 thin slices (60 g/2 oz) smoked leg ham

2 thin slices (60 g/2 oz) Swiss cheese

oil

Cream Sauce (optional)

¼ cup (60 ml/2 fl oz) strong chicken stock (broth)

3-4 tbsp cream

Open out veal loin on board and season with salt and pepper. Mix butter with mustard, parsley and spring onions and spread on each side of the bread. Place bread along centre of veal, top with ham and cheese slices and roll up. Tie securely with wet white string, season with salt and pepper and brush with oil.

Place roast on oiled barbecue grill directly over a drip pan containing 1 cup water. Roast indirect, hood down, for 1½-2 hours until cooked to taste. Remove to a platter, cover loosely with foil and stand for 10 minutes before carving. Serve sliced with Cream Sauce if desired, and barbecue-cooked accompaniments.

Cream Sauce: Place drip pan over direct heat and add strong chicken stock. Stir well to dissolve browned juices and stir in cream. Strain into sauceboat and serve with the veal.

Suggested BBQ accompaniments: Cook new potatoes and green beans by indirect heat, following directions for Barbecue-steamed New Potatoes (page

Swiss veal roast

90) and Barbecue-steamed Vegetables (page 89). Place potatoes alongside roast at beginning of cooking, add beans 20 minutes before end of cooking time.

MUSTARD CREAM RACK OF VEAL

Charcoal kettle: Indirect—Medium—Preheat not necessary
Gas kettle: Indirect—Hot—Preheat 8-10 minutes
Covered gas grill: Indirect—Hot—Preheat 8-10 minutes
Cooking time: 1½-2 hours
Serves: 6-8

1 rack of veal (veal rib roast) with 6-9 ribs

salt and freshly ground black pepper

2 tbsp melted butter

½ cup (125 ml/4 fl oz) dry white wine

½ cup (125 ml/4 fl oz) chicken stock (broth)

2 tbsp Dijon mustard

grated rind of 1 large orange

1 cup cream

Weight of veal rack varies with size of veal carcase, and can weigh 1.5-2.5 kg (3-5 lb), so choose size according to number of serves required. Season with salt and pepper and place rib side down in a greased roasting pan. Brush butter over rack. Mix wine and stock in a jug, mix mustard and orange rind in a small bowl. Take veal and other ingredients out to barbecue.

Place pan with veal on grill and cook indirect, hood down, for 30 minutes. Pour wine mixture over veal and continue to cook for further 30-45 minutes, depending on size of rack; baste occasionally with dish juices. Spread mustard-orange rind mixture over top and sides of veal and gently pour cream over the meat. Continue to cook for further 30-45 minutes, basting occasionally. Place veal onto a warm serving platter. Bring sauce to the boil over direct heat, scraping down brown bits on sides of dish; add a little stock if needed. Pour into sauceboat. Carve veal between rib bones and serve with the sauce and vegetable accompaniments of choice.

Suggested BBQ accompaniments: Ginger Orange Pumpkin (page 89), cooked indirect alongside veal; add after first 30 minutes. Steamed broccoli, cooked by direct heat while sauce is being completed, see Barbecue-steamed Vegetables (page 89).

VEAL WITH GRUYÈRE CRUST

Charcoal kettle: Indirect—Medium—Preheat not necessary
Gas kettle: Indirect—Medium—Preheat 8-10 minutes
Covered gas grill: Indirect—Medium—Preheat 8-10 minutes
Cooking time: about 3 hours
Serves: 8-10

1 veal leg roast, about 2.5 kg (5 lb)

1/3 cup (90 g/3 oz) butter

2 large onions, chopped

1 cup (250 ml/8 fl oz) dry white wine

1/2 cup (125 ml/4 fl oz) strong chicken stock (broth)

salt and freshly ground white pepper

1 cup (125 g/4 oz) grated Gruyère cheese

1/2 cup (30 g/1 oz) soft breadcrumbs

Veal with Gruyère crust

If butcher stocks light veal, ask for leg with chump (sirloin) removed, otherwise purchase shank end of a half-leg (veal round roast).

Melt butter in a frying pan, pour half the butter into a bowl and reserve. Add onion to pan and cook gently for 10 minutes until soft without browning. Add wine, stock, and salt and pepper to taste, bring to the boil and remove from heat. Brush a roasting pan with butter, put in the veal and brush leg with liquid from onion mixture. Mix cheese and crumbs and press firmly over top and sides of leg. Carefully spoon remaining butter over coating. Spoon onion mixture around veal, taking care not to disturb cheese coating.

Place pan on barbecue grill and cook indirect, hood down, turning pan occasionally to brown veal evenly. Gently baste veal with pan liquid about 3 times. Cook for about 3 hours until juices run clear, or check with meat thermometer (page 19). Remove veal to warm platter and stand in a warm place, uncovered, for 20 minutes. Place pan over direct heat, bring onion mixture to the boil and pour into sauceboat. Carve veal in thickish slices and serve with sauce and steamed asparagus. No other accompaniment is needed.

Suggested BBQ accompaniment: When boiling sauce over direct heat, cook asparagus alongside in a frying pan as directed for Barbecue-steamed Vegetables (page 89).

VEAL WITH PEPPERCORN CREAM SAUCE

All barbecues: Direct—Hot
Cooking time: 12-15 minutes
Serves: 6

6 escalopes of veal from loin, each about 125 g (4 oz)

1/2 cup (125 ml/4 fl oz) dry white wine

1/2 cup (125 ml/4 fl oz) chicken stock (broth)

2 tsp lemon juice

pinch salt

1/2 tsp sugar

1 tsp drained green peppercorns

1 tsp drained pink peppercorns

1 tbsp oil

1 tbsp butter

1 tbsp Beurre Manié (page 18)

1/2 cup (125 ml/4 fl oz) cream

For the escalopes, have butcher remove the eye meat from a loin of veal. If loin is large in diameter, have it sliced 2 cm (¾ in) thick, if small, have it sliced 4 cm (1½ in) thick, with slices butterflied (cut almost through and opened out). Assemble all ingredients, mixing the liquids with salt, sugar and peppercorns in a jug. Take out to barbecue.

Heat a large frying pan over direct heat, add oil and butter and when foaming subsides, brown veal quickly on each side, then continue to cook for further 2-3 minutes each side until juices run clear. Remove to a warm platter and keep warm, covered, at side of barbecue. Stir liquids and peppercorn mixture into pan juices, mashing peppercorns lightly with a fork. Stir in Beurre Manié, a little at a time, until sauce is thickened and bubbling. Stir in cream, add any juices from veal platter and simmer gently 1 minute. Pour over veal and serve immediately with boiled new potatoes and a tossed green salad.

Suggested BBQ accompaniment: Boil peeled new potatoes on the barbecue over direct heat before cooking the veal. Follow directions on page 90, they can complete cooking while veal is being cooked.

LAMB

Lamb every which way is possible in a covered barbecue, be it kettle or grill. The following recipes demonstrate the versatility of these outdoor cookers—versatility in the various cooking methods used and in the range of lamb cuts, from the inexpensive to the budget blow-out.

Because of the range of the recipes, you will find many suitable for family meals, ideal for cooking and eating outdoors on balmy days and evenings.

Roast leg of lamb is a perennial favourite. A true 'roast' should be placed directly on the oven rack with a dish on a lower rack to catch the drippings. Few of us do this because of the mess it makes of the oven, but with covered barbecue cooking, you can now enjoy a properly roasted leg of lamb. While it is recommended the lamb be turned for even browning, it is not really necessary, and a lot depends on your particular barbecue.

BUTTERFLIED LAMB WITH ROSEMARY

Charcoal kettle Indirect—Medium—Preheat not necessary
Gas kettle: Indirect—Hot—Preheat 8-10 minutes
Covered gas grill: Indirect—Hot—Preheat 8-10 minutes
Cooking time: 1½-2 hours
Serves: 6-8

1 leg lamb, about 2 kg (4 lb), boned and opened out (butterflied)

3 cloves garlic, slivered

2 sprigs fresh rosemary

¼ cup (60 ml/2 fl oz) white wine

2 tbsp lemon juice

2 tbsp olive oil

2 tsp honey

3 tsp Dijon mustard

freshly ground black pepper

Fold in sides and shank end of meat to make an evenly thick roast, held in shape with two long metal skewers passed crosswise through meat. Make incisions into fat and meat surfaces and insert garlic slivers and small brackets of rosemary leaves. Mix remaining ingredients in a shallow dish, add lamb and turn it to coat with marinade. Cover and leave at room temperature for 1-2 hours, or refrigerate for several hours, turning occasionally.

Drain lamb and reserve marinade. Place lamb on lightly oiled grill of preheated barbecue, directly above drip pan. Roast indirect, hood down, for 1½-2 hours until cooked to taste. Turn occasionally during cooking, brushing with reserved marinade.

When cooked to taste, remove to a platter and cover loosely with foil. Leave 10 minutes, remove skewers and slice to serve. If desired, fat can be drained from drip pan and the remaining marinade added with some hot stock. Stir to dissolve browned juices, place over direct heat and bring to the boil. Strain into a sauceboat and serve with the lamb. Roast potatoes and/or Green

Butterflied lamb with rosemary

Pasta Salad (page 96) can be served as accompaniments.

Suggested BBQ accompaniment: Arrange medium-sized peeled potatoes, brushed with oil, on grill around lamb at beginning of cooking; turn occasionally during cooking.

ROAST LAMB WITH FRUIT STUFFING

> *Charcoal kettle*: *Indirect—Medium—Preheat not necessary*
> *Gas kettle*: *Indirect—Medium—Preheat 8-10 minutes*
> *Covered gas grill*: *Indirect—Medium—Preheat 8-10 minutes*
> *Cooking time*: *2-2½ hours*
> *Serves*: *6*

1 boned lamb leg or forequarter, about 1.5-2 kg (3-4 lb)

juice of ½ lemon

salt

freshly ground black pepper

oil

Fruit Stuffing

¼ cup (30 g/1 oz) chopped dried apricots

2 tbsp sultanas (golden raisins)

hot water

1 tbsp butter

1 small onion, chopped

grated rind of 1 lemon

2 cups (125 g/4 oz) soft breadcrumbs

1 small egg, beaten

Open out lamb and place fat side down on board. Sprinkle meat with half the lemon juice, season lightly with salt and pepper and brush with oil. Spread stuffing on lamb and roll up. Tie securely with wet, white string. Rub with remaining lemon juice, season with salt and pepper and brush with oil.

Place on barbecue grill directly above drip pan containing 1 cup water. Cook indirect for 2-2½ hours, turning lamb occasionally to brown evenly. Remove to a platter, cover loosely with foil and leave for 15-20 minutes before carving. For barbecued accompaniments and

gravy, see directions given for Traditional Roast Lamb, page 56. Spiced Orange Beetroot (page 94) can be prepared instead of green peas.

Fruit Stuffing: Cover apricots and sultanas with hot water and soak for 15 minutes. Melt butter in a pan and cook onion gently until transparent. Remove from heat and add drained fruit, lemon rind and breadcrumbs. Mix lightly, then add enough beaten egg to combine, mixing lightly.

LAMB RACKS WITH HERB AND PINENUT CRUST

> *Charcoal kettle*: *Indirect—Medium—Preheat not necessary*
> *Gas kettle*: *Indirect—Hot—Preheat 8-10 minutes*
> *Covered gas grill*: *Indirect—Hot—Preheat 8-10 minutes*
> *Cooking time*: *50-70 minutes*
> *Serves*: *6*

6 lamb racks (best ends of neck), each with 3-4 ribs

juice of ½ lemon

Herb and Pinenut Crust

2 cups (125 g/4 oz) soft white breadcrumbs

2 tbsp melted butter or margarine

¼ cup (30 g/1 oz) pinenuts (pignolias)

4 tbsp chopped fresh herbs (parsley, thyme, rosemary, chives)

grated rind of 1 lemon

1 clove garlic, crushed

salt and pepper to taste

beaten egg to bind

Rosemary Madeira Sauce
(optional)

1 sprig fresh rosemary

1 tbsp flour

1 cup (250 ml/8 fl oz) chicken stock (broth)

2 tbsp Madeira

Remove fine skin covering racks and trim off some of the fat if excessive. If you prefer to trim off all the fat, then the underlying silvery membrane must

Lamb racks with herb and pinenut crust

also be removed, otherwise the crust will not stay in place. Sprinkle meat with lemon juice.

Place crust ingredients, except for egg, in a mixing bowl. Mix lightly to combine, then mix in just enough beaten egg to bind. Press crust mixture evenly on the racks, place crust side up in a dish and refrigerate, covered, for 1 hour or overnight.

Place lamb racks, with ribs down, on lightly oiled grill of preheated barbecue, directly above drip pan. Roast indirect, hood down, and cook for 50-60 minutes until cooked to taste. Serve immediately with vegetable accompaniments, and with the following sauce if desired.

Rosemary Madeira Sauce: Drain fat from drip pan, leaving about 1 tablespoon fat in pan. Place pan over direct heat and add rosemary sprig. Press rosemary with fork to release flavour as it cooks. Sprinkle in flour, stir well and cook until lightly browned. Stir in chicken stock and Madeira. Stir until thickened slightly and bubbling, strain into sauceboat and serve with the lamb.

Suggested BBQ accompaniments: Steamed carrots and snow peas (mangetout), see Barbecue-steamed Vegetables (page 89), both drained and tossed with melted butter, adding snipped chives to carrots.

DOWN-UNDER LAMB CUTLETS

Charcoal kettle: Indirect—Medium—Preheat 10-12 minutes
Gas kettle: Indirect—Hot—Preheat 10-12 minutes
Covered gas grill: Indirect—Hot—Preheat 10-12 minutes
Cooking time: 15-18 minutes
Serves: 4

8 large lamb rib cutlets

¼ cup (30 g/1 oz) slivered almonds

16 dried apricot halves

⅓ cup (90 ml/3 fl oz) fresh orange juice

1 tbsp oil

freshly ground black pepper

2 sheets frozen puff pastry, thawed

egg wash or milk to glaze

Ask butcher for cutlets which have not been flattened, with rib bones 'Frenched', i.e. trimmed of fat and gristle.

Toast almonds in a dry pan over medium heat, stirring occasionally; tip onto a plate to prevent them burning. Bring apricots to the boil in the orange juice, remove from heat and keep aside. Trim cutlets, brush with oil and season with pepper. Place well apart on 2 ungreased baking trays. Top each with a few toasted almonds and 2 soaked apricot halves. Cut 2 pastry sheets into quarters and place over filling, pressing pastry gently onto tray around each cutlet and pinching it in at the rib bone. Trim pastry, leaving a border of pastry around each cutlet. Decorate with shapes cut from remaining pastry, secure in place with dabs of water. Prepared cutlets may be covered and stored in the refrigerator for several hours or overnight. Glaze with egg wash or milk just before cooking.

Bake indirect in preheated hot barbecue, hood down, cooking the two trays together. Cook for 15-18 minutes or until pastry is browned and juices just begin to seep out onto trays—this indicates lamb is cooked to medium. Serve immediately, lifting each cutlet with a wide metal spatula.

Suggested BBQ accompaniments: Steamed carrots, steamed snow peas (mange-tout) and green peas, see Barbecue-steamed Vegetables (page 89).

Down-under lamb cutlets

TRADITIONAL ROAST LAMB

Charcoal kettle: Indirect—Medium—Preheat not necessary
Gas kettle: Indirect—Medium—Preheat 8-10 minutes
Covered gas grill: Indirect—Medium—Preheat 8-10 minutes
Cooking time: 2-2½ hours
Serves: 6

1 leg lamb, about 2 kg (4 lb)

salt

freshly ground black pepper

6 medium-sized potatoes, peeled

6 thick pieces pumpkin with skin left on

6 medium-sized onions, peeled

oil

2 cups (250 g/8 oz) frozen green peas

2 tbsp water

½ tsp sugar

Gravy for Your Roast (page 99)

mint sauce or jelly for serving

Wipe lamb with damp kitchen paper and season with salt and pepper. Prepare vegetables, soaking potatoes in cold water for 20 minutes to remove some of the starch (prevents discolouring during cooking). When ready to cook, brush lamb with oil; drain and dry potatoes and brush potatoes, pumpkin and onions with oil. Place peas in a foil food container, add water, sugar and salt if desired and cover with foil.

Place lamb on grill directly above drip pan. Roast indirect, hood down, for 1 hour, turning leg once. Arrange vegetables around lamb and cook for further 1-1½ hours until lamb is cooked to taste and vegetables are tender and browned. Turn lamb once more during cooking, turn vegetables occasionally to brown evenly. During last 15 minutes, place peas on the grill.

Remove lamb to carving platter, cover loosely with foil and allow to stand in a warm place for 15-20 minutes. Place roast vegetables in heatproof dish and keep warm on barbecue while making gravy as directed over direct heat. Carve lamb and serve with the vegetables, gravy and mint sauce or jelly.

LAMB BOULANGÈRE

Charcoal kettle: Indirect—Medium—Preheat not necessary
Gas kettle: Indirect—Hot—Preheat 8-10 minutes
Covered gas grill: Indirect—Hot—Preheat 8-10 minutes
Cooking time: 2-2½ hours
Serves: 6-8

1 leg lamb, about 2 kg (4 lb)

2 cloves garlic, slivered

Lamb boulangère

2 sprigs fresh rosemary, or ground rosemary

salt

freshly ground black pepper

2 tbsp oil

2 medium-sized onions, sliced

1 kg (2 lb) potatoes, peeled and quartered

2 small bay leaves

440 g (1 lb) can peeled tomatoes

Cut slits into skin of lamb and insert garlic slivers and small brackets of rosemary leaves. If fresh rosemary is not available, dust lamb lightly with ground rosemary. Season with salt and pepper and brush with oil.

Put remaining oil in a large roasting pan, add onions and potatoes and toss to coat with oil. Clear the centre of the dish and put in the lamb. Season vegetables with salt and pepper and scatter fresh rosemary and bay leaves on top. Chop the tomatoes and add to vegetables.

Place pan directly on grill of preheated barbecue. Roast indirect, hood down, for 2-2½ hours until cooked to taste. Turn leg over twice during cooking to brown evenly. If pan juices begin to scorch, add a little stock (broth) or water.

Remove lamb to serving platter, cover loosely with foil and leave to stand for 10 minutes. Keep vegetables hot in turned-off barbecue. To serve, slice the lamb and serve with the vegetables, spooning juices over lamb slices. Serve with crusty bread and a tossed green salad.

SMOKED LAMB ROSEMARY

Charcoal kettle: Indirect—Medium—Preheat 8-10 minutes
Gas kettle: Indirect—Hot—Preheat 8-10 minutes
Covered gas grill: Indirect—Hot—Preheat 8-10 minutes
Cooking time: 50-70 minutes
Serves: 6

6 lamb racks (best ends of neck), each with 3-4 ribs

2 tsp fresh or dried rosemary leaves

½ lemon

salt

freshly ground black pepper

1 tbsp oil

4 tbsp redcurrant jelly

large, woody sprig of fresh rosemary, well soaked

Pull off fine skin covering the lamb and trim off a little fat if necessary. Score fat into diamonds and insert rosemary leaves into the scoring. Rub racks all over with the half lemon, squeezing out juice as you go, then season with salt and pepper and brush meat surfaces with oil. Spread fat surfaces with half the redcurrant jelly.

Place lamb racks, fat side up, on barbecue grill, directly over drip pan containing 2 cups water. Break up soaked rosemary sprig into smaller pieces and place a third of these on a piece of foil. Place directly onto lava rocks on the lighted side of gas barbecue; for charcoal kettle, place some pieces on foil on top of the coals each side. Rosemary should smoulder rather than burn. Roast indirect, hood down, for 50-70 minutes until cooked to taste. Replenish rosemary as necessary to keep up the smoke; spread lamb once more with remainder of redcurrant jelly during cooking. Serve one rack per person with vegetable accompaniments.

Suggested BBQ accompaniments: Sugar-glazed New Potatoes (page 90); steamed asparagus or other green vegetable, see Barbecue-steamed Vegetables (page 89).

LAMB DINNER-IN-A-DISH

Charcoal kettle: Indirect—Medium—Preheat 6-8 minutes
Gas kettle: Indirect—Medium—Preheat 6-8 minutes
Covered gas grill: Indirect—Medium—Preheat 6-8 minutes
Cooking time: 1½-2 hours
Serves: 6-8

1.5 kg (3 lb) lamb shoulder chops

¼ cup (60 ml/2 fl oz) oil

salt

freshly ground black pepper

½ tsp dried marjoram leaves

½ tsp dried thyme leaves

1 tbsp chopped fresh parsley

2 medium-sized onions, sliced

1 medium-sized carrot, thinly sliced

4 large, ripe tomatoes, skinned and sliced

1 tsp sugar

750 g (1½ lb) old potatoes, sliced

1½ cups (185 g/6 oz) frozen green peas

water or stock (broth) as needed

Trim lamb and place in a large oiled roasting dish. Season with salt and pepper and sprinkle with herbs. Cover with onion and carrot slices and top with tomatoes. Sprinkle on half the oil and season with salt, pepper and sugar. Peel and cut potatoes into 5 mm (¼ in) slices and place in a bowl of water. Take dish of lamb, bowl of potatoes, remaining oil and the peas out to the barbecue.

Place filled baking dish (uncovered) on grill in preheated barbecue and cook indirect, hood down, for 45 minutes. Strew peas over dish contents, top with drained, sliced potatoes and brush remaining oil over potatoes. Continue to cook with hood down for further 45-60 minutes until lamb and vegetables are tender, adding a little water or stock to dish when necessary. Serve directly onto warmed plates, accompanied by hot bread.

Suggested BBQ accompaniment: Feta and Olive Bread Braid (page 111), added to barbecue during last 15-20 minutes of cooking lamb dinner.

LAMB PROVENÇALE

> **Charcoal kettle:** *Indirect—Medium—Preheat not necessary*
> **Gas kettle:** *Indirect—Medium—Preheat 8-10 minutes*
> **Covered gas grill:** *Indirect—Medium—Preheat 8-10 minutes*
> **Cooking time:** *2-2½ hours*
> **Serves:** *6*

1 leg lamb, about 2 kg (4 lb)

2 tbsp olive oil

2 cloves garlic, crushed

ground rosemary

1 tbsp finely chopped parsley

2 tsp chopped fresh thyme

salt

freshly ground black pepper

½ cup (125 ml/4 fl oz) chicken stock (broth)

¼ cup (60 ml/2 fl oz) white wine

1 tbsp additional chopped parsley and fresh thyme combined

Wipe lamb with damp kitchen paper and rub well with 2 teaspoons of the olive oil, the crushed garlic and a light sprinkle of ground rosemary. Mix the fresh herbs and press over the leg. Season with salt and pepper, cover and stand at room temperature for at least 30 minutes.

Oil grill of heated barbecue with a little olive oil, place leg on grill directly over drip pan containing 1 cup water. Roast indirect, hood down, for 2-2½ hours, turning leg occasionally. Drizzle occasionally with a little olive oil, and add water to drip pan as needed—there should be about 5 mm (¼ in) of liquid in it during cooking. When lamb is cooked to taste, remove to platter, cover loosely with foil and stand in a warm place for at least 15 minutes before carving.

Carefully remove drip pan and skim off excess fat. Place pan over direct heat, add stock and wine and stir well to dissolve baked-on juices. Bring to the boil and pour into sauceboat. Sprinkle additional fresh herbs over lamb and take to the table with the hot lamb juices. Serve with Ratatouille, a tossed salad of mixed greens and hot French bread.

Suggested BBQ accompaniment: Ratatouille (page 41), placed on the barbecue next to the lamb, after lamb has been cooking for 1 hour. French bread (baguettes) may be heated indirect for 6-8 minutes after lamb is removed—do not wrap in foil.

LAMB WITH MUSTARD SAUCE

> **All barbecues:** *Direct high heat, uncovered for initial cooking, then indirect as follows, finishing with direct high heat. (See pages 8 and 10 for details on combination direct and indirect cooking for charcoal and gas kettles.)*
> **Charcoal kettle:** *Indirect—Medium—Preheat 8-10 minutes*
> **Gas kettle:** *Indirect—Hot—Preheat 8-10 minutes*
> **Covered gas grill:** *Indirect—Hot—Preheat 8-10 minutes*
> **Cooking time:** *20-25 minutes*
> **Serves:** *6-8*

2-3 lamb eyes of loin, each about 600-800 g (1¼-1¾ lb)

freshly ground black pepper

2 tsp oil

3 tbsp butter

½ cup (125 ml/4 fl oz) dry white wine

½ cup (125 ml/4 fl oz) canned beef consommé, undiluted

2 tbsp grainy mustard such as Pommery

salt to taste

¼ cup (60 ml/2 fl oz) thick cream

The eye of lamb loin is seldom sold as a retail cut. Have the butcher bone out 2-3 lamb mid loins, trimming the eyes of all fat and gristle. You will also receive 2-3 fillets, which can be added to the recipe, or stored for another meal. Allow about 200 g (7 oz) raw lamb per serve. Season lamb with pepper.

Place a large frying pan, with heatproof handle, on barbecue grill heated to high. When pan is hot, add oil and 1 tablespoon of the butter. When foaming and beginning to brown, add lamb and brown quickly on all sides. Remove pan from heat and prepare barbecue for indirect cooking as above.

Place pan on grill and cook indirect, hood down, for 10-12 minutes—lamb should feel fairly resilient when pressed with tongs. Remove lamb to a warm

Lamb provençale

platter, cover loosely with foil and keep warm.

Place pan with cooking juices on grill over direct high heat and stir in wine, consommé and mustard. Stir well to lift browned sediment and boil to reduce a little. Adjust seasoning with salt and pepper, stir in cream, return to the boil. Finally, whisk in remaining butter, a little at a time, without allowing sauce to boil. Remove pan to cooler section of barbecue.

Cut lamb obliquely in thick slices. Spoon sauce onto 6-8 heated plates and overlap 3-4 slices of lamb onto sauce. Add vegetables and serve immediately.

Suggested BBQ accompaniments: Sugar-glazed New Potatoes (page 90) and steamed broccoli (see Barbecue-steamed Vegetables, page 89). Cook potatoes ahead of time and reheat in covered dish when cooking lamb indirect; cook broccoli with the lamb.

Italian-style lamb chops

PINEAPPLE-GLAZED LAMB RIBLETS

Charcoal kettle: Indirect—Medium—Preheat not necessary
Gas kettle: Indirect—Medium—Preheat 6-8 minutes
Covered gas grill: Indirect—Medium—Preheat 6-8 minutes
Cooking time: 1¼ hours
Serves: 6

2 kg (4 lb) lamb riblets (cut from breast)

salt and freshly ground black pepper

1 tsp grated fresh ginger

2 cloves garlic, crushed

1 large onion, grated

1 cup (250 ml/8 fl oz) pineapple juice

2 tbsp brown sugar, packed

2 tsp curry powder

¼ cup (60 ml/2 fl oz) water

Trim excess fat from riblets. Place in a single layer in a roasting dish and season with salt and pepper to taste. Mix remaining ingredients together in a jug and take out to barbecue with the dish of riblets.

Place uncovered dish on grill of heated barbecue and cook, hood down, for 30 minutes, turning riblets once. Drain off any fat. Pour pineapple mixture over

riblets and continue to cook indirect for a further 45 minutes or until fork-tender and well glazed, turning riblets occasionally during cooking. Remove dish from barbecue, tilt and let fat run to one end. Spoon off fat and discard. Pile riblets in a deep, warmed bowl and serve as part of a barbecue meal—they are an excellent finger food.

ITALIAN-STYLE LAMB CHOPS

All barbecues: Direct heat, uncovered for part of the cooking, then with hood down.
Cooking time: 20-25 minutes
Serves: 6

6 lamb chump chops, 2.5 cm (1 in) thick

2 cloves garlic, crushed

2 tbsp vermouth

1 tsp fresh or dried rosemary leaves

2 tbsp oil

1 medium-sized eggplant (aubergine)

1 large onion, finely chopped

2 large tomatoes, skinned and chopped

salt and freshly ground pepper to taste

½ tsp sugar

1 tbsp chopped fresh basil

6 slices mozzarella cheese

Trim chops and nick selvedge of each in two places. Marinate in a mixture of garlic, vermouth, rosemary and half the oil for 1 hour, turning now and then. Slice eggplant lengthwise into 6 slices, sprinkle with salt and leave 20 minutes, rinse and dry with kitchen paper.

Heat barbecue to medium with a grill and a hotplate in place. Drain chops and reserve marinade. Place chops on lightly oiled grill and cook 2-3 minutes each side until browned but not completely cooked. Meanwhile, place remaining oil on the hotplate and brown the eggplant on half the cooking surface. On a corner of the hotplate, fry the onion, tossing often, until softened, add tomato, seasoning, sugar and basil and toss occasionally to cook evenly, adding a little marinade to keep mixture moist.

Pile the cooked eggplant on the side of the hotplate and move the chops from the grill onto the hotplate. Scoop up the tomato mixture, divide equally onto each chop. Place a slice of cheese and a slice of eggplant on top of each. Put the hood down and cook for 3-4 minutes until cheese melts and lamb is cooked to taste—it should feel slightly resilient when pressed with tongs. Arrange on serving platter, garnish with basil sprigs. Serve with a tossed salad and a hot bread.

Suggested BBQ accompaniment: Prepare Mozzarella and Pepper Bread (page 114) and wrap loosely in foil because of the direct cooking involved; place on the side of the grill when cooking begins. It will be sufficiently heated by the time the lamb has finished cooking.

HERBED LAMB KEBABS

All barbecues: Direct heat, uncovered for part of the cooking, then with hood down.
Cooking time: 7-10 minutes
Serves: 6-8

1 kg (2 lb) boneless lamb from leg or shoulder

1 quantity Herb-wine Marinade (page 99)

fresh bay leaves

brackets of fresh rosemary leaves

fresh mushroom caps

cherry tomatoes

red and green (bell) peppers

2 tbsp oil

Trim lamb and cut into 2.5 cm (1 in) cubes. Prepare marinade as directed in a glass or ceramic bowl, add lamb and stir well. Cover and marinate for at least 2 hours, or for several hours in refrigerator. Stir occasionally.

Thread lamb onto flat metal skewers, alternating cubes with your choice of bay leaves, rosemary, mushroom caps, cherry tomatoes and pepper squares. Place marinade in a small saucepan and add the oil.

Heat barbecue to hot and place filled skewers on oiled grill. Cook until browned on all sides, basting kebabs frequently with marinade. Reduce heat to low or move to outer section of charcoal barbecue, put hood down and cook for 3-4 minutes. If lamb is slightly resilient when pressed with tongs, it is cooked to medium—do not overcook. Serve with rice pilaf, a tossed salad of mixed greens and crusty bread.

Suggested BBQ accompaniment: Eggplant Pilaf cooked by indirect heat (page 43). Keep warm at side of barbecue when kebabs are put on to cook.

SPICED LAMB KEBABS

All barbecues: Direct heat, Hot reducing to Medium-Hot if necessary
Cooking time: 4-5 minutes
Serves: 6-8

1 kg (2 lb) lamb cubes from shoulder or forequarter

1½ tsp salt

1 medium-sized onion, roughly chopped

1 clove garlic, chopped

1 cup (30 g/1 oz) roughly chopped flat-leaf parsley, packed

2 tbsp chopped mint

1 medium-sized potato, finely shredded

1 cup (60 g/2 oz) soft white breadcrumbs

1 egg

freshly ground black pepper

1 tsp ground cumin

½ tsp ground allspice

oil for cooking

Lamb should contain a little fat so that kebabs will be moist. Place cubes in two lots in food processor bowl, adding half the salt to each lot. Process until ground to a paste-like consistency, tipping into a bowl when processed. Add onion, garlic, parsley and mint to food processor and process to a thin paste. Add to lamb with remaining ingredients except oil. Mix well with a wooden spoon, then knead with hands until thoroughly blended. Mixture should stick to hands. Wash hands and keep them damp. Shape onto long, flat metal skewers, in ovals about 10 cm (4 in) long and 2 cm (¾ in) thick at centre. Two or three kebabs should fit on each skewer. Place on a baking tray, cover with plastic film and chill for 30 minutes or overnight.

Brush kebabs with oil and place on oiled barbecue grill over high heat or glowing coals. Turn frequently, brushing occasionally with oil, and cook for about 4-5 minutes. Push kebabs off skewers onto a heated platter. Serve as part of a barbecue meal with a pilaf and salads, or serve in the traditional manner in warmed pocket breads with Cos (romaine) lettuce leaves, diced tomato and cucumber and Tahini and Parsley Sauce (page 82).

Note: If preferred, lamb mixture may be shaped into large or small patties and cooked on well-heated and oiled barbecue hotplate or griddle. The small patties can be placed 2-3 to a pocket bread for serving traditionally.

LAMB AND COCONUT CURRY

Charcoal kettle: Indirect—Medium—Preheat not necessary
Gas kettle: Indirect—Low—Preheat 4-5 minutes
Covered gas grill: Indirect—Low—Preheat 4-5 minutes
Cooking time: 1½-2 hours
Serves: 6-8

1.5 kg (3 lb) boneless lamb from leg or shoulder

3 tbsp ghee (clarified butter) or oil

2 large onions, chopped

2 tsp grated fresh ginger root

1-2 red chillies, seeded and chopped

2 cloves garlic, crushed

1 tbsp curry powder

3 tbsp chopped coriander leaves (cilantro)

1 large ripe tomato, peeled and chopped

1 cup (250 ml/8 fl oz) canned coconut milk

2 tsp brown sugar

salt to taste

1 tsp garam masala or ground allspice

2 tbsp lemon juice

Herbed lamb kebabs

Lamb and coconut curry

Cooking can begin over direct heat on the barbecue, or do the initial cooking on the stove.

Trim lamb and cut into 2 cm (¾ in) cubes. Heat ghee in a large Dutch oven or flameproof casserole and add onion, ginger, chillies and garlic. Cook gently on low heat until onion is transparent—about 10-12 minutes. Stir in curry powder and cook gently for a further 5 minutes, stirring occasionally. Increase heat and add lamb cubes. Stir occasionally until lamb loses red colour, stir in remaining ingredients except for garam masala and lemon juice, adding salt to taste. If preparing in the kitchen, take out to barbecue at this stage.

Cover pan or casserole and cook by indirect heat, hood down, for 1½-2 hours until lamb is tender. Stir in garam masala and lemon juice, cover and simmer for a further 5 minutes. Serve with boiled rice and traditional curry accompaniments such as banana sprinkled with lemon juice and toasted coconut, sliced cucumber and chopped mint in yoghurt, and fruit chutney.

Suggested BBQ accompaniments: Cook the rice alongside the curry in the barbecue. Use 2-cup quantity and prepare according to directions for Barbecue-steamed Rice (page 95), indirect method. Place in barbecue after curry has cooked for 1 hour. If it cooks ahead of the curry, remove and keep warm near the barbecue. Wholemeal (whole wheat) flat breads, warmed over

direct heat for about 20 seconds each side, are an easy substitute for the traditional chapatis which usually accompany curries.

ROLLED LOINS WITH APPLE AND GINGER

Charcoal kettle: Indirect—Medium—Preheat 8-10 minutes
Gas kettle: Indirect—Medium—Preheat 8-10 minutes
Covered gas grill: Indirect—Hot—Preheat 8-10 minutes
Cooking time: 55-65 minutes
Serves: 6-8

2 lamb mid loins, boned, each about 1 kg (2 lb)

2 Granny Smith (green) apples, grated

1 tbsp butter

1 tbsp finely chopped preserved ginger

¼ cup (30 g/1 oz) chopped walnuts

salt and freshly ground black pepper

1 cup (250 ml/8 fl oz) apple juice or cider

1 tbsp syrup from ginger

½ cup (125 ml/4 fl oz) chicken stock (broth)

When purchasing the mid loins, ask butcher to leave sufficient 'skirt' so that loin can be rolled easily, and to bone them for you. Remove the fine skin covering the fat.

Cook grated apple in butter until softened, stir in preserved ginger and walnuts. Open out mid loins, fat side down, season lightly with salt and pepper. Spread each with apple mixture and roll up firmly. Tie securely with wet, white string and season with salt and pepper. If not required immediately, cover lamb and store in refrigerator overnight.

Place the two rolls in a roasting dish and add apple juice and ginger syrup. Put dish on grill of heated barbecue and cook indirect for 55–65 minutes, turning rolls occasionally to brown evenly. Add a little water to dish if juices show signs of scorching. When cooked to taste—preferably medium—remove rolls to platter, cover loosely with foil and stand for 10 minutes. Put roasting dish over direct heat, skim off fat and add stock.

Stir over heat to dissolve browned juices. Bring to the boil and strain into sauceboat. Remove strings from lamb and carve in thick slices. Serve on warm plates with the juices and vegetable accompaniments.

Suggested BBQ accompaniments: Gingered Sweet Potatoes (page 92) cooked indirect alongside the roasting dish, and placed in barbecue at the same time. Add green beans towards end of cooking; cook direct or indirect for 10–15 minutes—see Barbecue-steamed Vegetables (page 89).

HONEY-SOYA LAMB SHANKS

Charcoal kettle: Indirect—Medium—Preheat not necessary
Gas kettle: Indirect—Medium—Preheat 8-10 minutes
Covered gas grill: Indirect—Medium—Preheat 8-10 minutes
Cooking time: 1½ hours
Serves: 6-8

6-8 lamb foreshanks

double quantity Honey-soya Marinade (page 98)

½ cup (125 ml/4 fl oz) water

Ask butcher to leave the lamb shanks intact. Wipe with damp kitchen paper. Mix marinade ingredients as directed in a baking dish large enough to accommodate shanks in a single layer. Add shanks and turn to coat with marinade. Cover and marinate at room temperature for up to 2 hours, or refrigerate for several hours.

Place dish with shanks and marinade (uncovered) on grill in heated barbecue and cook indirect, hood down, for 1½ hours or until tender, turning shanks occasionally. Add water to dish halfway during cooking; it may be necessary to add a further amount of water as the dish liquid should not be allowed to scorch. Serve the shanks with steamed rice and stir-fried vegetables.

Suggested BBQ accompaniments: Cook the rice alongside the shanks in the barbecue. Use 2-cup quantity and prepare according to directions for Barbecue-steamed Rice (page 95), using indirect method. Place in barbecue after shanks have cooked for 1 hour. Leave shanks (covered) and rice on side where cooked, and cook Stir-fried Vegetables (page 93) over direct heat.

PORK AND HAM

With the range of cuts available, you will never be short of ideas for interesting barbecue meals featuring these meats. Recipes range from the traditional Roast Pork with Crackling untraditionally cooked under cover, to the expected barbecued pork ribs and ham steaks. There are slow-cooked casserole-type dishes, too, which require little preparation and even less attention when cooking.

During festive seasons and special holiday meals, the kitchen oven is often unable to cope with the amount of food fed into it. Have you ever thought of glazing the ham in the barbecue? The result is superb.

For all the pork roast recipes, consult the table on page 21 for further details on cooking times and internal temperatures.

Danish roast pork

DANISH ROAST PORK

> *Charcoal kettle: Indirect—Medium—Preheat 10-12 minutes*
> *Gas kettle: Indirect—Hot/Medium—Preheat 10-12 minutes*
> *Covered gas grill: Indirect—Hot/Medium—Preheat 10-12 minutes*
> *Cooking time: 1½-2 hours*
> *Serves: 6-8*

1 pork loin, boned and rolled, about 2 kg (4 lb)

1 small Granny Smith (green) apple, peeled and diced

juice of 1 lemon

8 pitted prunes

coarse salt

½ cup (125 ml/4 fl oz) dry white wine

½ cup (125 ml/4 fl oz) chicken stock (broth)

3 tbsp redcurrant jelly

¼ cup (60 ml/2 fl oz) cream

If possible purchase pork loin with rind (skin) in place and ask butcher to score it at 2 cm (¾ in) intervals. Have the loin rolled and tied firmly. With a ham knife, cut a tunnel through the centre of the roast. Toss diced apples with lemon juice. Using the handle of a wooden spoon, push prunes and diced apple pieces alternately into tunnel in pork. Dry pork with kitchen paper and rub with salt.

Place pork on oiled grill directly over drip pan containing 1 cup water. Cook indirect, hood down, for 25-35 minutes until rind bubbles and becomes crisp. Reduce heat to medium-hot in gas barbecues if vegetable accompaniments are not being cooked. Cook for further 1-1½ hours. Do not baste crackling or turn pork over during cooking. Remove pork to platter and leave uncovered in a warm place for 15 minutes. Remove drip pan and skim off excess fat. Place over direct heat and add wine, stock and redcurrant jelly. Bring to the boil and stir in browned juices from sides of dish. Stir in cream, heat through and pour into sauceboat. Serve pork with the sauce and vegetables of choice.

Roast pork with crackling

Suggested BBQ accompaniments: In gas barbecues, leave on hot. Prepare Spiced Red Cabbage with Apple (page 92) and Barbecue-steamed New Potatoes (page 90). Place on grill next to pork after 30 minutes.

ROAST PORK WITH CRACKLING

Charcoal kettle Indirect—Hot—Preheat 10-12 minutes
Gas kettle: Indirect—Hot/Medium—Preheat 10-12 minutes
Covered gas grill: Indirect—Hot/Medium—Preheat 10-12 minutes
Cooking time: 2½-3 hours
Serves: 8-10

1 half-leg of pork (fresh ham), bone in, about 3.5 kg (8 lb)

oil

coarse salt

4-5 whole apples (optional)

Pork leg should have the rind (skin) on it. Ask butcher to score rind at 1 cm (½ in) intervals across top and sides of leg.

Dry pork with kitchen paper, brush with oil and rub salt into rind. Place on grill directly over drip pan containing 2 cups water. Cook indirect, hood down, 30-45 minutes until rind bubbles and becomes crisp. Do not baste with oil or turn leg over at any time during cooking otherwise crackling will toughen; for gas kettle or covered gas grill, give leg a quarter turn occasionally to crisp the crackling evenly. When crackling is formed, reduce gas to medium; heat in charcoal kettle reduces as fire burns down. If cooking whole apples, rub with oil and place around pork after 2 hours.

When pork is cooked, remove to carving platter and keep in a warm place for 20 minutes—do not cover. Put apples in a covered dish. Make gravy according to directions for Gravy for Your Roast (page 99). To serve, lift off crackling in sections and cut in serving portions. Carve pork and place on warm plates, ladle on gravy and place crackling alongside. Add half an apple per serve, or serve with apple sauce and vegetables.

Suggested BBQ accompaniments: Scrub 2 medium-sized whole sweet potatoes, rub with oil, place on grill next to pork after 1 hour. Peeled potatoes (see

Roast Vegetables, page 88) may also be placed on grill for indirect cooking. With vegetables added, heat for gas barbecues may have to be increased to medium-hot. Cook a green vegetable by direct heat while making gravy.

CARMEN'S EASY BOSTON BAKED BEANS

Charcoal kettle: Indirect—Medium—Preheat not necessary
Gas kettle: Indirect—Medium—Preheat 8-10 minutes
Covered gas grill: Indirect—Medium—Preheat 8-10 minutes
Cooking time: 2 hours
Serves: 6-8

2 x 440 g (1 lb) cans baked beans in tomato sauce

1 large onion, chopped

½ cup (125 ml/4 fl oz) tomato ketchup

½ cup (125 ml/4 fl oz) water

2 tbsp treacle (molasses, see page 18)

1-2 tbsp brown sugar

250 g (8 oz) bacon pieces

Empty baked beans into a deep oven or casserole dish. Add remaining ingredients, adding 1 tablespoon brown sugar to begin with. Stir well, taste and add more brown sugar if necessary—amount depends on sweetness of beans and ketchup. Do not cover dish.

Place dish of beans on barbecue grill and cook indirect, hood down, for 2 hours. Liquid reduces during cooking, onion melts into sauce and beans absorb the flavours; stir once only if necessary. Serve beans straight from the dish with warm crusty bread and a tossed salad. Excellent served as a side dish for barbecued pork or beef ribs, with hamburgers and hot dogs.

PLUM-GLAZED AMERICAN SPARERIBS

Charcoal kettle: Indirect—Medium—Preheat 8-10 minutes
Gas kettle: Indirect—Hot—Preheat 8-10 minutes
Covered gas grill: Indirect—Hot—Preheat 8-10 minutes
Cooking time: 2 hours
Serves: 6

3 slabs American-style pork spareribs, about 2 kg (4 lb) in all

1 lemon or lime

salt and freshly ground black pepper

oil

1 quantity Plum Barbecue Sauce (page 101)

American-style pork spareribs come from the whole pork belly. Ask the butcher to remove the rib section in one piece, so that ribs are covered with a single layer of meat and a thin layer of fat. Halve the lemon or lime and rub over the slabs of ribs, squeezing out the juice as you rub. Rub also with salt and pepper and brush with oil. Put sauce in a pan.

Place spareribs on grill directly over drip pan containing 2 cups water. Cook indirect, hood down, for 30 minutes. Baste with sauce, turning ribs over, and continue to cook for further 1½ hours, turning and basting with sauce every 10-15 minutes. Keep sauce on side of grill to heat while ribs cook, and keep hood down. Test if cooked by cutting into meat—it should be crusty outside and tender within. To serve, pile on a warm platter and provide a sharp knife for cutting ribs off between the bones. Serve remaining hot Plum Barbecue Sauce separately. Serve as finger food, or serve as a main meal with a rice pilaf and a tossed green salad.

Suggested BBQ accompaniment: Prepare Orange and Currant Pilaf (page 94) and cook alongside ribs after ribs have cooked for 1½ hours.

APRICOT-GLAZED PORK RIBS

Charcoal kettle: Indirect—Medium—Preheat 8-10 minutes
Gas kettle: Indirect—Hot—Preheat 8-10 minutes
Covered gas grill: Indirect—Hot—Preheat 8-10 minutes
Cooking time: 1½ hours
Serves: 6

4 slabs pork back ribs, about 1-1.25 kg (4-4½ lb) in all

1 lemon or lime

salt and freshly ground black pepper

oil

1 quantity Apricot Barbecue Sauce (page 101)

Back ribs are available from butchers who prepare boneless pork rib loin. The chine bone (backbone) is sawn off, leaving slabs of curved top-rib bones. Halve the lemon or lime and rub over ribs, squeezing out juice as you rub. Rub also with salt and pepper and brush all over with oil. Place sauce in a pan.

Place ribs on grill directly over drip pan containing 2 cups water. Cook indirect, hood down, for 15 minutes. Baste with sauce, turn ribs over, and continue to cook for further 1¼ hours, turning and basting with sauce every 10-15 minutes. Give ribs an occasional brush with oil also. Keep sauce on side of grill to heat while ribs cook, and keep hood down. Test if cooked by cutting meat between rib bones—it should be crusty outside and tender within. To serve, pile on a warm platter and provide a sharp knife for cutting ribs off between the bones. Serve remaining hot Apricot Barbecue Sauce separately. Ribs are finger food, so provide plenty of paper napkins.

PORK SATAYS

All barbecues: Direct—Hot
Cooking time: 8-10 minutes
Serves: 6

750 g (1½ lb) boneless pork loin

1 medium-sized brown onion, grated

1 clove garlic, crushed

1 tsp ground ginger

1 tsp grated lemon rind

Left: Tacos with chilli con carne (see p. 48); right: Plum-glazed American spareribs

1 tsp ground coriander

2 tsp brown sugar

1 tsp turmeric

1 tbsp lemon juice

2 tbsp oil

1 quantity Satay Sauce (page 98)

Trim fat from pork and cut into 2 cm (¾ inch) cubes. Mix remaining ingredients except oil and Satay Sauce in a bowl, add pork and mix well. Cover and marinate at room temperature for up to 2 hours, or in refrigerator for several hours as necessary. Soak 18 bamboo skewers in water for 1 hour. When required to cook, thread 4-5 pieces of pork towards pointed end of each skewer. Take out to barbecue with oil and Satay Sauce.

Brush satays with oil and place on grill over hot barbecue. Turn and brush frequently with oil until nicely browned and just cooked through, about 8-10 minutes. Serve hot with Satay Sauce served separately; sauce need not be heated, but it may require thinning down with coconut milk or boiling water. Satays may be served as a starter to a meal as finger food, or as part of a main meal, in which case Gado Gado (page 42) would make an ideal accompaniment.

PORK WITH ORANGE-PORT SAUCE

All barbecues: *Direct—Hot reducing to Medium*
Cooking time: *12-15 minutes*
Serves: *6*

6 boneless pork mid loin chops

freshly ground black pepper

oil

grated rind of 1 orange

¾ cup (185 ml/6 fl oz) fresh orange juice

¼ cup (60 ml/2 fl oz) port

1 tbsp brown sugar

2 tsp French mustard

1 tsp chicken stock (bouillon) powder

3 tsp cornflour (cornstarch)

¼ cup (60 ml/2 fl oz) water

Pork with orange-port sauce

1 tbsp toasted, slivered almonds to garnish

Season pork with pepper, brush all over with oil and place on a plate. Mix orange rind and juice in a saucepan with port, brown sugar, mustard and chicken stock powder. In a small jug, blend cornflour with water. Take all ingredients out to barbecue.

Place saucepan on barbecue grill and bring liquid to the boil. Stir conflour and water mixture, and gradually stir into pan contents. Continue to stir until sauce boils and thickens. Leave at side of grill to simmer gently.

Oil heated hotplate or grill, add pork and cook quickly on each side to seal, reduce heat or move to cooler section of barbecue and continue to cook for about 3 minutes each side until just cooked through—pork should be barely pink inside and juicy. Arrange on a warm platter, pour sauce over and sprinkle with toasted almonds. Serve with warm, crusty bread and Burghul and Pumpkin Salad (page 95), or other salad of choice.

PORK SPARERIBS IN BARBECUE SAUCE

All barbecues: *Direct—Hot then Indirect—Medium*
Cooking time: *1½ hours*
Serves: *6-8*

1.5 kg (3 lb) pork spareribs

oil

2 cloves garlic, crushed

¼ cup (60 ml/2 fl oz) tomato ketchup

3 tbsp honey

1 tbsp brown sugar

1 tbsp dry sherry

1 tbsp chilli sauce

2 tbsp soya sauce

1 tbsp cider vinegar

¼ tsp five-spice powder or ground allspice

These pork spareribs should be cut from the whole pork belly in strips about 2.5 cm (1 in) wide and about 12 cm (5 in) long. Brush spareribs with oil and put on a plate. Mix remaining ingredients in a large roasting pan and take all out to barbecue.

Heat barbecue for direct cooking, and when very hot, place ribs on oiled grill and brown quickly, turning with tongs. Cook for about 10 minutes. Place spareribs in pan containing sauce ingredients and turn in the sauce. Change to indirect cooking and place pan on grill. Cook indirect, hood down, with medium setting for gas barbecues. Turn ribs occasionally during cooking, and cook for 1¼-1½ hours until meat is fork tender. Add a little water to pan if sauce reduces too much during cooking. Transfer ribs and sauce to a warm serving dish and serve with steamed rice.

Suggested BBQ accompaniment: Cook Barbecue-steamed Rice (page 95), using 1½-cup quantity of rice of choice. Cook indirect next to spareribs 30 minutes before ribs have finished cooking.

Chinese barbecued pork

CHINESE BARBECUED PORK

> *Charcoal kettle*: Indirect—Medium—Preheat 8-10 minutes
> *Gas kettle*: Indirect—Medium—Preheat 8-10 minutes
> *Covered gas grill*: Indirect—Medium—Preheat 8-10 minutes
> *Cooking time*: 30-40 minutes
> *Serves*: 6-8

1 kg (2 lb) boneless pork loin or fillets (tenderloins)

2 cloves garlic, crushed

1 tbsp oil

½ tsp sesame oil

½ tsp Chinese five-spice powder

2 tbsp soya sauce

3 tsp hoisin sauce

2 tbsp honey

2 tbsp dry sherry

2 drops red food colouring (optional)

Purchase loin in one piece; if using fillet, 2-3 will be required. Remove all fat and gristle from pork. If using loin, cut lengthwise into strips about 4 cm (1½ in) thick; fillets remain as they are. Mix remaining ingredients in a shallow dish, add pork and turn to coat with marinade. Cover and marinate for several hours or overnight in refrigerator.

Lift pork from marinade and place on oiled barbecue grill directly over drip pan containing 1 cup water. Cook indirect, hood down, for 30-40 minutes, basting often with marinade. Pork should be slightly underdone. Remove to a platter and stand for 10 minutes. Slice thinly and serve hot as part of a barbecue meal with Chinese plum sauce or hoisin sauce for dipping. May also be served cold, used in stir-fry dishes with vegetables, or added to fried rice.

CURRY-GLAZED PORK CHOPS

> *Charcoal kettle*: Indirect—Medium—Preheat not necessary
> *Gas kettle*: Indirect—Medium—Preheat 6-8 minutes
> *Covered gas grill*: Indirect—Medium—Preheat 6-8 minutes
> *Cooking time*: 45-55 minutes
> *Serves*: 6

6 pork forequarter (sparerib/blade) pork chops

1 tbsp butter or margarine

2 tbsp flour

3 tsp curry powder

1 tsp salt

½ tsp cinnamon

1 tbsp desiccated (unsweetened) coconut

¾ cup (185 ml/6 fl oz) chicken stock (broth)

2 tbsp tomato ketchup

½ cup (125 ml/4 fl oz) apple sauce

2 tbsp apricot jam

1 tbsp dried onion flakes (instant minced onion)

Trim excess fat from chops. Grease a large, shallow oven dish with butter. Mix flour with curry powder, salt, cinnamon and coconut. Coat chops with mixture and place in a single layer in dish. Mix remaining ingredients and pour over chops. Leave dish uncovered.

Place dish on barbecue grill. Cook indirect, hood down, for 45-55 minutes until fork-tender, turning chops halfway through cooking. Sauce should be considerably reduced and pork richly glazed by end of cooking time. Serve with steamed rice and curry accompaniments such as banana slices in lemon juice, cucumber slices mixed with yoghurt and crushed garlic, red onion slices moistened with a little vinegar.

Suggested BBQ accompaniment: Cook Barbecue-steamed Rice (page 95) alongside chops, using 1½-cup quantity of long-grain rice. Place in barbecue after pork has cooked for 30 minutes.

PORK FILLET WITH FRUIT AND MACADAMIAS

> *Charcoal kettle*: Indirect—Medium—Preheat 8-10 minutes
> *Gas kettle*: Indirect—Hot—Preheat 8-10 minutes
> *Covered gas grill*: Indirect—Hot—Preheat 8-10 minutes
> *Cooking time*: 1-1¼ hours
> *Serves*: 6

6 dried apricots, chopped

6 pitted prunes, chopped

½ Granny Smith (green) apple, chopped

2 tbsp chopped macadamia nuts

3 pork fillets (tenderloins), each about 500 g (1 lb)

2 tbsp melted butter

1 quantity Apricot Barbecue Sauce (page 101)

If apricots are very dry, soak in boiling water for 10 minutes then drain, otherwise soaking is not necessary. Mix apricots, prunes, apple and macadamia nuts. Cut a pocket in the side of each pork fillet and fill with the fruit and nut mixture. Secure openings with poultry pins and brush fillets with melted butter. Put sauce in a saucepan.

Place fillets on barbecue grill directly over drip pan containing 1 cup water. Place pan with sauce at side of grill. Cook indirect, hood down, for 1–1¼ hours. After first 15 minutes, baste fillets with sauce and turn them. Continue to baste and turn fillets every 10 minutes. Remove pork to a warm serving platter, cover loosely with foil and stand for 10 minutes. Remove pins and slice to serve. The apricot sauce should be reduced to a thick consistency by the end of cooking time; serve separately in a sauceboat. Serve with vegetables of choice.

Suggested BBQ accompaniments: Prepare Gingered Sweet Potatoes (page 92) and cook indirect alongside pork fillets. A green vegetable may be cooked by direct heat while pork fillets are standing; see Barbecue-steamed Vegetables (page 89).

PORK WITH CINNAMON APPLES

All barbecues: Direct—Hot reducing to Medium
Cooking time: 10-12 minutes
Serves: 6

6 pork butterfly steaks (chops)

freshly ground black pepper

1 red and 1 green apple

2 tbsp melted butter

oil

1 tsp cinnamon sugar

Trim excess fat from butterfly steaks. Season pork with pepper. Wash apples, halve, remove cores and cut into slender wedges. Place in a bowl, add melted butter and toss to coat. Take all ingredients out to barbecue.

Oil section of heated barbecue hotplate on which pork is to be cooked. Add pork and sear on each side. Place apples next to pork and toss them occasionally as the pork cooks. Reduce heat of barbecue and continue to cook pork more slowly, turning occasionally, until just cooked through; do not overcook. Sprinkle apples with cinnamon sugar, toss once more. Remove pork and apples to a warm platter and serve immediately with warm crusty bread and a vegetable or salad of choice.

Suggested BBQ accompaniment: Spiced Red Cabbage with Apple (page 92), cooked by direct heat 40 minutes before pork is placed on the barbecue.

Pork with cinnamon apples

CROWN ROAST OF PORK WITH GINGER STUFFING

> **Charcoal kettle:** *Indirect—Medium—Preheat 8-10 minutes*
> **Gas kettle:** *Indirect—Hot—Preheat 8-10 minutes*
> **Covered gas grill:** *Indirect—Hot—Preheat 8-10 minutes*
> **Cooking time:** *2-2½ hours*
> **Serves:** *6-8*

1 crown roast of pork (12-14 ribs)

salt and freshly ground black pepper

oil

Ginger Stuffing

2 tbsp butter or margarine

1 medium-sized onion, chopped

2 tsp grated fresh ginger

1 cup (125 g/4 oz) chopped untoasted cashew nuts

grated rind of 2 oranges

2 tbsp chopped preserved (candied) ginger

2 cups (125 g/4 oz) soft white breadcrumbs

1 egg, lightly beaten

Wipe crown roast with damp kitchen paper. Season inside and out with salt and pepper. Cut a round of heavy-duty foil to fit roast base and brush with oil. Stand roast on the foil. Prepare stuffing and fill centre of roast. Brush oil over outside of meat and ribs. Cover rib bones with pieces of foil.

Place roast on barbecue grill directly over drip pan containing 2 cups water. Cook indirect, hood down, for 2-2½ hours until cooked; pierce meat between rib bones—juices should be faintly pink. Lift onto a warm platter and remove foil from bones and base. Cover with foil and stand for 15 minutes. Make gravy, if desired, with juices from drip pan; see Gravy for Your Roast (page 99). Carve between rib bones and serve with vegetables of choice cooked beside the roast.

Ginger Stuffing: Heat butter in a frying pan, add onion and cook gently until soft. Add grated ginger and cashew nuts and cook, stirring often, until nuts are lightly browned. Remove from heat, cool and stir in remaining ingredients, adding enough beaten egg to bind. Season to taste with salt and pepper.

SMOKED PORK LOIN ROAST

> **Charcoal kettle:** *Indirect—Medium—Preheat not necessary*
> **Gas kettle:** *Indirect—Hot—Preheat 8-10 minutes*
> **Covered gas grill:** *Indirect—Hot—Preheat 8-10 minutes*
> **Cooking time:** *1½-2 hours*
> **Serves:** *6-8*

1 bone-in pork loin roast, about 2.5 kg (5 lb)

1 tsp dried thyme leaves

2 bay leaves, crumbled finely

1 tsp salt

½ tsp freshly ground black pepper

2 tsp Dijon mustard

2 tbsp melted butter

3 cups (250 g/8 oz) hickory chips, soaked

Pork should have the rind (skin) removed, but fat layer should remain intact. Mix thyme, bay leaves, salt, pepper and mustard, and rub into fat and meat of pork. Brush with melted butter, cover and stand for 1-2 hours. Prepare 4 foil 'logs' with the soaked hickory chips (see page 15).

Place pork fat side up on barbecue grill directly over drip pan containing 2 cups water. Place 2 hickory 'logs' directly on lava rocks or on each side of charcoal fire in kettle. Cook pork indirect, hood down, for 1½-2 hours, adding remaining 2 hickory 'logs' when first 2 are reduced to ash. Remove pork to a warm platter, cover loosely with foil and stand for 15 minutes. Carve the pork and serve with vegetable accompaniments of choice.

Suggested BBQ accompaniments: Prepare Potatoes Boulangère (page 91), and cover securely with foil. Cook indirect alongside pork, leaving on foil for entire cooking time to protect from smoke. Potatoes will not brown, but they still taste good. Barbecue-roasted Peppers (page 94) are also excellent served with the pork; they may be prepared before cooking the pork, or a day or two beforehand and held in the refrigerator. Bring to room temperature before serving.

CIDER-GLAZED HAM STEAKS

> **All barbecues:** *Direct—Hot*
> **Cooking time:** *6-8 minutes*
> **Serves:** *6*

3-6 ham steaks, about 1 cm (½ in) thick

2 tbsp brown sugar

2 tsp mustard powder

1 cup (250 ml/8 fl oz) apple cider

4 whole cloves

2 tbsp melted butter

Quantity of ham steaks depends on size of cut; if large steaks from the leg, only 3 would be required. Mix brown sugar and mustard to break up lumps. Place in a glass or ceramic shallow dish and stir in apple cider. Add whole cloves and ham steaks, turn steaks to coat with marinade. Cover and marinate for 2 hours at room temperature, turning steaks occasionally. Take out to barbecue with the melted butter in a small bowl.

Cook steaks on oiled barbecue grill or hotplate over a hot fire. Add melted butter to marinade and baste ham during cooking. Cook for about 3-4 minutes each side. Serve hot with accompaniments of choice.

Suggested BBQ accompaniments: Whole baked sweet potatoes and jacket potatoes, cooked direct beforehand. Wedges of cantaloupe melon, grilled beside the ham and basted with the marinade. See table, page 25.

HAM STEAKS WITH RAISIN SAUCE

> **All barbecues:** *Direct—Hot*
> **Cooking time:** *15-20 minutes*
> **Serves:** *6*

3-6 ham steaks, about 1 cm (½ in) thick

2 tbsp melted butter

Raisin Sauce

¾ cup (125 g/4 oz) seeded raisins

½ cup (125 ml/4 fl oz) sweet sherry

¼ cup (90 g/3 oz) redcurrant jelly

⅛ tsp ground allspice

grated rind of 1 orange

½ cup (125 ml/4 fl oz) water

3 tsp cornflour (cornstarch)

Quantity of ham steaks depends on size of cut; if large steaks from the leg, only 3 would be required. Brush butter over steaks and place on a flat dish. Mix sauce ingredients in a saucepan. Take all out to barbecue.

Place saucepan with sauce ingredients on grill of hot barbecue and stir constantly until thickened and bubbling. Leave to simmer gently at side of grill. Place ham steaks on grill and cook for about 2-3 minutes each side until lightly browned. Arrange ham steaks on a warm platter, spoon on some of the sauce and serve remainder separately in a sauceboat. Serve with vegetable accompaniments of choice.

Suggested BBQ accompaniments: Frozen corn cobs; wrap in foil and cook direct on barbecue (see table, page 25). Potatoes previously boiled in their skins; slice diagonally in 2 cm (¾ in) slices, brush with melted butter, season and heat on the barbecue grill for 3-4 minutes each side.

BAKED SHERRY-GLAZED HAM

Charcoal kettle: *Indirect—Medium—Preheat not necessary*
Gas kettle: *Indirect—Hot—Preheat 8-10 minutes*
Covered gas grill: *Indirect—Hot—Preheat 8-10 minutes*
Cooking time: *2½ hours*
Serves: *20-25*

1 cooked leg ham, about 5 kg (10 lb)

whole cloves

1 cup (150 g/5 oz) brown sugar

3 tsp mustard powder

1 cup (250 ml/8 fl oz) dry sherry

Cut skin around shank of ham so that this portion is left on. Peel off remaining skin and reserve. Score fat on top and sides of ham in diamonds and insert a whole clove in the centre of each diamond. Mix brown sugar with mustard to break up lumps and add enough sherry to make a thick paste.

Baked sherry-glazed ham

Place ham on oiled grill directly over 1 or 2 large drip pans. Cook indirect, hood down, for 2 hours. After the first hour, spoon a little of the sherry over the ham every 15 minutes, retaining about ¼ cup. After 2 hours, spread brown sugar mixture over the fat and continue to cook, hood down, for further 30 minutes until nicely glazed, drizzling with remaining sherry towards end of cooking. In some barbecues, it may be necessary to shield sides of ham with foil to prevent scorching. When ham is ready, lift onto serving platter with 2 strong cooking forks. Stand for 20-30 minutes before carving.

To store leftover ham, cover cut surface with reserved ham skin and wrap ham in a clean cloth. Store in refrigerator and use within 2 weeks, changing cloth each 2-3 days.

Fruit-glazed Ham: In place of sherry, use same quantity of orange, pineapple or apple juice, or apricot nectar; prepare and cook as above.

Note: For barbecues such as the gas kettle, a half-leg of ham or a more compact boned leg may fit more easily than a whole leg. Check size before purchase. Cook for 1½ hours before glazing.

POULTRY

All too often poultry is ruined by cooking it too quickly. Chicken, in particular, becomes dry and stringy if subjected to constant high heat. With indirect cooking, chicken is moist and tender, just as it should be. Cooking times for poultry can vary considerably according to the type of barbecue used, so check degree of cooking with a meat thermometer (see page 22) when cooking whole birds.

Don't forget the covered barbecue when preparing that special festive or holiday repast—cook your turkey or goose to perfection while the rest of the meal is cooked in the kitchen.

ROAST MARSALA QUAILS

> *Charcoal kettle: Indirect—Medium—Preheat not necessary*
> *Gas kettle: Indirect—Hot—Preheat 8-10 minutes*
> *Covered gas grill: Indirect—Hot—Preheat 8-10 minutes*
> *Cooking time: 35-45 minutes*
> *Serves: 4-6*

12 quails

1 quantity Marsala Marinade

1 tbsp balsamic vinegar or 2 tsp red-wine vinegar

¼ cup (60 g/2 oz) butter or margarine, melted

Marsala Sauce (see Drumsticks in a Basket, page 70)

Rinse the body cavities of the quails and place upright in a colander to drain. Dry with kitchen paper, tuck wings behind breast and truss legs with white string. Prepare marinade as directed using olive oil. Add the vinegar. Pour into a large plastic bag placed in a large dish. Add quails, seal bag with tie and turn bag over to distribute marinade. Leave in refrigerator for 2-3 hours or overnight, turning bag over occasionally.

Drain marinade into a small saucepan. Brush barbecue grill with melted butter and place quails on grill directly over drip pan containing 1 cup water. Put pan of marinade on same side as quails. Brush quails with butter and cook indirect, hood down, for 35-45 minutes. Turn and baste quails often during cooking, basting with marinade and occasionally with butter. To test, cut into quail breast—it should be slightly pink near bone when cooked. Serve the quail with Marsala Sauce made as directed for Drumsticks in a Basket. Serve with vegetables of choice or a tossed salad such as Green Salad with Cashew Dressing (page 97).

DRUMSTICKS IN A BASKET

> *Charcoal kettle: Indirect—Medium—Preheat not necessary*
> *Gas kettle: Indirect—Hot—Preheat 8-10 minutes*
> *Covered gas grill: Indirect—Hot—Preheat 8-10 minutes*
> *Cooking time: 1-1¼ hours*
> *Serves: 6*

1 quantity Marsala Marinade

12-18 chicken drumsticks

Bread Basket (page 112)

Marsala Sauce (optional)

2 tsp chicken stock (bouillon) powder

2 tsp cornflour (cornstarch)

¼ cup (60 ml/2 fl oz) water

salt to taste

Mix marinade ingredients, according to directions, in a large plastic container with a tight seal. Add chicken, seal and shake to coat. Leave to marinate at room temperature for no more than 1 hour, or in refrigerator for several hours or overnight. Shake container occasionally to distribute marinade.

Drain marinade into a small saucepan. Place chicken on oiled grill of barbecue, directly over drip pan containing 1 cup water. Put marinade on side of grill next to chicken. Cook indirect, hood down, for 1-1¼ hours. Turn and baste chicken often during cooking. During last 10 minutes, clear a space on the grill and wipe with a wad of kitchen paper. Place prepared Bread Basket on grill and heat as directed. When heated, pile drumsticks in basket and cover with lid. Leave on the grill to keep warm if making sauce. Place bread basket of drumsticks in a serving basket and serve hot. The Bread Basket can serve as a delicious accompaniment.

Marsala Sauce: If possible, remove drip pan and pour contents into remaining marinade. Skim off excess fat and add stock powder. Bring to the boil over direct heat, mix cornflour into water and stir into simmering marinade. Stir until bubbling, adding salt to taste and a little more water if necessary. Strain into a sauceboat and serve alongside the drumsticks.

MARSALA MARINADE

> *Makes: about 1½ cups*

1 cup (250 ml/8 fl oz) Marsala

¼ cup (60 ml/2 fl oz) olive or other salad oil

grated rind of 1 lemon

¼ cup (60 ml/2 fl oz) lemon juice

2 cloves garlic, crushed

2 tsp chopped fresh thyme or marjoram

2 tsp chopped fresh rosemary

1 tbsp chopped parsley

2 tbsp chopped spring onions (scallions)

½ tsp freshly ground black pepper

Combine ingredients in a glass or ceramic dish in which food is to be

Left: Roast marsala quails; right: Drumsticks in a basket

marinated. If fresh herbs are not available, use 1 teaspoon each of dried thyme (or marjoram) and rosemary; parsley should be fresh. Use to marinate poultry or veal, or as directed in recipes.

ROAST CHICKEN WITH SAGE POTATOES

Charcoal kettle: Indirect—Medium—Preheat not necessary
Gas kettle: Indirect—Hot—Preheat 8-10 minutes
Covered gas grill: Indirect—Hot—Preheat 8-10 minutes
Cooking time: 1½-2 hours
Serves: 4-5

Cooking aids available for covered barbecues are many and varied, and it is up to you which ones you choose.

However, there is one which is recommended for its versatility—the roasting rack, illustrated on page 17. It is a practical alternative to rotisserie cooking.

1 chicken, about 1.5 kg (3 lb)
salt and freshly ground black pepper
1 lemon, halved
20 fresh sage leaves
2 tbsp oil
1 kg (2 lb) medium-sized old potatoes

Clean out fat from chicken cavity, rinse and dry with kitchen paper. Season cavity with salt and pepper, chop one half of the lemon and place in cavity with 4 sage leaves. Truss the chicken loosely so that body cavity remains open. Rub with lemon half, squeezing out juice as you rub, season with salt and pepper and brush well with oil.

Insert the prongs of the roast rack into the cavity of the chicken so that chicken is breast side up.

Peel and quarter potatoes, place in a large roasting pan and add remaining oil and sage leaves, and salt and pepper to taste. Toss well to coat potatoes with oil. Stand rack with chicken in centre of pan, with potatoes under and around chicken.

Place pan on barbecue grill and cook indirect, hood down, for 1½-2 hours until chicken is cooked when tested. During cooking, turn and reposition potatoes so that they brown evenly, and baste chicken with pan drippings. Remove chicken to a warm platter, surround with the potatoes and serve immediately with a tossed salad.

Note: Failing a roast rack, place the chicken in the centre of the pan with potatoes around it. Turn chicken twice during cooking and increase cooking time by 30 minutes.

Roast turkey with mushroom stuffing

ROAST TURKEY WITH MUSHROOM STUFFING

Charcoal kettle: Indirect—Medium—Preheat not necessary
Gas kettle: Indirect—Medium—Preheat 8-10 minutes
Covered gas grill: Indirect—Medium—Preheat 8-10 minutes
Cooking time: 3½-4 hours
Serves: 10-12

1 turkey, about 5-6 kg (11-13 lb)

salt and freshly ground black pepper

½ cup (125 g/4 oz) butter or margarine, melted

Mushroom Stuffing

60 g (2 oz) bacon, chopped

¼ cup (60 g/2 oz) butter or margarine

1 large onion, finely chopped

½ cup (60 g/2 oz) chopped celery

chopped liver from turkey (optional)

125 g (4 oz) mushrooms, chopped

grated rind of 1 lemon

2 tbsp lemon juice

2 tbsp chopped parsley

1 tbsp chopped fresh thyme or 1 tsp dried thyme leaves

6 cups (375 g/12 oz) soft white breadcrumbs

2 medium-sized eggs, beaten

Clean out turkey cavities, rinse and dry with kitchen paper. Prepare stuffing (see below) and fill crop and body cavity loosely. Truss turkey and season with salt and pepper. Brush all over with melted butter.

Place turkey, breast side up, on barbecue grill directly over 1-2 drip pans, each containing about 2 cups water. Shield each side of turkey with foil. Cook indirect, hood down, for 3½-4 hours, basting occasionally with remaining melted butter. Shield top of breast with foil if it browns too quickly. Remove foil 30 minutes before end of cooking time. Remove to a warm platter, cover with foil and stand for 20 minutes before carving. Make gravy with juices from drip pan(s) if desired, following directions for Gravy for your Roast (page 99) using double the amount of ingredients given. Serve turkey with gravy, cranberry sauce and vegetable accompaniments of choice.

Mushroom Stuffing: Put bacon in a large heated frying pan and cook until browned. Add butter, onion and celery and cook gently until onion is soft. Add liver if used, stir until colour changes, then add mushrooms and cook for 2-3 minutes. Remove from heat and add remaining ingredients except eggs. Toss until well mixed, then bind with beaten eggs, mixing lightly. Season to taste with salt and pepper.

Suggested BBQ accompaniments: Vegetable accompaniments may be added to barbecue if using a charcoal kettle or a large gas grill. Suggestions—roast potatoes, see Roast Vegetables (page 88), Gingered Sweet Potatoes (page 92).

CHICKEN AND PRUNE PUFFS

Charcoal kettle: Indirect—Medium—Preheat 8-10 minutes
Gas kettle: Indirect—Hot—Preheat 8-10 minutes
Covered gas grill: Indirect—Hot—Preheat 8-10 minutes
Cooking time: 20-25 minutes
Serves: 6

6 large chicken breast halves, skinned

12 pitted prunes

grated rind of 1 lemon

1 tbsp lemon juice

¼ tsp ground cinnamon

salt and freshly ground black pepper

12 sheets fillo pastry

⅓ cup (90 ml/3 fl oz) melted ghee (clarified butter)

Cut a pocket into the thick side of each half-breast. Toss pitted prunes gently with lemon rind, juice and cinnamon to distribute flavourings. Insert 2 prunes in each breast. Season chicken lightly with salt and pepper.

Brush a sheet of fillo pastry with melted butter, top with another sheet, butter top and fold in half across the length to give almost a square of pastry. Brush lightly with butter, place a chicken breast towards one corner, and wrap like a parcel, folding in sides. Place seam side down on a greased baking tray and repeat with remaining ingredients. Brush tops and sides of parcels with remaining melted butter. Cover with plastic film (wrap) and leave in refrigerator for several hours if necessary, but bring to room temperature for 1 hour before cooking.

Place tray of chicken parcels on barbecue grill and cook indirect, hood down, for 20-25 minutes. Chicken is cooked when juices begin to seep through pastry onto tray. Serve immediately with vegetable accompaniments of choice.

Suggested BBQ accompaniment: Prepare Butternut Nutmeg Pumpkin (page 93) and put on to cook before the chicken. While chicken is cooking, scoop out the flesh into an ovenproof dish, mash to a purée and return to barbecue to heat after chicken has cooked for 10 minutes.

BAKED CITRUS CHICKEN

Charcoal kettle: *Indirect—Medium—Preheat not necessary*
Gas kettle: *Indirect—Medium—Preheat 6-8 minutes*
Covered gas grill: *Indirect—Medium—Preheat 6-8 minutes*
Cooking time: *1½-2 hours*
Serves: *6*

2 kg (4 lb) chicken pieces

grated rind of 2 oranges

grated rind of 1 lemon or lime

1 tsp mustard powder

1½ tsp salt

¼ tsp ground rosemary

2 tbsp brown sugar, packed

2 tbsp melted butter or margarine

1½ cups (375 ml/12 fl oz) fresh orange juice

juice of 1 lemon or lime

2 tbsp Beurre Manié (page 18)

Leave skin on chicken pieces. Mix orange and lemon or lime rinds with mustard, salt, rosemary and half the brown sugar. Rub into chicken, place pieces in a single layer in an oven dish greased with butter, and leave for 30 minutes. Mix juices with remaining brown sugar and pour over chicken. Drizzle on remainder of melted butter. Take out to barbecue with Beurre Maniè in a small dish.

Place dish of chicken on barbecue grill and cook indirect, hood down, for 1½-2 hours. Turn chicken over twice during cooking so that chicken browns evenly. When tender, move dish to direct heat and heap chicken to one side of dish. Stir Beurre Manié into sauce a little at a time and stir until lightly thickened and bubbling. Turn chicken in the sauce and serve from the dish or transfer to a platter. Serve with a rice dish and a tossed green salad.

Suggested BBQ accompaniment: Prepare Orange and Currant Pilaf (page 94) and add to barbecue after chicken has cooked for 1 hour.

APRICOT CHICKEN WINGS

Charcoal kettle: *Indirect—Medium—Preheat not necessary*
Gas kettle: *Indirect—Medium—Preheat 8-10 minutes*
Covered gas grill: *Indirect—Medium—Preheat 8-10 minutes*
Cooking time: *45-50 minutes*
Serves: *6-8*

2 kg (4 lb) chicken wings

1 cup (250 ml/8 fl oz) Apricot Barbecue Sauce (page 101)

Leave chicken wings whole. Place in a glass or ceramic bowl and pour on Apricot Barbecue Sauce. Toss well to coat with sauce. Cover and marinate at room temperature for up to 2 hours, or refrigerate for several hours.

Put chicken wings and sauce in a large metal roasting pan and place on barbecue grill. Cook indirect, hood down, for 45-50 minutes, turning wings occasionally. Sauce will reduce to a thick glaze by the end of cooking time. Serve hot as finger food or as part of a main meal.

Baked citrus chicken

ROAST CHICKEN WITH CURRANT RICE STUFFING

> *Charcoal kettle: Indirect—Medium—Preheat not necessary*
> *Gas kettle: Indirect—Hot—Preheat 8-10 minutes*
> *Covered gas grill: Indirect—Hot—Preheat 8-10 minutes*
> *Cooking time: 2-2½ hours*
> *Serves: 4-6*

1 chicken, about 1.75 kg (3½ lb)

salt and freshly ground black pepper

¼ cup (60 g/2 oz) butter or margarine, melted

Currant Rice Stuffing

2 tbsp butter or margarine

1 small onion, chopped

2 tbsp pinenuts (pignolias)

½ cup (100 g/3½ oz) long-grain rice

2 tbsp currants

1 tbsp chopped parsley

¼ tsp ground allspice

¾ cup (185 ml/6 fl oz) water

Clean chicken cavity if necessary. Rinse, drain well and dry chicken inside and out with kitchen paper. Fill cavity with stuffing (see below) and truss chicken. Season with salt and pepper and brush half the butter all over chicken. Take out to barbecue with remaining butter.

Place chicken on barbecue grill directly over drip pan containing 1 cup water. Cook indirect, hood down, for 2-2½ hours, basting occasionally with remaining butter. Remove to a warm platter, cover with foil and let stand for 10 minutes before serving with accompaniments of choice.

Currant Rice Stuffing: Melt butter in a frying pan, add onion and cook gently until soft. Add pinenuts and cook until lightly browned. Stir in rice, currants, parsley and allspice. Add water, stir well, cover and simmer gently for 10 minutes until water is absorbed. Cool before stuffing chicken.

Suggested BBQ accompaniment: Prepare Hot Herbed Tomatoes (page 91) and add to barbecue 30 minutes before chicken completes cooking. Pesto Breads (page 110) go well with the chicken; heat after chicken and tomatoes are removed.

Roast chicken with currant rice stuffing

OVEN-FRIED CHICKEN

> *Charcoal kettle: Indirect—Medium—Preheat 8-10 minutes*
> *Gas kettle: Indirect—Hot—Preheat 8-10 minutes*
> *Covered gas grill: Indirect—Hot—Preheat 8-10 minutes*
> *Cooking time: 1-1¼ hours*
> *Serves: 6*

2 kg (4 lb) chicken pieces

¼ cup (30 g/1 oz) plain (all-purpose) flour

¼ cup (30 g/1 oz) dry breadcrumbs

1 tsp salt

1 tsp lemon pepper seasoning

1 tbsp finely chopped parsley

¼ tsp ground rosemary leaves

¼ tsp ground sage leaves

2 eggs, beaten

2 tbsp milk

¼ cup (60 g/2 oz) butter or margarine, melted

¼ cup (60 ml/2 fl oz) oil

Use breast halves, legs and thighs with skin and bone. Wipe dry with kitchen paper. In a pie dish mix flour with crumbs, salt, lemon pepper and herbs until thoroughly combined. In another dish, beat eggs and milk. Dip chicken pieces in egg wash, then coat with flour mixture, dusting off excess. Place on a tray and chill for 1 hour. Mix melted butter and oil in a large metal roasting pan. Take all out to barbecue.

Place roasting pan on barbecue grill and heat, hood down, until butter mixture is hot. Add chicken pieces and spoon butter mixture over chicken. Cook indirect, hood down, for 1-1¼ hours, until golden brown and cooked through, turning chicken occasionally. Remove chicken pieces to a warm platter and serve immediately with a selection of salads.

CHICKEN LEGS WITH PISTACHIOS

> *Charcoal kettle: Indirect—Medium—Preheat not necessary*
> *Gas kettle: Indirect—Hot—Preheat 8-10 minutes*
> *Covered gas grill: Indirect—Hot—Preheat 8-10 minutes*
> *Cooking time: 1-1¼ hours*
> *Serves: 6*

6 chicken legs with thighs attached (Marylands)

salt and freshly ground black pepper

2 tsp Dijon mustard

2 tbsp lemon juice

¼ cup (60 ml/2 fl oz) oil

Pistachio Stuffing

2 tbsp butter or margarine

2 spring onions (scallions), chopped

¾ cup (90 g/3 oz) shelled pistachio nuts

½ tsp dried tarragon

1 cup (60 g/2 oz) soft white breadcrumbs

Purchase large chicken Marylands, otherwise it will be difficult to form pockets for stuffing. Loosen skin from the top of the thigh, opening a pocket across top of thigh and part-way down leg. Use fingers and the handle of a teaspoon. Fill with stuffing and secure skin in place with wooden cocktail picks or poultry pins. Season with salt and pepper. Cover and chill for several hours if necessary. Mix mustard with lemon juice and oil in a small pan.

Place chicken pieces on oiled barbecue grill directly over drip pan. Baste with mustard mixture and cook indirect, hood down, for 1–1¼ hours, turning and basting occasionally. Serve with potatoes and a tossed salad.

Pistachio Stuffing: Melt butter in a small pan, add spring onion and cook gently until soft. Place in bowl of food processor and add remaining ingredients. Process to a coarse paste, seasoning with a little salt and pepper.

Suggested BBQ accompaniment: Prepare Hasselback Potatoes (page 90) and place on barbecue 15 minutes before adding the chicken.

TURKEY WITH CRANBERRY-LIME GLAZE

Charcoal kettle: Indirect—Medium—Preheat not necessary
Gas kettle: Indirect—Hot—Preheat 8-10 minutes
Covered gas grill: Indirect—Hot—Preheat 8-10 minutes
Cooking time: 1½-2 hours
Serves: 6-8

1 boneless turkey roast, about 1 kg (2 lb)

salt and freshly ground black pepper

Turkey with cranberry-lime glaze

¼ cup (60 g/2 oz) butter or margarine

1 cup (250 ml/8 fl oz) Cranberry-lime Sauce and Glaze (page 100)

2 tsp cornflour (cornstarch)

1 cup (250 ml/8 fl oz) chicken stock (broth)

Boneless turkey roast is often available rolled, netted and frozen; thaw for 24 hours in refrigerator and leave in netting. If boneless turkey breast is not available, use a 1-1.5 kg (2-3 lb) turkey half-breast with skin removed. Season turkey roast with salt and pepper and brush all over with melted butter. Put ½ cup of the sauce in a small pan and stir in remaining melted butter to use as a glaze. Mix remaining sauce in a bowl with the cornflour.

Place turkey roast on greased barbecue grill directly over drip pan containing 1 cup water. Cook indirect, hood down, for 30 minutes, turning turkey to brown evenly. Brush lightly with glaze and continue to cook for further 1-1½ hours, turning and brushing with glaze each 15 minutes or so. Check degree of cooking with meat thermometer (see table, page 22). When cooked, remove to a warm platter, cover loosely with foil and stand for 15 minutes.

Carefully remove drip pan and place over direct heat. Add stock and heat, stirring in any browned juices. Bring to the boil, then stir in sauce–cornflour mixture and any remaining glaze, and keep stirring until lightly thickened and bubbling. Pour into sauceboat. Slice turkey and serve with the sauce and vegetables of choice.

Suggested BBQ accompaniments: Butternut Nutmeg Pumpkin (page 93) and potatoes baked in their jackets. Place on barbecue with turkey.

DUCK WITH PLUM GLAZE

> *Charcoal kettle: Indirect—Medium—Preheat 8-10 minutes*
> *Gas kettle: Indirect—Hot—Preheat 8-10 minutes*
> *Covered gas grill: Indirect—Hot—Preheat 8-10 minutes*
> *Cooking time: 2-2½ hours*
> *Serves: 8*

2 ducks, each about 2 kg (4 lb)

salt and freshly ground black pepper

1 cooking apple, quartered

1 lemon, sliced

½ cup (125 ml/4 fl oz) red wine

Plum Glaze

½ cup (175 g/5 oz) plum jam, sieved

¼ cup (60 ml/2 fl oz) water

2 tbsp red wine vinegar

2 tsp chilli sauce

¼ tsp ground ginger

¼ tsp ground allspice

Remove any internal fat from ducks, dry with kitchen paper and season cavities with salt and pepper. Divide apple and lemon between ducks, secure opening with poultry pins and truss. Prick skin well with a fine skewer and season with salt and pepper. Prepare glaze and take out to barbecue in its pan.

Place ducks on barbecue grill directly over drip pan containing 2 cups water. Cook indirect, hood down, for 2-2½ hours. After ducks have cooked for 1 hour, brush with glaze, and repeat every 20 minutes or so. When cooked, remove to a board, cover with foil and stand 15 minutes. Meanwhile put pan with remaining glaze over direct heat, add wine and bring to the boil. Boil gently for 5 minutes until syrupy. Remove stuffing from ducks and discard. Halve the ducks, arrange on a warm platter and coat with sauce. Serve with vegetables of choice.

Plum Glaze: Put sieved plum jam in a small pan with remaining glaze ingredients and heat, stirring often, until smooth.

Suggested BBQ accompaniment: Steamed snow peas (mange-tout) cooked over direct heat when making the sauce; see Barbecue-steamed Vegetables (page 89).

ROAST GOOSE WITH CHESTNUTS AND APPLES

> *Charcoal kettle: Indirect—Medium—Preheat 8-10 minutes*
> *Gas kettle: Indirect—Medium—Preheat 8-10 minutes*
> *Covered gas grill: Indirect—Medium—Preheat 8-10 minutes*
> *Cooking time: 3½-4 hours*
> *Serves: 8-10*

1 goose, about 4 kg (9 lb)

1 lemon

salt and freshly ground black pepper

2 tbsp butter

2 apples and 125 g (4 oz) chestnuts for serving

Stuffing

250 g (8 oz) chestnuts

1 small onion, chopped

2 tbsp butter

3 cooking apples, peeled and diced

Clean out body cavity of goose, removing any internal fat. Rinse cavity and dry inside and out with kitchen paper. Squeeze a little lemon juice into cavity and sprinkle in a little salt and pepper. Fill cavity with stuffing, sew up opening or secure with poultry pins. Truss the goose and rub all over with lemon juice and salt and pepper. Prick the skin all over with a fine skewer so that fat can be released during cooking.

Place goose, breast side up, on barbecue grill directly over drip pan containing 1 cup water. Shield sides with foil and cook indirect, hood down, for 3½ hours or until cooked when tested. Remove foil towards end of cooking. Place goose on a warm platter, cover with foil and let stand for 20 minutes. Place a frying pan over direct heat and add butter. Slice apples and brown slices on each side, place on platter with goose. Add prepared chestnuts to pan and fry for 3-4 minutes, tossing often until heated through. Arrange around goose. Serve with vegetables of choice.

Stuffing: To shell chestnuts (for stuffing and garnish), cut through shell at each end, place in a pan with water to cover and boil for 10 minutes. Take pan off heat. Remove a few chestnuts at a time and peel off shells and skins.

Break chestnuts for stuffing in half (reserve remainder for garnish). Heat butter in a frying pan, add onion and cook gently until softened. Add chestnut pieces and cook for further 5 minutes. Remove from heat and add diced apples.

Suggested BBQ accompaniments: Roast potatoes, see Roast Vegetables (page 88) and Spiced Red Cabbage with Apple (page 92). Add to barbecue after goose has been cooking for 2 hours.

POUSSINS WITH GINGER LIME BUTTER

> *All barbecues: Direct—Medium*
> *Cooking time: 18-22 minutes*
> *Serves: 6*

3 poussins (spatchcocks), each about 500 g (1 lb)

grated rind and juice of 2 limes

1 tsp grated fresh ginger

2 tsp honey

2 tbsp oil

salt and freshly ground black pepper

1 quantity Ginger Lime Butter (page 100)

Poussins are very young chickens. Split the poussins and cut off the backbones with poultry shears. Mix lime rind and juice with ginger, honey and oil. Place poussin halves in a dish and brush all over with lime mixture. Season with salt and pepper, cover and leave for 1 hour, or refrigerate for several hours.

Place poussins on barbecue grill and cook, covered, for 18-22 minutes, turning and basting frequently with remaining marinade. When cooked, pile onto a warm platter and serve with Ginger Lime Butter and a selection of salads.

MANGO CHICKEN ROLLS

> *All barbecues: Direct—Hot reducing to Medium-low*
> *Cooking time: 12-15 minutes*
> *Serves: 8*

8 large chicken breast halves, skinned

Roast goose with chestnuts and apples

chicken and mango slices to a warm platter and spoon on remaining glaze. Serve with a rice pilaf and a tossed salad.

Suggested BBQ accompaniment: Prepare Carrot Pilaf (page 94), cooking it by direct heat before cooking chicken. Keep warm until chicken is cooked.

SMOKED LEMON-HONEY CHICKEN

> *Charcoal kettle: Indirect—Medium—Preheat 8-10 minutes*
> *Gas kettle: Indirect—Hot—Preheat 8-10 minutes*
> *Covered gas grill: Indirect—Hot—Preheat 8-10 minutes*
> *Cooking time: 1½-2 hours*
> *Serves: 4*

1 chicken, about 1.5 kg (3 lb)

1 lemon, halved

salt and freshly ground black pepper

4 tsp honey

¼ cup (60 g/2 oz) butter, melted

4 cups (250 g/8 oz) hickory chips, soaked (see page 15)

Clean chicken cavity if necessary. Rinse, drain well and wipe inside and out with kitchen paper. Chop one lemon half and place in cavity with a sprinkling of salt and pepper and drizzle in 1 teaspoon of the honey. Squeeze remaining lemon half and reserve 1 tablespoon of the juice in a small bowl. Truss chicken, rub remainder of juice on the outside and season with salt and pepper. Brush half the butter all over chicken, place on a plate, cover and refrigerate for at least 1 hour, although flavour is better if set aside for several hours or overnight. Mix remaining honey into reserved lemon juice. Drain soaked hickory chips and make into 4 foil 'logs'.

Place 2 foil 'logs' on glowing coals of charcoal kettle or on lava rock of gas barbecues. Place chicken on barbecue grill directly over drip pan containing 2 cups water. Cook indirect, hood down, for 1½-2 hours, basting occasionally with remaining butter. Add 2 more 'logs' when first lot has stopped releasing smoke. About 15 minutes before end of cooking time, baste chicken with lemon-honey mixture. When chicken is cooked, remove to a warm platter, cover with foil and stand for 10 minutes. Serve with salad and warm, crusty bread.

2 fresh mangoes or 16 canned mango slices

salt and freshly ground black pepper

2 tbsp melted butter or margarine

1 tsp Dijon mustard

2 tbsp sieved orange marmalade

½ cup (125 ml/4 fl oz) fresh orange juice

2 tbsp port

Flatten chicken breasts between two sheets of plastic film (wrap), taking care not to tear holes in flesh. Peel fresh mangoes and slice each into 8 wedges; drain canned mangoes if used. Place a slice of mango on each chicken breast and roll up. Secure with wooden cocktail picks and season rolls with salt and pepper. Mix remaining ingredients in a small saucepan for a glaze.

Heat barbecue with hotplate or griddle in place. Place glaze on side of barbecue to heat gently. Brush mango rolls with glaze and cook on hotplate, turning rolls to brown evenly, about 4-5 minutes. Brush with glaze during cooking. Move to cooler part of hotplate or reduce heat on gas barbecue and cook, hood down, for 8-10 minutes until chicken is cooked through. During last 3 minutes of cooking, add remaining mango slices to hotplate to heat. Remove

Spiced Chinese chicken wings

SPICED CHINESE CHICKEN WINGS

Charcoal kettle: Indirect—Medium—Preheat not necessary
Gas kettle: Indirect—Medium—Preheat 8-10 minutes
Covered gas grill: Indirect—Medium—Preheat 8-10 minutes
Cooking time: 40-45 minutes
Serves: 6-8

2 kg (4 lb) chicken wings

1 quantity Honey-soya Marinade and Baste (page 98)

Leave chicken wings whole, or separate at the joints, storing the wing-tips for stock. Have Honey-soya Marinade in a glass or ceramic bowl, add chicken wings and toss well to coat. Cover and marinate at room temperature for up to 2 hours, or refrigerate for several hours.

Place chicken wings and marinade in a large metal roasting pan. Place on barbecue grill and cook indirect, hood down, for 40-45 minutes, turning wings occasionally. Serve hot, piled in a large bowl, as finger food. If desired, wings may be removed from dish and placed briefly over direct heat to make them more crisp—take care not to burn them.

CHICKEN DRUMSTICKS TERIYAKI

Charcoal kettle: Indirect—Medium—Preheat not necessary
Gas kettle: Indirect—Hot—Preheat 8-10 minutes
Covered gas grill: Indirect—Hot—Preheat 8-10 minutes
Cooking time: 1-1¼ hours
Serves: 6

1 quantity Teriyaki Marinade (page 100)

¼ cup (60 ml/2 fl oz) pineapple juice

1 tbsp oil

12-18 chicken drumsticks

Mix marinade ingredients, according to directions, in a large plastic container with a tight seal. Stir in pineapple juice and oil. Add chicken, seal and shake to coat. Leave to marinate at room temperature for no more than 1 hour, or in refrigerator for several hours or overnight. Shake container occasionally to distribute marinade.

Drain marinade into a small saucepan. Place chicken on oiled grill of barbecue, directly over drip pan containing 1 cup water. Put marinade on side of grill next to chicken. Cook indirect, hood down, for 1-1¼ hours. Turn and baste chicken often during cooking. Pile drumsticks on a warm platter and pour over any remaining hot marinade. Serve as finger food or as part of a main meal.

COCONUT CHICKEN SATAYS

> **All barbecues:** *Direct—Hot reducing to Medium*
> **Cooking time:** *6-8 minutes*
> **Serves:** *6*

750 g (1½ lb) boned and skinned chicken breasts

1 quantity Coconut and Lemon Grass Sauce (page 99)

1 tbsp soya sauce

12 long bamboo skewers

Cut chicken breasts into 2 cm (¾ in) cubes. Put a third of the Coconut and Lemon Grass Sauce in a bowl, stir in soya sauce and add cubed chicken. Toss well to coat, cover and marinate for 1 hour in refrigerator. Soak bamboo skewers in cold water for 1 hour. Thread 6-7 pieces of chicken onto each skewer and take out to barbecue with remaining marinade and the remainder of the Coconut and Lemon Grass Sauce in a small pan.

Place the pan of sauce on the side of the grill to heat through. Cook chicken skewers on grill over a hot fire for 6-8 minutes until just cooked through, turning and basting often with marinade. Pile satays onto a warm platter and pour sauce into a bowl. Serve with boiled rice and a salad of tomato and cucumber slices sprinkled with chopped spring onions (scallions).

Suggested BBQ accompaniment: Cook 1½-cup quantity of short-grain rice by direct heat before cooking the satays. See Barbecue-steamed Rice, page 95.

TANDOORI CHICKEN SMOKED WITH MESQUITE

This famous Indian chicken dish is traditionally cooked in a clay oven called a tandoor. The cylindrical clay oven is fired with charcoal, and the smoky wood flavour adds a dimension to the chicken that is difficult to duplicate in the domestic kitchen. If you cook the chickens over a direct charcoal fire, the yoghurt marinade burns and spoils the flavour. By smoke-cooking the Tandoori Chicken by indirect heat, the flavour is as close as you can get to the real thing, even in a gas grill.

> **Charcoal kettle:** *Indirect—Medium—Preheat 10-12 minutes*
> **Gas kettle:** *Indirect—Hot—Preheat 10-12 minutes*
> **Covered gas grill:** *Indirect—Hot—Preheat 10-12 minutes*
> **Cooking time:** *1¾-2¼ hours*
> **Serves:** *6*

3 chickens, each about 1 kg (2 lb)

2 cloves garlic, crushed

2 tsp grated fresh ginger

1½ tsp each salt and cumin

1 tsp each turmeric, paprika and white pepper

½ tsp each cinnamon, cardamom and chilli powder

1/8 tsp ground cloves

¾ cup (185 ml/6 fl oz) natural yoghurt

2 tbsp lime or lemon juice

½ cup (125 g/4 oz) ghee or clarified butter

2 cups (125 g/4 oz) mesquite chips, soaked

lime or lemon wedges for serving

Remove skin from chickens. Cut deep slashes into the breasts, thighs and legs. In a bowl mix garlic, ginger, salt, spices, yoghurt and lime or lemon juice. Put chickens in a shallow glass or ceramic dish and rub yoghurt mixture into slashes, then coat with remaining mixture. Cover and marinate in refrigerator for 3-4 hours at least. Make 2 foil 'logs' with the drained mesquite chips (see page 16).

Have a large drip pan in place with 3-4 cups water before preheating barbecue. Remove chickens from marinade and brush off excess, leaving a thin coating. Quickly brush grill with ghee and add chickens. Cook indirect, hood down, for 15 minutes. Put mesquite 'logs' onto charcoal or lava rock, brush chickens with ghee and marinade and continue to cook for 1½-2 hours. Turn chickens and brush alternately with ghee and marinade during cooking. The ghee keeps the flesh moist. Serve chickens on a warm platter with lime or lemon wedges, a tomato, cucumber and red-onion salad, and bread.

Suggested BBQ accompaniment: Stack and wrap 6-8 white pita breads in foil and heat package in barbecue during last 10 minutes of cooking the chickens. Pita bread is a good substitute for naan, an Indian bread.

Coconut chicken satays

SEAFOOD

Seafood, fish in particular, is a food which should be included more frequently in our diet. While we are happy to order it in restaurants, we are reluctant to prepare it at home because of its rather distinctive smell. Cooking it outdoors solves that problem, and cooking it undercover gives more scope to the types of recipe that can be prepared.

While you might want to try recipes, remember that simple is best when it comes to seafoods. Fish smelling fresh from the sea needs little more than anointment with oil or butter, a quick sear on the barbecue and a squeeze of lemon to serve it at its best.

CHILLI CRAB

All barbecues: Direct—Hot reducing to Medium
Cooking time: 8-10 minutes
Serves: 4

| 2 live crabs, each about 500 g (1 lb) |
| 1 tbsp salted black beans |
| 2 cloves garlic, crushed |
| 1 tsp grated fresh ginger |
| 1-2 red chillies, seeded and finely chopped |
| 2 tsp sugar |
| ½ cup (125 ml/4 fl oz) water |
| ¼ cup (60 ml/2 fl oz) tomato ketchup |
| ¼ cup (60 ml/2 fl oz) peanut oil |
| 4 spring onions (scallions), sliced |

Scrub crabs while still tied, then place in freezer for 10 minutes or so to stun them. Chop in half with a cleaver or heavy knife and clean out grey fibrous tissue and stomach contents; rinse well. Chop body into four pieces, leaving legs attached. Remove large claws and crack in several places with flat side of cleaver; crack legs lightly.

Rinse black beans and place in a bowl. Mash well with a fork and stir in garlic, ginger and chilli to taste. Mix sugar into water and add tomato ketchup. Place all ingredients on a tray and take out to barbecue.

Place a wok or large frying pan on the barbecue grill, add oil and heat well. Add black bean mixture and stir-fry for 1-2 minutes, add crab pieces and stir-fry quickly until colour begins to change. Stir in tomato ketchup mixture. Reduce heat to medium or move wok to cooler section of barbecue and cook, hood down, for 5 minutes or until crab pieces are red and cooked through. Add spring onions, toss well and serve immediately with boiled rice.

Suggested BBQ accompaniment: Prepare Barbecue-steamed Rice (page 95); use 1-cup quantity of short-grain rice and follow Chinese Boiled Rice instructions. Cook by direct heat before cooking the crab, and keep warm at side of grill.

Chilli crab

MUSSELS MARINIÈRE

*All barbecues: Direct—Hot reducing to
Medium*
Cooking time: 20-25 minutes
Serves: 4-6

2 kg (4 lb) mussels

1 bay leaf

4 parsley stalks

2 sprigs fresh thyme

1 tbsp butter

6 spring onions (scallions), chopped

2 cups (500 ml/16 fl oz) dry white wine

freshly ground black pepper

2 tbsp Beurre Manié (page 18)

1 tbsp finely chopped parsley

Scrub mussels well with a stiff brush and remove beards by tugging downwards towards pointed end. Discard any mussels that are not tightly closed. Tie bay leaf, parsley and thyme together with white string. Prepare remaining ingredients and take all out to barbecue.

Place a wide saucepan or Dutch oven on the barbecue, add butter and spring onions and cook for 1 minute. Add bunch of herbs, wine and pepper to taste and bring to the boil. Add mussels, cover pan tightly and cook for 5 minutes, shaking pan occasionally, until mussels are opened.

With a slotted spoon remove mussels to a large heatproof bowl, leaving pan of cooking liquid to simmer at the side of the barbecue. Discard any mussels which have not opened. Remove top shells from mussels and discard. Cover prepared mussels and keep warm at side of barbecue.

Remove bunch of herbs from simmering liquid and discard. Gradually stir Beurre Manié into liquid until lightly thickened. Simmer for 1 minute. Divide mussels between 4-6 deep plates, spoon sauce over and sprinkle lightly with chopped parsley. Serve immediately with crusty French bread.

Note: The first section of the recipe, up to end of the second paragraph, is the basic method for steaming mussels. Use when steamed mussels are required for any recipe. Mussels and cooking liquid can be transferred to a bowl, covered and chilled until required.

Mussels marinière

BARBECUED LOBSTER TAILS

All barbecues: Direct—Hot
Cooking time: 11-15 minutes
Serves: 6

6 uncooked frozen lobster tails, each
    about 250 g (8 oz)

½ cup (125 g/4 oz) butter or
    margarine

¼ cup (60 ml/2 fl oz) lemon juice

2 tbsp finely chopped parsley

salt and freshly ground black
    pepper

paprika

lemon wedges and parsley to
    garnish

Thaw lobster tails in refrigerator for 12-18 hours. Cut each side of soft shell underneath tails with kitchen scissors and remove. Make 2-3 shallow incisions into lobster meat on each tail. Run a skewer through the length of each tail to keep them flat. Melt butter in a small pan and mix with lemon juice, parsley and salt and pepper to taste. Brush some of the butter mixture onto lobster meat.

Place lobster tails, shell down, on barbecue grill and cook until shells turn red—about 5 minutes. Brush meat again with butter mixture, turn and grill for further 5-8 minutes on meat side until flesh turns white. Turn meat side up, brush once more with butter and sprinkle lightly with paprika. Cook for further 1-2 minutes, remove skewers and place on a warm platter. Spoon on any remaining butter mixture, garnish with lemon wedges and parsley and serve with salad.

Chilli prawns with coconut

CHILLI PRAWNS WITH COCONUT

> *All barbecues*: *Direct—Medium*
> *Cooking time*: *6 minutes*
> *Serves*: *6 as starter, 4 as main meal*

1 quantity Coconut and Lemon Grass Sauce (page 99)

1.5 kg (3 lb) medium-sized raw prawns (shrimp)

2 tbsp oil

2 cups (125 g/4 oz) shredded, unsweetened coconut

2 tbsp crushed, roasted peanuts (optional)

Prepare Coconut and Lemon Grass Sauce and place half the sauce in a bowl to cool. Peel the prawns, leaving tails on. De-vein, rinse and dry with kitchen paper. Add prawns to bowl of sauce and toss well to coat. Cover and marinate in refrigerator for 1 hour. Leave remaining sauce in pan in which it was cooked.

Place pan of sauce on side of barbecue grill to simmer gently. Put half the oil in a large frying pan, place on grill and heat. Add coconut and stir-fry until lightly golden. Tip out into a dish and keep aside. Add remaining oil to pan and heat well. Remove prawns from marinade with draining spoon and add to pan. Stir-fry over medium heat until they turn pink (about 3 minutes). Moisten with a little of the marinade as they cook. Take care not to overcook the prawns or they will toughen. Place coconut on 4-6 warm plates, top with prawns and sprinkle with peanuts if desired. Serve with the hot sauce served separately.

BARBECUED FISH WITH TAHINI AND PARSLEY SAUCE

> *All barbecues*: *Direct—Hot*
> *Cooking time*: *6-8 minutes*
> *Serves*: *6*

6 whole whiting or bream, each about 375 g (12 oz)

3 tbsp olive oil

salt and freshly ground black pepper

Tahini and Parsley Sauce

2 cloves garlic, chopped

½ tsp salt

½ cup (125 ml/4 fl oz) tahini (sesame seed paste)

about ½ cup (125 ml/4 fl oz) cold water

½ cup (125 ml/4 fl oz) lemon juice

3 tbsp finely chopped parsley

If whiting or bream are unavailable, choose other fish suitable for cooking whole on the barbecue grill. Gut and scale fish, rinse well and dry with kitchen paper. Place in a shallow dish, rub well with olive oil and season with salt and pepper.

For easier handling, place fish in an oiled hinged fish basket, or place directly on oiled barbecue grill. Cook over a hot fire for 4-5 minutes on first side, turn and cook for 2-3 minutes or until flesh flakes when tested at thickest part. Brush with olive oil during cooking. Remove carefully from basket, or lift off grill with two wide spatulas. Place on a warm serving dish. Serve with Tahini and Parsley Sauce, tossed salad and bread.

Tahini and Parsley Sauce: Put chopped garlic onto a plate and crush to a smooth paste with salt, working it in with the flat edge of a knife blade. Transfer to a bowl, stir in tahini and beat well with a wooden spoon. Gradually beat in water and lemon juice alternately, adding enough water to give a creamy sauce. Stir in parsley and adjust seasoning with more salt if necessary.

COCONUT BAKED FISH

> *Charcoal kettle*: *Indirect—Medium—Preheat not necessary*
> *Gas kettle*: *Indirect—Hot—Preheat 8-10 minutes*
> *Covered gas grill*: *Indirect—Hot—Preheat 8-10 minutes*
> *Cooking time*: *45-55 minutes*
> *Serves*: *6*

1 whole snapper, about 2 kg (4 lb)

1 tbsp grated onion

½ tsp grated fresh ginger

1 small clove garlic, crushed

¼ tsp chilli powder

1 tsp salt

1 quantity Coconut and Lemon Grass Sauce (page 99)

oil

Gut and scale the snapper, rinse thoroughly and dry with kitchen paper. Cut 3 shallow, diagonal slashes into the flesh on each side. Mix grated onion with ginger, garlic, chilli powder and salt. Rub into slashes and cavity of fish, place in an oiled baking dish, cover and leave in refrigerator for 1 hour. Prepare Coconut and Lemon Grass Sauce and leave in its pan.

Place uncovered baking dish with fish on barbecue grill and spoon on half the sauce. Cook indirect, hood down, for 45-55 minutes until flesh flakes when tested just behind the head. Add a little water to dish during cooking if sauce begins to scorch. Towards end of cooking, place pan of sauce on grill next to the fish and let it simmer gently. Serve the fish with the sauce, boiled rice and a salad of sliced cucumber, onion and tomato.

Suggested BBQ accompaniment: Prepare Barbecue-steamed Rice (page 95), using 1½-cup quantity of short-grain rice, and place in barbecue next to fish after fish has been cooking for 30 minutes.

MEDITERRANEAN FISH CASSEROLE

> *Charcoal kettle: Indirect—Medium—Preheat not necessary*
> *Gas kettle: Indirect—Hot—Preheat 8-10 minutes*
> *Covered gas grill: Indirect—Hot—Preheat 8-10 minutes*
> *Cooking time: 1½ hours*
> *Serves: 6*

1.5 kg (3 lb) fish cutlets (steaks)

juice of 1 lemon

salt and freshly ground black pepper

½ cup (125 ml/4 fl oz) olive oil

1 large onion, sliced

1 medium-sized carrot, thinly sliced

½ cup (60 g/2 oz) chopped celery

1 tbsp chopped celery leaves

3 large ripe tomatoes, peeled and chopped

½ cup (125 ml/4 fl oz) dry white wine

½ tsp sugar

lemon slices and chopped parsley for serving

Choose cutlets from snapper, mackerel, cod, hake, halibut or striped bass, according to the fish available. Wipe cutlets with damp kitchen paper, sprinkle with lemon juice, salt and pepper and leave aside.

In a large frying pan, heat oil and add onion, carrot and celery. Cook gently for 10-12 minutes, stirring often, until onion is transparent. Add celery leaves, tomatoes, wine and sugar, cover and simmer for 20 minutes. Spread some of the sauce in an ovenproof dish, add fish cutlets and sauce in layers, finishing with sauce. Cover with foil or lid.

Mediterranean fish casserole

Casserole may be set aside in refrigerator for 2-3 hours if necessary.

Place casserole on barbecue grill and cook indirect, hood down, for 1 hour or until fish flakes when tested. Remove foil or lid after 40 minutes, and complete cooking, basting top of fish occasionally with sauce. Serve from the dish with crusty bread and a tossed green salad.

FISH STEAKS WITH TAPENADE

> *All barbecues: Direct—Hot*
> *Cooking time: 8-10 minutes*
> *Serves: 6*

6 fish steaks or cutlets, each about 250 g (8 oz)

salt and freshly ground black pepper

1 lemon, halved

olive oil

Tapenade

45 g (1½ oz) can anchovy fillets in oil

12 black olives, pitted

1 clove garlic, chopped

1 tbsp drained capers

1 tsp Dijon mustard

1 tbsp brandy

1 tbsp lemon juice

¼ cup (60 ml/2 fl oz) olive oil

Select swordfish steaks or snapper, striped bass or halibut cutlets (steaks), according to availability. Wipe with kitchen paper and season lightly with salt and pepper, squeeze on a little lemon juice and brush with olive oil. Let stand for 15 minutes.

Oil barbecue grill and cook fish over a hot fire, brushing frequently with olive oil. Cook for 4-5 minutes each side until flesh flakes—do not overcook. Lift onto a warm serving platter and garnish with lemon wedges. Serve with the Tapenade served separately, warm, crusty bread and a tossed salad.

Tapenade: Drain anchovies and place in a food processor or blender jar and add remaining ingredients except oil. Process until smooth, and continue to process while gradually adding the oil. Transfer to a sauceboat and leave at room temperature until required for serving.

FISH IN BUTTER SAUCE

> *Charcoal kettle: Indirect—Medium—Preheat not necessary*
> *Gas kettle: Indirect—Hot—Preheat 8-10 minutes*
> *Covered gas grill: Indirect—Hot—Preheat 8-10 minutes*
> *Cooking time: 25-30 minutes*
> *Serves: 6*

6 whole whiting or mullet, each about 375 g (12 oz)

6 small sprigs fresh parsley

1 onion, sliced

1 lemon, sliced

salt and freshly ground black pepper

¼ cup (60 ml/2 fl oz) dry white wine

Butter Sauce

½ cup (125 g/4 oz) butter

1 tbsp finely chopped shallot or white onion

1 small clove garlic, crushed

1 tbsp finely chopped parsley

If whiting or mullet are unavailable, choose other serving-sized fish with tender, sweet flesh suitable for poaching. Gut and scale fish, rinse well and leave whole. Place a sprig of parsley and a slice each of onion and lemon in cavity of each fish. Arrange fish side by side in a greased ovenproof dish, season with salt and pepper and pour wine into dish. Cover with foil.

Place dish on barbecue grill and cook indirect, hood down, for 25-30 minutes until flesh flakes. Check if cooked just below the head, using the point of a knife. Remove the flavourings from body cavities and transfer fish to a serving dish. Pour over Butter Sauce and serve immediately, garnished with lemon slices and parsley.

Butter Sauce: Over direct heat, melt butter in a small saucepan, add shallot and cook gently for 5-6 minutes. Add garlic and parsley and cook 1 minute. Pour over fish.

Suggested BBQ accompaniment: Barbecue-roasted Peppers (page 94), cooked by direct heat before cooking the fish.

SARDINES IN VINE LEAVES

> *All barbecues: Direct—Hot*
> *Cooking time: 4-6 minutes*
> *Serves: 4-6 as a first course*

24 fresh sardines

salt

24 fresh or preserved grape vine leaves

½ cup (125 ml/4 fl oz) olive oil

1 lemon

freshly ground black pepper

lemon wedges for serving

Gut sardines, leaving heads on, and rub off fine scales with kitchen paper. Rinse well and dry thoroughly with kitchen paper. Spread sardines in a single layer in a dish and sprinkle lightly with salt. Leave for 20 minutes. Rinse vine leaves in cold water and cut off stems. Place a vine leaf on work surface, shiny side down, and brush with olive oil. Place a sardine across base of leaf, squeeze on a little lemon juice and season with pepper. Roll up firmly. Repeat with remaining sardines. Rolls may be placed on a tray, covered and set aside in refrigerator for several hours or overnight if necessary.

Place sardines in an oiled, hinged wire basket and brush well with oil. Barbecue over a hot fire for 2-3 minutes each side until leaves are charred and sardines are cooked. Serve onto small plates with lemon wedges. Sardines are unwrapped and lemon juice squeezed on before eating. The vine leaves are not eaten.

Note: If a hinged basket is not available, thread sardines onto pairs of soaked bamboo skewers, placing skewers about 2 cm (¾ in) apart. Thread 4-6 sardines on each pair of skewers. Oil and cook as above and remove from skewers for serving.

Fish in butter sauce

SMOKED TROUT

Charcoal kettle: Indirect—Low—Preheat 8-10 minutes
Gas kettle: Indirect—Low—Preheat 8-10 minutes
Covered gas grill: Indirect—Low—Preheat 8-10 minutes
Cooking time: 45-60 minutes
Yield: 1 x 500 g (1 lb) cleaned trout weighs about 350 g (12 oz) after smoking

2-3 cleaned trout, each about 500 g (1 lb)

1 kg (2 lb) coarse-grained pickling salt

3 cups (185 g/6 oz) hickory chips, soaked

Leave heads on trout, but they should be scaled and gutted with gills removed, with the body cavities cleaned of any traces of blood. Dry well with kitchen paper. Place a layer of salt in a shallow glass or ceramic dish, add the fish side by side with space between fish. Fill cavities with salt and cover fish completely with remaining salt. Cover dish and leave in refrigerator for 6-8 hours. The salting extracts about 10 per cent of the moisture from the fish. In the meantime, soak wood chips in cold water for 1-2 hours.

Rinse fish well in cold water to remove salt, dry well with kitchen paper. Make 2 foil 'logs' with the hickory chips, as described on page 16. Prepare a low fire in charcoal kettle (page 6).

When barbecue is covered or lit for preheating, place a drip pan containing 3 cups water directly under grill. Place 1 'log' on coals each side of charcoal kettle, or 2 'logs' on top of lava rocks on section of gas barbecue which is to stay lit for duration of cooking.

Oil barbecue grill and place trout on grill for indirect cooking; elevate trout in gas kettle or grill as described on page 14, placing fish on warming rack in grill or using a wire cake rack on top of a roasting rack in kettle. This allows more smoke to circulate around fish. Smoke-cook for 45-60 minutes. In gas barbecues, turn fish over after the top develops the bronzed sheen typical of smoked fish—after about 35 minutes. Fish is cooked when juices begin to ooze through skin on top. Fish may be served hot or cool. Wrap in waxed or greaseproof paper, overwrap with foil and store in refrigerator; use within 1 week.

Salmon with ginger lime butter, shown with Devilled tomato butter (page 101) and Lemon and herb butter (page 100)

SALMON WITH GINGER LIME BUTTER

All barbecues: Direct—Medium-hot
Cooking time: 6-8 minutes
Serves: 6

6 salmon cutlets (steaks), each about 250 g (8 oz)

grated rind and juice of 1 lime

1 tsp grated fresh ginger

2 tbsp oil

salt and freshly ground black pepper

1 quantity Ginger Lime Butter (page 100)

Wipe salmon with damp kitchen paper and place in a shallow dish. Mix lime rind, juice, ginger and oil and brush onto each side of cutlets. Season lightly with salt and pepper, cover and stand for 20 minutes or so.

Cook salmon on greased barbecue hotplate or grill for about 3-4 minutes each side until salmon is opaque and flakes with a fork. Brush with lime mixture from dish during cooking and take care not to overcook salmon as it can become dry. Lift on to warm plates. Serve with Ginger Lime Butter and simply cooked vegetables of choice.

Suggested BBQ accompaniments: New potatoes (peeled), see Barbecue-steamed New Potatoes (page 90); and asparagus, broccoli or snow peas (mange-tout), see Barbecue-steamed Vegetables (page 89). Cook by direct heat on barbecue grill. Cook potatoes before the salmon; put the green vegetable on at the same time as the salmon.

SMOKED TROUT IN FILLO WITH HORSERADISH-DILL SAUCE

> **Charcoal kettle:** *Indirect—Medium—Preheat 8-10 minutes*
> **Gas kettle:** *Indirect—Hot—Preheat 8-10 minutes*
> **Covered gas grill:** *Indirect—Hot—Preheat 8-10 minutes*
> **Cooking time:** *10-15 minutes*
> **Serves:** *8 as a first course*

2 smoked trout, each about 350 g (12 oz)

8 small sprigs fresh dill

8 sheets fillo pastry

¼ cup (60 g/2 oz) butter, melted

additional dill sprigs to garnish

Horseradish-dill Sauce

1½ cups (375 ml/12 fl oz) sour cream

2 tsp chopped fresh dill

2 tbsp prepared horseradish

salt and freshly ground white pepper

Carefully remove skin from trout and lift fillet from bones on each side of fish. Cut each fillet across in halves. Brush a sheet of fillo pastry with butter and fold in half to give almost a square of pastry. Brush top with butter and place a trout fillet across one corner. Top fillet with a sprig of dill and wrap into a parcel, folding in sides. Place seam side down on a greased baking tray. Repeat with remaining fillets and pastry. Brush tops of parcels with butter. At this stage, parcels may be covered with plastic film (wrap) and left in refrigerator for up to 24 hours if necessary.

Place baking tray of parcels on barbecue grill and cook indirect, hood down, for 10-15 minutes, until puffed and lightly coloured. Spoon Horseradish-dill Sauce in the centre of 6 warm plates and place a trout parcel in the middle. Garnish with dill and serve immediately as a first course.

Horseradish-dill Sauce: In a small saucepan, mix sour cream with dill, horseradish and salt and pepper to taste. Place on grill alongside tray of trout parcels to heat. Stir well before serving.

Paella

PAELLA

In Spain paella is often cooked outside on a charcoal fire, and by all means put the whole recipe together at the barbecue if you like, but it is easier on the cook if the first stage is completed at the kitchen stove.

> **Charcoal kettle:** *Indirect—Medium—Preheat not necessary*
> **Gas kettle:** *Indirect—Hot—Preheat 8-10 minutes*
> **Covered gas grill:** *Indirect—Hot—Preheat 8-10 minutes*
> **Cooking time:** *50-60 minutes*
> **Serves:** *8-10*

8-10 mussels, scrubbed and bearded

250 g (8 oz) peeled, raw prawns (shrimp)

1 cooked lobster, about 500 g (1 lb)

1 chicken, about 1.5 kg (3 lb)

2-3 smoked chorizo sausages

½ cup (125 ml/4 fl oz) olive oil

125 g (4 oz) cleaned squid hoods (optional)

1 large onion, finely chopped

2 cloves garlic, chopped

1 green (bell) pepper, cut in strips

2½ cups (500 g/1 lb) long-grain rice

425 g (15 oz) can peeled tomatoes, chopped

1 cup (125 g/4 oz) frozen green peas

¼ tsp powdered saffron

salt and freshly ground black pepper

2 cups (500 ml/16 fl oz) chicken stock (broth)

3 cups (750 ml/24 fl oz) boiling water

8-10 canned artichoke hearts, halved

Prepare mussels and leave in colander covered with a damp cloth. De-vein prawns, rinse well and drain. Split lobster, rinse, slice tail with shell, crack claws and legs. Set aside prawns and lobster in refrigerator. Cut chicken into small serving-sized pieces and dry well. Slice chorizos 1 cm (½ in) thick.

Use a 35 cm (14 in) paella pan, flat-based wok, large frying pan or metal roasting pan about 6 cm (2½ in) deep. Place over high heat with half the oil. When hot, add chicken and chorizos and brown on each side. Remove to a plate. Add squid rings if used and fry for 2 minutes, add to chicken. Add remaining oil to pan with onion, garlic and pepper strips and cook, stirring often, for 5 minutes. Return chicken, chorizos and squid to pan, add rice and cook for a further 2-3 minutes, tossing often. Add tomatoes and their liquid, peas, saffron and salt and pepper to taste. Stir in the chicken stock and bring to the boil. Reduce heat to low, stir once more, then cook, covered with a large pan lid or baking tray, until stock is absorbed (about 8-10 minutes). Place artichoke hearts on top and take out to barbecue with prepared seafoods.

Place pan on barbecue grill, stir in the boiling water and spread rice evenly in pan. Cook indirect, hood down, for 15 minutes. Arrange prawns, mussels and lobster on top and continue to cook indirect for further 15-20 minutes until seafood is cooked and rice is tender—do not stir once cooking begins in barbecue. Remove from barbecue, cover with foil and let stand for 5 minutes. Serve from the pan with lemon wedges, warm, crusty bread and a tossed green salad.

Drain fish, retaining marinade. Brush fish with oil and cook on oiled hotplate or grill, basting often with marinade. Cook for 3-4 minutes each side. Serve hot with accompaniments of choice. The Burghul and Pumpkin Salad (page 95) complements the orange-flavoured fish.

browns; for charcoal kettle, move flan over direct heat. Test to see if cooked by inserting a knife in the centre—it should come out clean when flan is cooked. Let stand for 5 minutes before slicing in wedges to serve with a salad.

ORANGE-GINGER FISH CUTLETS

> **All barbecues**: *Direct—Medium-hot*
> **Cooking time**: *6-8 minutes*
> **Serves**: *6-8*

6-8 fish cutlets (steaks), each about 250 g (8 oz)

grated rind of 1 orange

¾ cup (185 ml/6 fl oz) fresh orange juice

1 tsp grated fresh ginger

¼ tsp ground ginger

2 tbsp honey

1 tbsp oil

Choose cutlets from snapper, cod, hake or striped bass, according to the fish available. Wipe cutlets with damp kitchen paper. Mix orange rind and juice with fresh and ground ginger and honey in a flat dish, add fish and coat with marinade. Cover and marinate in refrigerator for at least 2 hours or overnight if necessary.

Orange-ginger fish cutlets

SEAFOOD FLAN

> **Charcoal kettle**: *Indirect—Medium—Preheat 10-12 minutes*
> **Gas kettle**: *Indirect—Medium—Preheat 10-12 minutes*
> **Covered gas grill**: *Indirect—Medium—Preheat 10-12 minutes*
> **Cooking time**: *50-55 minutes*
> **Serves**: *6*

1 unbaked 23 cm (9 in) Rich Shortcrust Pastry flan case (page 38)

large white onion, sliced

2 tbsp butter

2 tbsp plain (all-purpose) flour

½ cup (125 ml/4 fl oz) cream

½ cup (125 ml/4 fl oz) milk

2 large eggs, beaten

1 tsp dried dill tips

1/8 tsp nutmeg

salt and freshly ground black pepper

6 each shelled oysters and scallops

125 g (4 oz) cooked, shelled prawns (shrimp)

125 g (4 oz) cooked lobster meat, chopped

125 g (4 oz) cooked crab meat, flaked

See page 39 for illustration. Prepare flan case as directed in Rich Shortcrust Pastry recipe (page 38), lining a 23 cm (9 in) flan dish with half the pastry. Chill flan case in refrigerator until filling is ready.

In a frying pan, cook onion gently in butter until soft, stir in flour and cook gently for 2 minutes. Add cream and milk and stir until thickened and bubbling. Leave aside until cool, then stir in beaten eggs, dill, nutmeg and salt and pepper to taste. Add seafood and mix in gently. Pour filling into flan case.

Place flan on barbecue grill and bake indirect, hood down, for 40-45 minutes, rotating if necessary during cooking to brown evenly. When filling is nearly set (after 35 minutes), turn burner on to low under flan so that base of pastry

TUNA-CURRY IMPOSSIBLE PIE

> **Charcoal kettle**: *Indirect—Medium—Preheat 6-8 minutes*
> **Gas kettle**: *Indirect—Medium-hot—Preheat 6-8 minutes*
> **Covered gas grill**: *Indirect—Medium-hot—Preheat 6-8 minutes*
> **Cooking time**: *50-55 minutes*
> **Serves**: *4-6*

¼ cup (60 g/2 oz) butter or margarine

1 large onion, chopped

½ cup (60 g/2 oz) chopped celery

½ green (bell) pepper, chopped

3 tsp curry powder

425 g (15 oz) can tuna chunks in brine

juice of ½ lemon

1 tsp salt

3 eggs

½ cup (60 g/2 oz) self-raising flour

¼ cup (60 ml/2 fl oz) liquid from tuna

1¼ cups (310 ml/10 fl oz) milk

Melt butter in a frying pan and pour half of the butter into a mixing bowl. Add onion, celery and pepper to butter in pan and cook gently for 10 minutes until onion is transparent. Stir in curry powder and cook, stirring occasionally, for 2 minutes. Remove pan from heat and stir in tuna, lemon juice and salt. Spread in the base of a greased 25 cm (10 in) ceramic pie plate. To melted butter in bowl add eggs, flour and tuna liquid and beat well with a balloon whisk until smooth. Add milk and beat for 1 minute. Pour over tuna mixture. Pie can stand for up to 1 hour if necessary before cooking.

Place pie on barbecue grill and cook indirect, hood down, for 40-45 minutes, rotating dish halfway during cooking to brown evenly. Pie is cooked when a knife inserted in centre comes out clean. Let stand for 5 minutes, then cut into wedges and serve with a tossed salad. Natural yoghurt mixed with chopped cucumber makes a pleasant accompaniment to the pie.

VEGETABLES, RICE AND SALADS

With undercover barbecue cooking, a wider range of accompaniments can be cooked alongside the main course. The Vegetable and Fruit cooking table on page 25 should be consulted for most of the standard accompaniments.

Many of the dishes can be cooked by direct or indirect heat. For indirect cooking, the heat of the barbecue is governed by the main food being cooked, and timing given is for Hot or Medium temperatures, the longer time for Medium heat.

While you can use foil pans or do the usual foil wrap for many vegetables, with indirect cooking, oven dishes may be used so that the foods can go straight to the table. Flameproof dishes and saucepans with heatproof handles can be used for direct cooking if you prefer. There are lots of choices—that's the beauty of cooking undercover!

Stir-fried asparagus with walnuts

STIR-FRIED ASPARAGUS WITH WALNUTS

All barbecues: *Direct—Hot*
Cooking time: *6-8 minutes*
Serves: *6*

18-24 spears green asparagus

1 tbsp peanut or corn oil

½ cup (60 g/2 oz) walnut quarters

1 tsp grated fresh ginger

1 clove garlic, crushed

2 tsp soya sauce

1-2 tbsp water

1 tsp sesame oil

Rinse asparagus and break off woody ends. Slice each spear diagonally in 3 pieces. Heat oil in a large frying pan over direct heat (or use a wok). Add walnut pieces and fry, stirring occasionally, until lightly coloured. Add ginger and garlic, fry for 1 minute, then add soya sauce and asparagus. Stir-fry for 3-4 minutes, sprinkling in a little water now and then to create steam. When asparagus is crisp-tender, stir in sesame oil and serve immediately.

ROAST VEGETABLES

Crisp, brown roast potatoes, as good to taste as those cooked in fat with a fraction of the calories! Other root vegetables and pumpkin can also be roasted. Because vegetables go straight onto the grill, they can be positioned wherever there is space. Choose vegetables from the list supplied, in amounts to suit catering requirements and the capacity of your barbecue grill.

All barbecues: *Indirect—Hot*
Cooking time: *1-1½ hours*

old potatoes, peeled	
pumpkin or butternut pumpkin (squash)	
small onions	
large carrots	
large parsnips	
oil	
salt and freshly ground pepper (optional)	

Leave potatoes whole or cut in halves or quarters, but keep pieces fairly large. Scrub pumpkin skin, remove seeds and fibres, cut into chunks, leaving skin on. Potato and pumpkin pieces should be about 125 g (4 oz) in weight. Peel onions, trimming off root close to base. Peel carrots and parsnips and cut into thick chunks. Brush vegetable pieces with oil and season with salt and pepper if desired. Place around meat joint or poultry being roasted by indirect heat. Cook indirect, hood down, until tender, turn occasionally during cooking. The vegetables do not have to be positioned over drip pan.

Ginger orange pumpkin

GINGER ORANGE PUMPKIN

> **All barbecues:** *Indirect—Hot/Medium*
> **Cooking time:** *1-1¼ hours*
> **Serves:** *6*

1 kg (2 lb) butternut pumpkin (squash)	
1 large orange	
½ cup (125 ml/4 fl oz) water	
¼ cup (60 g/2 oz) butter or margarine	
1 tbsp honey	
1 tsp ground ginger	

Cut pumpkin in 1 cm (½ in) slices and remove seeds and skin. Arrange slices, overlapping, in a greased ovenproof dish. Using a paring knife, cut thin strips of rind from orange, taking care not to include pith. Cut rind into julienne strips and boil in water for 5–6 minutes until tender. Drain, rinse and keep aside.

Melt butter in a small saucepan, stir in honey and ginger. Juice the orange and add to the butter mixture. Pour over the pumpkin slices and take out to the barbecue with the orange strips in a small container. Cook by indirect heat alongside other foods, basting slices with dish juices occasionally. When lightly browned and almost tender, sprinkle on orange strips and complete cooking. Serve from the dish as an accompaniment to roast meats or poultry—it is very good with pork, chicken or duck.

BARBECUE-STEAMED VEGETABLES

> **All barbecues:** *Direct—Hot; Indirect—Hot/Medium*

Suitable vegetables, prepare as normal

asparagus	green peas
broccoli	snow peas
Brussels sprouts	(mange-tout)
green beans	sugar peas
cabbage	baby squash
carrot	zucchini
cauliflower	(courgettes)

Direct: Bring a small amount of water to the boil in a saucepan with heatproof handle, place on barbecue grill; use a frying pan for asparagus spears. Add vegetable with a sprinkling of salt and/or a little sugar if appropriate for vegetable being cooked. Cook direct, uncovered or partly covered with lid, until cooked to taste. Drain and toss with a little melted butter, chopped fresh herbs, a squeeze of lemon juice, a sprinkling of toasted sesame seeds or caraway seeds, according to vegetable.

Indirect: Preheating is not necessary as the barbecue would already be heated. Temperature is selected according to the main food being cooked. Most of the vegetables listed above can be cooked, except for broccoli, Brussels sprouts, green cabbage and cauliflower, as the longer cooking in an enclosed container causes unpleasant flavour, smell and colour. Place prepared vegetable in an oven dish or foil pan, or on heavy-duty foil for wrapping. Sprinkle with salt and/or sugar and add 2-3 tablespoons water. Cover securely with lid or foil, or wrap securely. Cook indirect, hood down, for twice the normal time a particular vegetable would require. Serve as for vegetables cooked by direct heat.

Hasselback potatoes

potatoes, cut-side up. Season with salt and pepper and baste well with butter mixture. Take out to barbecue with the cheese and paprika.

Cook by indirect heat, hood down, alongside other foods, basting occasionally with butter mixture. When golden brown and almost tender, sprinkle tops with Parmesan and a dusting of paprika. Complete cooking and serve hot with roast meats or poultry.

BARBECUE-STEAMED NEW POTATOES

All barbecues: Direct—Hot/Medium;
Indirect—Hot/Medium
Cooking time: 25-60 minutes
Serves: 6-8

1 kg (2 lb) small new potatoes

1 cup (250 ml/8 fl oz) water

salt to taste

Wash potatoes well, leave skins on or scrape if desired. Place in saucepan with heatproof handle, or flameproof casserole dish or foil pan; add water. Add salt to taste, cover with lid or foil and cook direct or indirect, hood down, until tender—potatoes cooked indirect in medium barbecue can take up to 1 hour. Drain and finish in the following ways:

Sugar-glazed New Potatoes: Drain potatoes. In pan or dish in which potatoes were cooked, heat 2 tablespoons butter with 2 tablespoons brown sugar and 1 tablespoon honey over direct heat. When bubbling, add potatoes and toss until coated. Cover and keep hot until needed, tip into serving dish and serve hot.

Herbed New Potatoes: Scrape potatoes before cooking. Place drained potatoes in serving dish, add 2 tablespoons butter, 1 tablespoon finely chopped chives and 1 tablespoon chopped parsley, toss gently and serve.

Hot Potato Salad: In a large, heated frying pan, cook 125 g (4 oz) chopped bacon slices until browned and crisp. Remove from heat and add hot, drained potatoes (halved if desired), 2 tablespoons balsamic or red wine vinegar, 2 tablespoons chopped spring onions (scallions) and 2 teaspoons each

VEGETABLE KEBABS

All barbecues: Direct—Medium
Cooking time: 10-12 minutes
Serves: 6

2 zucchini (courgettes)

3 yellow baby squash

3 small onions

1 small red (bell) pepper

1 small green (bell) pepper

12 button mushrooms

1 quantity Simple Lemon Baste (page 100)

Cut zucchini crosswise into chunks; halve baby squash; peel onions and quarter; seed peppers and cut into squares; brush any soil from mushrooms (do not wash) and trim stems. Thread vegetables alternately onto 6 flat metal skewers. Brush well with Simple Lemon Baste and cook on grill of barbecue over direct medium heat, turning and basting often until crisp-tender. Serve with barbecued meats and poultry cooked by direct heat.

HASSELBACK POTATOES

All barbecues: Indirect—Hot/Medium
Cooking time:1¼-1½ hours
Serves: 4-6

8-12 medium-sized old potatoes

¼ cup (60 g/2 oz) butter or margarine

2 tbsp oil

salt

freshly ground black pepper

2 tbsp grated Parmesan cheese

paprika

Choose oval-shaped potatoes of even size. Peel and cut a strip of potato off the base of each so that they sit flat. With a thin-bladed knife, cut each potato from rounded side into slices 5 mm (¼ in) thick, cutting almost to, but not through, the base—potatoes should remain intact. Place in a bowl of cold water and leave for 30 minutes. Drain well and dry with kitchen paper.

Heat butter and oil until butter foams. Pour into an ovenproof dish and add chopped fresh dill and parsley. Toss with the bacon and rendered bacon drippings, adding 1-2 tablespoons salad oil if bacon is very lean. Turn into a warm bowl to serve.

POTATOES BOULANGÈRE

> **All barbecues**: Indirect—Hot/Medium
> **Cooking time**: 1¼-1½ hours
> **Serves**: 6

1 kg (2 lb) old potatoes

¼ cup (60 g/2 oz) butter or margarine, melted

2 medium-sized onions, sliced

salt and freshly ground black pepper

Peel potatoes and cut into 5 mm (¼ in) slices. Soak in cold water for 20-30 minutes, drain and dry slices in a cloth. Put melted butter in a shallow oven dish, add onions and toss in butter until coated and slices have separated into rings. Add potato slices and toss to mix with the onions. Season with salt and pepper and cover dish with foil.

Place dish on grill of heated barbecue and cook indirect, hood down, for 45 minutes, remove foil and cook for further 30-45 minutes until tender and lightly browned on top. Use heat required for main food being cooked. Serve at the table from the dish.

HOT HERBED TOMATOES

> **All barbecues**: Direct—Medium or Direct, then Indirect—Medium
> **Cooking time**: 15-25 minutes
> **Serves**: 6-8

8-12 ripe tomatoes

¼ cup (60 g/2 oz) butter or margarine

1 clove garlic, crushed

¼ cup (30 g/1 oz) finely chopped celery

½ tsp salt

freshly ground black pepper

1 tsp sugar

2 tbsp snipped chives

2 tbsp finely chopped parsley

1 tbsp finely chopped fresh oregano or ½ tsp dried oregano leaves

2 tbsp chopped fresh basil or 1 tsp dried basil

Select even-sized, rather small tomatoes. Place in a bowl and cover with boiling water. Leave 30 seconds, drain and remove skins. Return to bowl for taking out to barbecue.

Place a flameproof dish or frying pan over medium, direct heat, add butter and when foaming, add garlic and celery and cook gently for 3-4 minutes to soften celery. Add tomatoes, stem end down, baste with butter mixture and sprinkle with salt, pepper, sugar and herbs. Cover with lid or foil and simmer over direct medium heat for 10 minutes, or cook indirect for 15-20 minutes, depending on heat of barbecue. Serve hot with roast or barbecued meats or poultry.

CAULIFLOWER WITH CREAMED CORN SAUCE

> **All barbecues**: Indirect—Hot/Medium
> **Cooking time**: 25-35 minutes
> **Serves**: 6-8

1 medium-sized cauliflower

salted water

½ stick celery or ¼ cup (60 ml/2 fl oz) milk

310 g (10 oz) can cream-style corn

4 chopped spring onions (scallions)

¼ tsp ground nutmeg

freshly ground black pepper

½ cup (60 g/2 oz) shredded natural Cheddar cheese

2 tsp grated Parmesan cheese

paprika

Remove heavy leaves from cauliflower, leaving some of the tender leaves in place, and trim the base so that it sits flat. Cut a deep cross into the base of the thick stem. Bring a large pan of salted water to the boil and add whole cauliflower with celery stick or milk—either ingredient preserves the cauliflower's flavour. Return to the boil and boil for 5 minutes until barely cooked—it should be crisp-tender. Drain off water and run cold water into pan to arrest cooking. Lift out cauliflower and drain well in colander.

Tip creamed corn into a bowl and stir in spring onions, nutmeg, pepper to taste and the Cheddar cheese. Place cauliflower upright in an ovenproof dish and coat with corn mixture. Sprinkle on Parmesan cheese and dust lightly with paprika. At this stage, cauliflower may be covered and stored in refrigerator for several hours or overnight.

Place uncovered dish on grill of barbecue and cook indirect, hood down, for 25-35 minutes until heated through and golden brown on top. Serve hot from dish.

Hot herbed tomatoes

ZUCCHINI PROVENÇALE

> **All barbecues:** *Indirect—Hot/Medium*
> **Cooking time:** *1¼-1½ hours*
> **Serves:** *6*

500 g (1 lb) zucchini (courgettes)

salt

425 g (15 oz) can tomatoes

1 tsp garlic granules (flakes)

2 tbsp chopped parsley

1 tsp chopped fresh marjoram or ½ tsp dried marjoram leaves

½ tsp sugar

freshly ground black pepper

2 medium-sized onions, sliced

2 tbsp olive oil

¾ cup (90 g/3 oz) shredded natural Cheddar cheese

1 large, ripe tomato, skinned

Wash and trim zucchini and cut obliquely into 1 cm (½ in) slices. Place in a colander, sprinkle liberally with salt and toss to distribute. Leave for 30 minutes, then rinse and drain.

Chop the canned tomatoes, place in a bowl with their liquid, add garlic granules, herbs, sugar and pepper to taste, and mix. Brush a casserole dish with oil and place a layer of zucchini in the base. Top with some of the tomato mixture and a few slices of onion and drizzle with a little olive oil. Repeat layers until these ingredients are used, placing half the cheese in a layer when dish is half-filled. Slice the tomato and place on top, then sprinkle with remaining cheese. Dish may be covered and refrigerated overnight at this stage.

Place uncovered dish on barbecue grill and cook indirect, hood down, for 1¼-1½ hours until zucchini is tender. Serve as an accompaniment to beef, veal, lamb or poultry.

GINGERED SWEET POTATOES

> **All barbecues:** *Indirect—Hot/Medium*
> *or Direct—Medium*
> **Cooking time:** *1-1½ hours*
> **Serves:** *6-8*

2 medium-sized sweet potatoes, each about 375 g (12 oz)

2 tbsp melted butter or margarine

2 tbsp chopped preserved ginger

2 tbsp water

Choose the orange-coloured sweet potatoes for preference. Peel and cut into 1 cm (½ in) slices. Brush a medium-sized foil pan or casserole dish with some of the melted butter and layer the sweet potato slices with chopped ginger. Add water and pour remaining butter on top, cover tightly with foil or lid.

Place on grill and cook indirect, hood down, for 1-1½ hours, depending on amount of other foods being cooked and the heat required for those foods. Sweet potatoes may also be cooked by direct medium heat in a foil pan or flameproof dish. Serve with pork, ham, lamb, veal or poultry.

Orange Sweet Potatoes: Replace preserved ginger with 2 tablespoons orange marmalade, add a light dusting of ground ginger and use orange juice in place of the water. Prepare, cook and serve as above.

SPICED RED CABBAGE WITH APPLE

> **All barbecues:** *Direct—Medium* or
> *Indirect—Hot/Medium*
> **Cooking time:** *50-60 minutes*
> **Serves:** *6*

1 medium-sized red cabbage

½ cup (125 ml/4 fl oz) prepared apple sauce

2 tbsp red wine vinegar

¼ cup (60 ml/2 fl oz) dry red wine

2 tbsp brown sugar

pinch each ground cloves and nutmeg

2 tbsp melted butter or margarine

Zucchini provençale

Rinse cabbage, remove core and shred finely. Place in a flameproof casserole dish and add remaining ingredients. Mix well and cover with lid.

Place on barbecue grill and cook direct or indirect, hood down, for 50-60 minutes until tender. Stir at least once during cooking. Heat for indirect cooking is determined by main food being cooked. Serve with roast duck, goose or pork, barbecued pork chops or sausages.

STIR-FRIED VEGETABLES

All barbecues: *Direct—Hot*
Cooking time: *10-12 minutes*
Serves: *6-8*

2 small onions
1 medium-sized carrot
185 g (6 oz) broccoli
½ Chinese cabbage
125 g (4 oz) snow peas (mange-tout)
1 cup (90 g/3 oz) sliced small mushrooms
1 cup (90 g/3 oz) bean sprouts
2 tbsp peanut or corn oil
1 clove garlic, crushed
1 tsp grated fresh ginger
water
1 tbsp light soya sauce
1 tbsp dry sherry
½ tsp sugar
salt and freshly ground pepper

Cut out roots of peeled onions, quarter and separate into leaves; slice carrot thinly; cut broccoli into small florets; cut cabbage into pieces; trim snow peas; wipe mushrooms with a damp cloth before slicing; nip off any dark ends on bean sprouts.

Heat oil in a large frying pan or wok set over direct high heat. Add garlic and ginger and stir-fry for a few seconds. Add onion, carrot and broccoli and stir-fry for 3-4 minutes, sprinkling in a little water to create steam—this helps to soften vegetables. Add cabbage, snow peas and mushrooms, stir-fry for further 2-3 minutes, again sprinkling in a little water as necessary. Add bean sprouts, toss over heat for a minute or so, then stir in soya sauce, sherry and sugar, season to taste with salt and pepper. Transfer to a deep serving bowl

Stir-fried vegetables

and serve immediately to accompany Chinese-style barbecued meats, poultry and seafoods.

BUTTERNUT NUTMEG PUMPKIN

All barbecues: *Indirect—Hot/Medium*
Cooking time: *1-1½ hours*
Serves: *6*

½ butternut pumpkin (squash), about 1 kg (2 lb)
2 tbsp melted butter or margarine
ground nutmeg

Scrub the skin of the pumpkin, remove seeds and fibres with a spoon. With a sharp knife, make deep cuts on the flat section of the pumpkin in a diamond pattern, taking care not to cut close to the skin. Put melted butter in the hollow and brush butter over cut surface. Sprinkle with ground nutmeg.

Place cut side up on barbecue grill and cook indirect, hood down, for 1-1½ hours, occasionally brushing melted butter over pumpkin. Heat of barbecue and cooking time depends on main food being cooked. When tender, remove to a serving dish and scoop pumpkin out of skin to serve. Serve with roast beef, veal, lamb, pork or poultry.

Butternut Orange Pumpkin: Omit nutmeg and add grated rind of 1 orange, 1 tablespoon orange juice and 2 teaspoons brown sugar to the melted butter. Sprinkle pumpkin with ground ginger. Brush during cooking with orange-butter mixture.

Carrot pilaf

ORANGE AND CURRANT PILAF

> **All barbecues:** *Indirect—Hot/Medium*
> **Cooking time:** *18-20 minutes*
> **Serves:** *6-8*

2 cups (420 g/14 oz) long-grain white rice

2 tbsp butter

grated rind of 1 orange

2 tbsp currants

1 tsp salt

3½ cups (875 ml/28 fl oz) boiling water

2 tbsp toasted pinenuts (pignolias) to garnish

Rinse rice until water runs clear, drain well. Place in casserole dish and add butter, orange rind, currants and salt. Pour on boiling water, stir and cover tightly. Place on barbecue grill and cook indirect, hood down, for 18-20 minutes. Remove and stand for 5-10 minutes. Fluff up with fork, sprinkle with toasted pinenuts and serve immediately.

Carrot Pilaf: In place of orange rind, currants and pinenuts, use 2 medium-sized, shredded carrots, ½ teaspoon cracked black peppercorns and 2 teaspoons chicken stock (bouillon) powder. Add to rice with the butter and salt, complete and cook as above. If desired, pilaf may be pressed into an oiled ring cake pan and inverted onto platter for serving. Serve with natural yoghurt.

Pepper and Tomato Pilaf: In place of orange rind, currants and pinenuts, use 1 tablespoon dried onion flakes (instant minced onion), 2 tablespoons each chopped red and green pepper (bell pepper), 1 large ripe tomato, skinned and chopped, and freshly ground black pepper to taste. Add to rice with the butter and salt, complete and cook as above.

CORN IN HUSKS

> **All barbecues:** *Indirect—Hot/Medium*
> **Cooking time:** *25-35 minutes*

corn cobs with husks

butter, salt and pepper for serving

Allow 1 cob per serve, more if there is sufficient space on barbecue to cook them. Heat of barbecue and time depends on main food being cooked; if only the corn is being cooked, use medium heat.

Strip off dry outer husks, leaving a good layer of the inner, light green husks. Tear strips off discarded husks to use as ties. Carefully pull back husks on cobs and remove silk. Replace husks and tie in place with husk strips. Soak in cold water for 30 minutes or up to 2 hours if time allows.

Place on grill of heated barbecue and cook, indirect, hood down, for 25-35 minutes, turning cobs occasionally. Wear heavy gloves to remove husks and pile cobs onto serving platter. Serve with butter, salt and pepper, to be added to individual taste.

BARBECUE-ROASTED PEPPERS

> **All barbecues:** *Direct—Hot*
> **Cooking time:** *20-25 minutes*
> **Serves:** *6-8*

½ cup (125 ml/4 fl oz) olive oil

1 clove garlic, quartered

6-8 large red (bell) peppers

1-2 green (bell) peppers (optional)

½ tsp salt

Put olive oil in a jug with the garlic and leave for several hours. Remove garlic and keep oil aside.

For colour contrast, 1-2 green peppers may be included. Wash peppers if necessary, leave intact and place on grill of heated barbecue. Cook direct, hood down, for 20-25 minutes, turning peppers every 5 minutes. When skins are blackened and blistered, remove and place in a paper bag. Close bag and leave for 10 minutes.

Remove skins, wipe off any flakes with kitchen paper. Halve, cut out stems and scrape out seeds. Cut into 2.5 cm (1 in) strips and place in a bowl. Sprinkle with salt and pour on garlic-flavoured oil. Serve with barbecued meats, poultry and fish. Peppers may also be cut into julienne strips and used as a garnish for salads and vegetable dishes.

SPICED ORANGE BEETROOT

> **All barbecues:** *Indirect—Hot/Medium*
> **Cooking time:** *1-1½ hours*
> **Serves:** *6-8*

6 medium-sized beetroot (beets)

2 thinly peeled strips orange rind

6 whole allspice berries

½ tsp salt

2-3 tbsp water

2 tbsp each butter and orange juice for serving

Trim stalks from beetroot, leaving 4 cm (1½ in) of stalks attached to each beetroot. Scrub well, taking care not to puncture skin. Place in a foil pan or on a large piece of heavy-duty foil. Add orange rind, allspice berries, salt and water. Seal with foil or wrap securely. Place on barbecue grill and cook indirect, hood down, for 1-1½ hours. Heat and time depends on other foods being cooked at the same time. When tender, tip out onto a dish and remove skins and stalks. Slice or quarter and place in serving dish. Toss with butter and orange juice and serve hot.

POTATO SALAD

Cooking time: 20-25 minutes
Serves: 6-8

1 kg (2 lb) new potatoes

6 spring onions (scallions), chopped

2 tbsp chopped parsley

2-3 tsp chopped fresh dill or mint

½ cup (125 ml/4 fl oz) mayonnaise

½ cup (125 ml/4 fl oz) sour cream

1 tbsp white wine vinegar

1 tsp prepared English mustard

Wash potatoes and boil in their jackets in lightly salted water until tender. Drain in a colander, run cold water over them and leave until cool. Leave whole if small, otherwise cut into thick slices. Mix remaining ingredients together, reserving about 2 tablespoons of the combined, chopped spring onions and herbs. If very thick, thin down with a little water.

Spoon a little of the mayonnaise dressing in the base of a serving bowl, add a layer of potatoes and cover with more of the dressing. Repeat with potatoes and dressing until ingredients are used. Sprinkle reserved herbs on top, cover and chill until required.

BARBECUE-STEAMED RICE

To cook rice successfully, the ratio of water to rice is important; while double the amount of water is used for up to 1½ cups of rice, the ratio of water decreases if more rice is used. Weights given for rice are averages and they include white, brown, short- and long-grain varieties. It is important to use the same system of measures—either cups *or* metric *or* imperial—for both rice and liquid. For serving a crowd, it is suggested that no more than 2 cups of raw rice be cooked in one utensil.

Potato salad

Regarding yield, rice triples in volume when cooked.

All barbecues: Indirect—Hot/Medium
Cooking time: 18-20 minutes (white)
40-50 minutes (brown)

Serves	Raw rice	Boiling water
3-4	1 cup (210 g/7 oz)	2 cups (500ml/16 fl oz)
5-6	1½ cups (315 g/10½ oz)	3 cups (750 ml/24 fl oz)
6-8	2 cups (420 g/14 oz)	3½ cups (875 ml/28 fl oz)

Rinse rice in a strainer under cold water until water runs clear. Drain and place in a casserole dish. Add salt to taste and 1-2 tablespoons butter if desired. Pour on boiling water, stir, cover tightly and place on grill in hot or medium heated barbecue. Cook indirect, hood down, until water is absorbed and rice is tender. Stand for 5-10 minutes, fluff up with fork and serve.

Alternative cooking method:

All barbecues: Direct—Medium

Use quantities as above and place in a flameproof casserole dish or Dutch oven. Cover and bring to the boil over direct heat, move to side of grill and continue to cook slowly until tender.

Chinese Steamed Rice: To prepare 'clinging' rice for serving with Chinese-style dishes, use short-grain white rice and rinse only briefly if necessary. Omit salt and butter and cook as above, using indirect or direct method.

BURGHUL AND PUMPKIN SALAD

Cooking time: 10-15 minutes
Serves: 6-8

1.5 kg (3 lb) pumpkin or butternut pumpkin (squash)

salt

½ cup (90 g/3 oz) burghul (bulgar)

½ cup (30 g/1 oz) chopped flat-leaf parsley

4 spring onions (scallions), chopped

2 tbsp cider vinegar

½ cup (125 ml/4 fl oz) salad oil

freshly ground black pepper

Peel pumpkin, remove seeds and fibre and cut flesh into 2 cm (¾ in) cubes. Place in top part of steamer, sprinkle lightly with salt and steam over boiling water for 10-15 minutes until tender. Do not overcook. Turn onto a tray so that it can cool quickly.

Put burghul into a fine sieve and rinse under cold water. Tip into a salad bowl and leave for 15-20 minutes until burghul absorbs the moisture, swelling and softening in the process. Add parsley and spring onions to burghul, mix well, then stir in vinegar, oil and pepper to taste. Add cooled pumpkin and toss gently to combine, taking care not to break up pumpkin. Cover and chill for up to 2 hours before serving.

TABOULEH

Serves: 6-8

¾ cup (125 g/4 oz) burghul (bulgar)

6 spring onions (scallions), finely chopped

2 cups (125 g/4 oz) chopped flat-leaf parsley

2 tbsp finely chopped fresh mint

¹/₃ cup (90 ml/3 fl oz) olive oil

2 tbsp lemon juice

1 tsp salt

freshly ground black pepper

2 medium-sized firm, ripe tomatoes

Cos (romaine) lettuce leaves for serving

Put burghul in a fine sieve and rinse under cold water. Tip into a bowl and leave for 15-20 minutes until it swells and softens. Add spring onions and mix in with a wooden spoon, pressing with spoon to release onion flavour into the burghul. Add parsley and mint and toss lightly. Beat oil with lemon juice, salt and pepper to taste and pour over salad. Cover and refrigerate until required, overnight if necessary. Just before serving, peel the tomatoes, halve crosswise, remove seeds and dice the flesh. Mix into the salad and serve in a bowl lined with Cos lettuce leaves.

GREEN PASTA SALAD

Cooking time: 7-8 minutes
Serves: 6-8

250 g (8 oz) green tagliatelle (long ribbon pasta)

lightly salted water

½ cup (125 ml/4 fl oz) olive oil

6-8 young silverbeet (Swiss chard) leaves

1 cup (90 g/3 oz) bean sprouts

²/₃ cup (90 g/3 oz) black Greek-style olives

1 clove garlic, crushed

½ tsp salt

2 tbsp white wine vinegar

freshly ground black pepper

Boil tagliatelle in salted water for 7-8 minutes until barely tender. Drain in a colander, run cold water through pasta, then return to pan and cover with cold water. Leave until pasta cools, drain again in colander and tip into a large salad bowl. Add 2 tablespoons olive oil and toss to coat strands. This prevents cold pasta from sticking.

Wash silverbeet leaves, remove white stalks and cut out white ribs from leaves. Drain, wrap in a tea-towel and chill until crisp and dry. Rinse bean sprouts and nip off any dark ends, drain well. Gently break silverbeet leaves into smallish pieces and add to pasta with the sprouts. Toss ingredients gently to combine and scatter olives over top.

Crush garlic and mix to a paste with ½ teaspoon salt. Place in a dressing jug and add remaining oil and vinegar. Beat well until combined, add pepper to taste. Add dressing and toss salad just before serving.

ZUCCHINI SALAD

Cooking time: 3 minutes
Serves: 6-8

500 g (1 lb) zucchini (courgettes)

½ cup (125 ml/4 fl oz) olive oil

2 tbsp white wine vinegar

1 clove garlic, crushed

salt and freshly ground black pepper

2 tbsp finely chopped parsley

2 tbsp finely chopped green (bell) pepper

2 tbsp finely chopped red (bell) pepper

2 tbsp chopped spring onions (scallions)

1 tbsp chopped dill-pickled cucumber

Wash zucchini, trim and slice thinly. Cook in boiling, salted water for 3 minutes, drain immediately in a colander and run cold water through to arrest the cooking. Drain thoroughly.

Put olive oil in a bowl and whisk in vinegar, garlic, and salt and pepper to taste. Stir in remaining ingredients. Place zucchini in salad bowl, pour on dressing and toss gently to coat zucchini with the dressing. Cover and chill until required. Salad may be chilled overnight if necessary.

SPINACH AND BACON SALAD

Serves: 6-8

500 g (1 lb) young spinach or silverbeet (Swiss chard) leaves

125 g (4 oz) bacon slices

2 hard-boiled eggs

Tabouleh

Dressing

½ cup (125 ml/4 fl oz) olive oil

2 tbsp balsamic or red wine vinegar

1 clove garlic, crushed (optional)

½ tsps powdered mustard

½ tsp sugar

salt and freshly ground black pepper

Remove stalks from spinach or silverbeet before weighing leaves.

Rinse leaves gently, drain well and roll in a tea-towel. Place in refrigerator to crisp.

Chop bacon into small squares and fry in a heated pan until lightly browned and crisp, stirring often. Drain on kitchen paper. Shell and chop the eggs and make the dressing.

Gently break crisp spinach leaves into pieces and pile in a large salad bowl, sprinkling leaves intermittently with bacon pieces and chopped egg. Cover and chill until required. Just before serving, add dressing and toss salad.

Dressing: Put ingredients into a screw-topped jar, adding salt and pepper to taste. Seal and shake vigorously until combined, transfer to a dressing jug.

Spinach and bacon salad

GREEN SALAD WITH CASHEW DRESSING

Serves: 6-8

125 g (4 oz) snow peas (mange-tout)

1 butterhead (bibb) lettuce

1 mignonette lettuce

2 cups (60 g/2 oz) watercress sprigs

2 ripe avocados

¹/₃ cup (60 g/2 oz) salted cashew nuts

Cashew Dressing

2 tbsp salted cashew nuts

½ cup (125 ml/4 fl oz) salad oil

2 tbsp balsamic or red wine vinegar

1 tbsp lemon juice

freshly ground black pepper as desired

Nip off ends of snow peas and place in a colander. Pour boiling water over them, then hold under cold water to cool. Drain well. Rinse lettuce, drain well, wrap in a tea-towel and place in refrigerator to crisp.

Put lettuce leaves in a salad bowl, add snow peas and watercress sprigs. Peel and seed avocados and cut into slender wedges. Arrange over the greens. Sprinkle with salted cashew nuts. Prepare dressing and place in a jug. Add dressing and toss salad lightly just before serving.

Cashew Dressing: Put cashew nuts in bowl of food processor and process until finely ground. Add remaining ingredients, process until creamy.

CAESAR SALAD

Cooking time: 3-4 minutes
Serves: 6-8

2 small Cos (romaine) lettuces

½ loaf French bread (large oval like Vienna) for croûtons

½ cup (125 ml/4 fl oz) olive oil

1 tbsp butter

2 cloves garlic, quartered

6-8 canned anchovy fillets

1 egg

2 tsp Worcestershire sauce

2 tbsp lemon juice

¹/₃ cup (45 g/1½ oz) grated Parmesan cheese

freshly ground black pepper

Separate lettuce leaves and rinse gently. Drain well, wrap in a tea-towel and crisp in refrigerator.

Trim crusts from bread, cut into 1 cm (½ in) cubes. Put half the oil into a frying pan, add butter and heat until butter foams, add garlic and cook until golden. Remove garlic with a slotted spoon and discard, add bread cubes and fry, tossing occasionally, until golden brown and crisp. Remove and drain on kitchen paper. Drain anchovy fillets and chop finely. Put egg in a small saucepan of boiling water and simmer for 1 minute to coddle.

To finish salad, gently break larger lettuce leaves into smaller pieces and place in salad bowl with the small leaves. Season with freshly ground pepper, break egg over lettuce, add Worcestershire sauce and lemon juice and toss to coat leaves with the soft egg. Pour on remaining oil, add croutons, anchovies and Parmesan cheese, toss gently. Serve immediately.

Note: Salad ingredients may be prepared ahead and arranged on a tray. The bread cubes can be fried and the egg coddled on the barbecue over direct heat.

MARINADES, SAUCES, BASTES AND BUTTERS

Adding flavour by means of a marinade, sauce, baste or butter is part and parcel of barbecue cooking. Marinating foods in an aromatic mixture enhances flavour and tenderises to a certain degree, but it takes time to derive the full benefit. However, by marinating food for a short time, then using the marinade as a baste, the marinade flavour is maximised. On the other hand, a sauce or baste adds flavour at the point of cooking, ideal for instant barbecues. Then again, a sauce or baste can be thinned down and used as a marinade too. There are no hard and fast rules.

Flavoured butters are handy for melting onto barbecued meat or seafoods. While it is recommended that butter be used because of its excellent flavour, table margarine may be substituted if preferred.

BARBECUE SAUCE AND BASTE

Cooking time: 15 minutes
Makes: about 2 cups

¼ cup (60 ml/2 fl oz) oil

1 tbsp dried onion flakes (instant minced onion)

1 tsp garlic granules (flakes)

1 cup (250 ml/8 fl oz) tomato ketchup

¾ cup (185 ml/6 fl oz) water

1 tbsp cider vinegar

2 tbsp Worcestershire sauce

1 tbsp treacle (molasses see page 18)

2 tsp brown sugar

1 tsp mustard powder

Put oil in a saucepan with onion flakes and garlic granules and cook gently for 2–3 minutes to brown lightly—do not allow to burn. Add remaining ingredients, mixing the brown sugar with the mustard to break up lumps before adding to the pan. Bring to a simmer and simmer gently, uncovered, for 10 minutes, stirring occasionally. Cool and store in a sealed jar in refrigerator for up to 1 month. Use as a sauce or baste for beef, burgers, sausages and meat loaf, or as directed in recipes. It is excellent for beef or pork ribs.

HONEY-SOYA MARINADE AND BASTE

Makes: about ½ cup

1 tsp grated fresh ginger root

2 cloves garlic, crushed

2 tbsp soya sauce

2 tsp hoisin sauce (optional)

2 tbsp dry sherry

2 tbsp honey

½ tsp Chinese five-spice powder or cinnamon

1 tsp sesame oil

Mix ingredients together in dish in which food is to be marinated, or in a small heatproof pan if using as a baste on the barbecue. Use for chicken pieces or pork, or as directed in recipes.

SATAY SAUCE

Cooking time: 10 minutes
Makes: about 2 cups

8 cm (3 in) piece lemon grass cut from base or 1 tsp grated lemon rind

1 tbsp oil

1 medium-sized brown onion, grated

2 cloves garlic, crushed

2 tsp grated fresh ginger root

¼ tsp chilli powder or to taste

1 tsp ground cumin

½ tsp ground coriander

1 cup (250 ml/8 fl oz) canned coconut milk

1 cup (250 g/8 oz) crunchy peanut butter

2 tbsp soya sauce

1 tbsp lemon juice

3 tsp brown sugar

If using lemon grass, slice thinly, then pound to a paste with a pestle. Heat oil in a saucepan, add onion, garlic, ginger and lemon grass or grated lemon rind and fry gently for 4–5 minutes. Add spices and cook gently for 1–2 minutes. Stir in coconut milk, bring slowly to the boil, then add remaining ingredients. Stir until smooth, simmer gently for 1 minute and remove from heat. If not required immediately, sauce will store in a sealed jar in the refrigerator for up to 2 weeks. Use as a sauce for beef, chicken or pork satays, or as directed in recipes; thin down with coconut milk or water to use as a marinade and baste.

TOMATO-CHILLI SAUCE

> **Makes:** *about 2 cups*

425 g (15 oz) can peeled tomatoes

¼ cup (60 ml/2 fl oz) tomato ketchup

1 tbsp red wine vinegar

2 tbsp chilli sauce

2 tbsp oil

salt and freshly ground pepper

Chop the tomatoes and place in a pan with their liquid. Stir in remaining ingredients, adding salt and pepper to taste. Warm on the side of the barbecue and serve warm with barbecued beef, sausages, burgers and lamb.

COCONUT AND LEMON GRASS SAUCE

> **Cooking time:** *18 minutes*
> **Makes:** *about 1½ cups*

8 cm (3 in) piece lemon grass (see note)

1 medium-sized red onion or 5-6 shallots, chopped

1 clove garlic, chopped

1 tbsp chopped fresh ginger

1-3 red chillies, seeded and chopped

2 tbsp cooking oil

1 tbsp chopped fresh coriander (cilantro)

1 cup (250 ml/8 fl oz) thick canned coconut milk

1 tbsp lime juice

1 tbsp light soya sauce

¼ tsp turmeric

Slice the lemon grass as finely as possible so that it can be ground more readily (it tends to be fibrous). Place in bowl of food processor with onion or shallots, garlic, ginger and chillies to taste. Process to a paste. Heat oil in a saucepan, add lemon grass-onion

Chicken wings in honey-soya marinade, and popular Asian ingredients

mixture and fry gently for 5 minutes, stirring often. Add remaining ingredients and simmer gently for 10 minutes. Use as a sauce or baste for fish or chicken, or as directed in recipes. May be stored in refrigerator in a sealed jar for up to 1 week.

Note: Cut lemon grass from bottom section of stalk just above the root, if present; this is the only part used. If fresh lemon grass is not available, substitute 12 pieces dried lemon grass (available from Asian food stores) or 1 teaspoon grated lemon rind.

HERB-WINE MARINADE

> **Makes:** *about 1½ cups*

1 cup (250 ml/8 fl oz) dry white wine

½ cup (125 ml/4 fl oz) olive oil

½ tsp cracked white peppercorns

1 tbsp white wine vinegar

1 clove garlic, crushed

1 small onion, sliced (optional)

1 tbsp finely chopped fresh herbs (see note)

Mix all ingredients together in dish in which food is to be marinated. Omit onion if using for seafoods. Use for lamb, veal, chicken, shellfish and fish, or as directed in recipes.

Note: Use a mixture of herbs to complement the food, such as:

    lamb—thyme, parsley, rosemary, mint

    veal—marjoram, tarragon, parsley, sage

    chicken—marjoram, thyme, parsley, tarragon

    seafoods—dill, marjoram, parsley, chervil.

GRAVY FOR YOUR ROAST

If you like to use meat and poultry drippings to make a gravy or sauce, it is possible if using a gas kettle or covered gas grill. Of course it is also possible if using a charcoal kettle, but it can be quite an effort as well as hazardous, as the drip pan is not easily removed while the coals are still hot.

> **Cooking time:** *about 5 minutes*

meat or poultry drippings

1-2 tbsp plain (all-purpose) flour

1-1½ cups (250-375 ml/8-12 fl oz) water

beef or chicken stock (bouillon) powder to taste

salt and pepper

Wearing thick gloves and using tongs, carefully remove drip pan from under the grill; it will be necessary to remove the grill, or move it aside. Place grill over direct heat and put drip pan on it. Skim off excess fat and discard. Stir flour into meat drippings and cook over direct heat, stirring often, for 1-2 minutes. Add water, stirring constantly, until thickened and bubbling. Stir in suitable stock powder to taste, adjust seasoning with salt and pepper and boil for 1 minute. Pour into gravy boat.

Note: Amount of flour and liquid depends on number of serves required.

SIMPLE LEMON BASTE

Makes: about ½ cup

1/3 cup (90 ml/3 fl oz) olive oil or melted butter

grated rind of ½ lemon

2 tbsp lemon juice

1 clove garlic, crushed

2 tsp finely chopped parsley

1 tsp chopped fresh marjoram or ½ tsp dried marjoram leaves

freshly ground black pepper

Put all ingredients in a small heatproof pan and beat well to combine. Place on side of barbecue grill to warm slightly and use as a baste for fish, chicken and vegetables.

RED WINE MARINADE

Makes: about 1½ cups

1 cup (250 ml/8 fl oz) dry red wine

¼ cup (60 ml/2 fl oz) oil

2 cloves garlic, crushed

2 tbsp balsamic or red wine vinegar

1 small brown onion, sliced

2 bay leaves, crumbled

1 tsp chopped fresh thyme

1 tbsp chopped parsley

1 tsp chopped fresh tarragon or ½ tsp dried tarragon

½ tsp cracked black peppercorns

Combine all ingredients in dish in which food is to be marinated. Use for beef, pork and game, or as directed in recipes.

TERIYAKI MARINADE

Makes: about 1 cup

½ cup (125 ml/4 fl oz) light soya sauce

1 clove garlic, crushed

1 tsp grated fresh ginger

¼ cup dry sherry

1 tbsp sugar

1 tbsp honey

1½ tsp lemon juice

2 tsp treacle (molasses, see page 18)

Mix all ingredients together in dish in which food is to be marinated. Use for chicken, beef and pork. After food has been marinated, add 1 tablespoon oil and use the marinade to baste the chicken or meat.

CRANBERRY-LIME SAUCE AND GLAZE

Makes: about 2½ cups

1 cup (350 g/12 oz) cranberry sauce

½ cup (175 g/6 oz) lime marmalade

grated rind of 2 limes

½ cup (125 ml/4 fl oz) lime juice

1 tbsp Dijon mustard

2 tbsp melted butter (for glaze)

Put all ingredients except for butter in bowl of food processor and process until smooth. Transfer to sauceboat and serve as a sauce for chicken, turkey, pork or ham. To use as a glaze for similar meats while cooking, mix the butter into ½ cup of the prepared sauce. The sauce will keep in a sealed jar in the refrigerator for 1-2 weeks.

LEMON AND HERB BUTTER

Makes: about 1¼ cups

1 cup (250 g/8 oz) butter at room temperature

2 tbsp chopped watercress

2 tbsp chopped parsley

2 tbsp chopped spring onions (scallions)

1 clove garlic, crushed

grated rind of 1 lemon

2 tbsp lemon juice

2 tsp grained mustard

Cream butter in a bowl, but do not overbeat as yellow colour should be retained. Prepare the herbs and spring onions, chopping them roughly to measure. Place in food processor bowl with garlic and lemon rind and process to a coarse purée. Add to creamed butter with lemon juice and mustard and mix well to combine. Transfer to butter crock, cover and chill. Alternatively, shape into 2 rough logs on 2 pieces of foil, roll up firmly and smooth into a roll. Twist ends to seal and chill until firm. Use for seafood, chicken, lamb and veal.

GINGER LIME BUTTER

Makes: about 1¼ cups

1 tbsp drained, chopped cooked spinach (optional)

grated rind of 2 limes

1 tbsp chopped flat-leaf parsley

1 tbsp chopped fresh ginger

3 tbsp lime juice

1 cup (250 g/8 oz) butter at room temperature

salt and finely ground white pepper

Spinach gives the butter a pleasant green colour without adding flavour. Frozen chopped spinach is ideal as it has been blanched and usually has a good colour. Otherwise, cook some fresh spinach, only with water clinging to leaves, just long enough to wilt. Drain, chop, drain again and measure.

Place spinach (if used), lime rind, parsley and ginger in bowl of food processor and process until puréed. Add lime juice and butter and process until smooth and light. Add salt and pepper to taste, process briefly to mix. Adjust flavour with more lime juice if necessary; butter should taste fairly strongly of lime. Transfer to butter crock, cover and chill until required. Use for barbecued seafoods, poultry and veal, or as directed in recipes.

Apricot barbecue sauce and Plum barbecue sauce

DEVILLED TOMATO BUTTER

Makes: about 1¼ cups

1 cup (250 g/8 oz) butter at room temperature

1 tbsp tomato paste

½ tsp caster (superfine) sugar

3 tsp chilli sauce

½ tsp Worcestershire sauce

paprika (optional)

Cream butter in a bowl. Beat in remaining ingredients, except paprika, until combined. Transfer to butter crock, cover and chill. If desired, dust top lightly with paprika for serving. Alternatively, shape into two rough logs on two pieces of foil, roll up and smooth the rolls. If desired, press rolls on work surface to form 'square' or 'triangular' rolls. Twist ends of foil and chill until firm. Use on barbecued beef, chicken and seafoods, or melt some over Barbecue-steamed Rice (see page 95).

PLUM BARBECUE SAUCE

Cooking time: 18 minutes
Makes: about 1½ cups

½ cup (175 g/6 oz) plum jam

1 medium-sized onion, grated

2 tbsp oil

1 cup (250 ml/8 fl oz) red wine

¼ cup (60 ml/2 fl oz) red wine vinegar

3 tsp French mustard

3 tsp chilli sauce

2 tbsp tomato ketchup

If jam has large pieces of fruit, push through a sieve or purée in food processor; measure after puréeing.

In a saucepan, cook onion gently in oil for 5 minutes. Add remaining ingredients and stir occasionally until combined. Reduce heat and simmer gently for 10 minutes. Use as a sauce for chicken, duck, pork, lamb, beef or veal. To use as a baste, add 1 tablespoon oil to ½ cup of the sauce. Store in a sealed jar in the refrigerator for up to 2 weeks.

APRICOT BARBECUE SAUCE

Cooking time: 18 minutes
Makes: about 1½ cups

½ cup (175 g/6 oz) apricot jam

1 medium-sized brown onion, grated

2 tbsp oil

1 cup (250 ml/8 fl oz) apricot nectar

2 tbsp Worcestershire sauce

1 tbsp cider vinegar

¼ tsp ground allspice

¼ tsp ground cinnamon

10 drops Tabasco sauce

If jam has large pieces of fruit, push through a sieve or purée in food processor; measure after puréeing.

In a saucepan, cook onion gently in oil for 5 minutes. Add remaining ingredients, stirring often until jam has melted. Reduce heat and simmer gently for 10 minutes. Use as a sauce to accompany pork, chicken, lamb or veal, or as a baste for these meats (thin down with a little water or apricot nectar if necessary). Sauce will keep for 2–3 weeks in a sealed jar in the refrigerator.

DESSERTS

No barbecue meal is complete without a sweet ending. The covered barbecue allows for a far greater variety of desserts to enter your repertoire, particularly if you have a penchant for hot puddings other than fruit wrapped in foil packets or impaled on skewers. You will find the desserts are easy to put together and, because the trend today is for minimum-fuss cooking, conventional oven directions have also been given. The desserts are just as suitable for meals served at the dinner table as they are for alfresco eating. And there will sometimes be occasions when the barbecue will be so busy with the main meal, you might have to cook in advance.

If your barbecue is a charcoal kettle, you will often find that, when cooking is completed, there is still enough heat to cook something else. Amongst the desserts, and in the Breads and Cakes chapter, you will find many recipes which can be put together quickly and cooked in the residual heat—why waste it!

FRUIT SALAD WITH HOT ORANGE SYRUP

Cooking time: *6-8 minutes*
Serves: *6-8*

3 oranges

1 punnet (250 g/8 oz) strawberries

3 kiwi fruit (Chinese gooseberries)

Fruit salad with hot orange syrup

½ pineapple

2 bananas

Hot Orange Syrup

½ cup (125 ml/4 fl oz) fresh orange juice

2 tbsp sugar

1 tbsp brown sugar, packed

1 tbsp Grand Marnier

blanched julienne orange shreds

Peel wide strips of rind from 1 orange thinly so that there is no pith on strips. Cut strips into julienne shreds, place in a pan with water to cover and boil for 3 minutes. Drain and keep aside.

Cut the pith from the first orange and peel remainder, removing all pith. Slice thickly and cut into chunky pieces. Place in a large glass bowl. Wash strawberries gently and drain well. Hull and halve if large. Peel kiwi fruit and slice. Remove skin and core from pineapple and cut into chunks. Peel and slice bananas. Add these fruits to oranges and toss lightly to mix. Cover and chill until required.

In a pan mix orange juice, sugars, Grand Marnier and reserved orange zest. Take out to barbecue with fruit salad.

When ready to serve, put pan of orange mixture over direct heat and stir until boiling. Boil gently for 4-5 minutes until reduced by a third. Spoon hot syrup over cold fruit salad and serve with cream or vanilla ice-cream.

PEPPERED PINEAPPLE WITH ORANGE SAUCE

All barbecues: *Direct—Hot reducing to Medium*
Cooking time: *5-7 minutes*
Serves: *6*

1 medium-sized pineapple

freshly ground black pepper

½ cup (90 g/3 oz) brown sugar, packed

grated rind of 1 orange

¾ cup (185 ml/6 fl oz) fresh orange juice

1 tbsp lemon juice

¼ cup (60 g/2 oz) butter

¼ cup (60 ml/ 2 fl oz) crème de cacao liqueur

vanilla ice-cream for serving

Remove skin from pineapple and cut in 6 slices, discarding ends. Remove core from slices. Sprinkle slices lightly with black pepper. Mix brown sugar and orange rind with orange and lemon juice in a jug. Place butter in a large frying pan and crème de cacao in a small pan. Take all out to barbecue.

Place frying pan over direct high heat and heat until butter stops foaming. Add pineapple slices and cook until pineapple is lighty browned on each side. Add sugar-juice mixture and leave to boil gently, moving pan to cooler section of barbecue or reduce heat to medium. Warm crème de cacao on the barbecue without overheating. Flame the crème de cacao and pour over pineapple. Shake pan until flames die down and serve pineapple onto individual plates with the sauce. Serve immediately with ice-cream.

Honeyed apple charlotte

out and feel the knife blade immediately. If quite hot, the pudding is cooked. Stand for 5-10 minutes, then turn out onto serving dish. Serve warm with Whipped Cinnamon Cream.

Whipped Cinnamon Cream: Whip cream to soft peaks, fold in sugar and cinnamon and place in serving bowl. Chill until needed.

HONEYED APPLE CHARLOTTE

Charcoal kettle: Indirect—Medium—Preheat not necessary
Gas kettle: Indirect—Medium-hot—Preheat 6-8 minutes
Covered gas grill: Indirect—Medium-hot—Preheat 6-8 minutes
Cooking time: 50-60 minutes
Serves: 6-8

1 x 780 g (28 oz) can unsweetened pie apple

¼ cup (90 g/3 oz) honey

3 tbsp sultanas (golden raisins)

1 tsp grated lemon rind

½ tsp ground cinnamon

⅛ tsp ground cloves

8-10 slices stale white bread, crusts removed

½ cup (125 g/4 oz) butter, melted

Whipped Cinnamon Cream

1 cup (250 ml/8 fl oz) cream

1 tbsp caster (superfine) sugar

½ tsp cinnamon

Turn pie apple into a bowl and add two-thirds of the honey, reserving remainder. Add sultanas, lemon rind and spices and mix well. Cut trimmed bread into strips to fit a charlotte mould or 18 x 8 cm (7 x 3 in) deep round cake pan or soufflé dish. Put melted butter in a shallow dish and dip in bread to coat each side, placing strips close together around sides and on base of mould as they are coated. Add filling and cover with remaining butter-coated bread. Drizzle reserved honey on top. Charlotte may be set aside for 1-2 hours at this stage if necessary.

Place on barbecue grill and cook indirect, hood down, for 50-60 minutes until top is golden brown and centre is hot. Test by plunging a thin knife blade in the centre, leave for 2-3 seconds, pull

BAKED APPLES

Charcoal kettle: Indirect—Medium—Preheat 6-8 minutes
Gas kettle: Indirect—Hot—Preheat 6-8 minutes
Covered gas grill: Indirect—Hot—Preheat 6-8 minutes
Cooking time: 35-45 minutes
Serves: 6

6 large green cooking apples

½ cup (125 g/4 oz) sugar

1 cup (250 ml/8 fl oz) white wine

1 cup (250 ml/8 fl oz) water

¼ cup (60 g/2 oz) butter or margarine

Raisin and Pecan Stuffing

⅓ cup (60 g/2 oz) brown sugar, packed

¼ cup (30 g/1 oz) chopped pecan nuts

½ cup (90 g/3 oz) chopped seeded raisins

grated rind of 1 lemon

½ tsp cinnamon

pinch ground cloves

Wash apples and core with apple corer. With the point of a sharp knife, score skin around the middle of each apple. Stand apples upright in an ovenproof dish and fill centres with stuffing (see below). Stir sugar into wine and water until dissolved and pour into dish. Place a piece of butter on top of each apple.

Place dish of apples on barbecue grill and cook indirect, hood down, for 35-45 minutes, basting occasionally with wine syrup. Serve hot, with syrup poured over each apple, and accompany with whipped cream.

Raisin and Pecan Stuffing: Mix ingredients together until combined.

Conventional oven: Preheat and bake at 180-190°C (350-375°F/Gas 4) for 35-40 minutes.

BANANAS IN RUM SYRUP

All barbecues: Direct—Hot
Cooking time: 6-8 minutes
Serves: 6

¾ cup (185 ml/6 fl oz) canned pineapple juice

1 tbsp brown sugar, packed

¼ cup (60 ml/2 fl oz) rum

12 small firm bananas

¼ cup (60 g/2 oz) butter

whipped cream for serving

Mix pineapple juice and brown sugar in a jug and stir to dissolve sugar. Put rum in a small pan. Take out to barbecue with bananas and butter.

Peel bananas just before required. Place a large frying pan or metal baking pan over direct heat and add butter. When foaming subsides, add bananas and cook quickly to lightly brown bananas each side. By the time the last banana goes in, the first is ready for turning. Add pineapple mixture to pan and simmer bananas, spooning syrup over them, and cook long enough only to warm them through. Do not let bananas become mushy. Warm the rum, ignite and pour over bananas. As soon as flames die down, serve bananas and syrup onto individual plates, 2 bananas per serve, and accompany with whipped cream.

MANGOES IN CHAMPAGNE

Serves: 6

3 mangoes

6 tsp Grand Marnier liqueur

1 chilled bottle (750 ml/26 fl oz) brut champagne

Peel and slice mangoes. Divide between 6 stemmed dessert glasses or champagne saucers and sprinkle 1 teaspoon Grand Marnier over mangoes in each glass. Place on a tray and chill until required. To serve, take out to barbecue table with the champagne and fill each glass with champagne just before serving. While this makes a refreshing ending to a meal, it can also be served as a starter for breakfast or brunch.

Mangoes in champagne

CHOCOLATE DESSERT WITH BERRY COULIS

Charcoal kettle: Indirect—Medium—Preheat 5-6 minutes
Gas kettle: Indirect—Medium—Preheat 5-6 minutes
Covered gas grill: Indirect—Medium—Preheat 5-6 minutes
Cooking time: 60-65 minutes
Serves: 8-10

1¼ cups (310 g/10 oz) sugar

¼ cup (30 g/1 oz) cocoa powder

1 cup (250 ml/8 fl oz) water

½ cup (125 g/4 oz) butter or margarine

½ tsp bicarbonate of soda (baking soda)

1½ cups (185 g/6 oz) self-raising flour

2 eggs, beaten

1 tsp vanilla essence

icing (confectioners') sugar for dusting

whipped cream for serving

Berry Coulis

2 punnets (500 g/1 lb) strawberries or raspberries

caster (superfine) sugar

Place sugar and sifted cocoa in a medium-sized saucepan. Stir in water, add butter and soda and bring to the boil, stirring occasionally. Boil gently for 5 minutes, remove from heat and cool completely. Grease a round 20 cm by 5 cm (8 in by 2 in) deep cake pan, line base with a round of baking paper or foil and grease lining. Chill and dust with a little flour.

Using a balloon whisk, stir sifted flour into cooled chocolate mixture with eggs and vanilla. Pour into prepared pan and cover top securely with well-greased foil. Cake may be set aside for up to 30 minutes before baking if necessary.

Place on grill in heated barbecue and bake indirect, hood down, for 45 minutes, remove foil and cook for further 10-15 minutes or until cooked when tested. Let stand for 10 minutes before turning out onto serving plate. Remove lining paper and dust top with icing sugar. Serve warm, cut in slices, with Berry Coulis and whipped cream.

Berry Coulis: Rinse berries only if absolutely necessary, draining well. Hull strawberries if used. Purée the berries and stir in sugar to taste. Pour into a jug for serving.

Conventional oven: Preheat and bake at 180-190°C (350-375°F/Gas 4) for 50-60 minutes.

CHOCOLATE SELF-SAUCING PUDDING

> *Charcoal kettle: Indirect—Medium—Preheat not necessary*
> *Gas kettle: Indirect—Medium—Preheat 6-8 minutes*
> *Covered gas grill: Indirect—Medium—Preheat 6-8 minutes*
> *Cooking time: 40-45 minutes*
> *Serves: 6*

1 cup (125 g/4 oz) self-raising flour

2 tbsp cocoa powder

½ cup (125 g/4 oz) caster (superfine) sugar

½ cup (125 ml/4 fl oz) milk

1 egg

2 tbsp melted butter or margarine

½ cup (90 g/3 oz) brown sugar, packed

2 tbsp cocoa powder, extra

1¼ cups (310 ml/10 fl oz) boiling water

Sift flour and cocoa powder into a mixing bowl. Stir in sugar. Add milk, egg and melted butter and beat with a balloon whisk until smooth. Pour into a greased 8-cup ovenproof dish and spread evenly. In a small bowl, mix brown sugar with extra cocoa powder, breaking up lumps. Sprinkle evenly over batter in dish. Pudding can be set aside up to 1 hour before baking if necessary.

Just before cooking the pudding, pour boiling water carefully over the surface. Place on barbecue grill and cook indirect, hood down, for 40-45 minutes until pudding is firm in the centre with chocolate sauce formed in the base of the dish. Serve hot or warm with cream or ice-cream.

Conventional oven: Preheat and bake at 180-190°C (350-375°F/Gas 4) for 40-45 minutes.

Baked carrot pudding

BAKED CARROT PUDDING

> *Charcoal kettle: Indirect—Medium—Preheat 5-6 minutes*
> *Gas kettle: Indirect—Medium—Preheat 5-6 minutes*
> *Covered gas grill: Indirect—Medium—Preheat 5-6 minutes*
> *Cooking time: 55-60 minutes*
> *Serves: 8*

250 g (8 oz) frozen sliced carrots

⅓ cup (90 g/3 oz) butter or margarine, melted

¾ cup (185 g/6 oz) caster (superfine) sugar

½ cup (30 g/1 oz) soft white breadcrumbs

2 eggs

½ cup (90 g/3 oz) chopped seeded raisins

1 tsp mixed spice or ½ tsp ground allspice

1½ cups (185 g/6 oz) self-raising flour

2 tbsp milk

Grease an 18 cm (7 in) fluted or plain ring cake pan with butter; chill, then dust with flour, shaking out excess.

Thaw carrots, place in food processor bowl and process to a coarse purée. Alternatively, cook carrots in a little water until tender, drain well and mash to a purée. Place puréed carrot in mixing bowl with warm, melted butter, sugar and crumbs and stir until sugar is dissolved. Beat in eggs, raisins and spice. Fold in flour alternately with milk. Pour into prepared cake pan and cover top securely with greased foil.

Place pan on barbecue grill and cook indirect, hood down, for 55-60 minutes, removing foil for last 10 minutes of cooking. Stand for 5 minutes before turning out onto serving platter. Serve hot or warm with custard or cream.

Conventional oven: Preheat and bake at 160-180°C (325-350°F/Gas 3) for 55-60 minutes, removing foil for last 10 minutes of cooking.

Upside-down cake

Place cake on barbecue grill and bake indirect, hood down, for 35-40 minutes until cooked when tested. Stand for 5 minutes before turning out onto serving plate. Serve warm with cream.

Conventional oven: Preheat and bake at 180-190°C (350-375°F/Gas 4) for 30-35 minutes.

BREAD AND BUTTER CUSTARD

Charcoal kettle: Indirect—Medium—Preheat not necessary
Gas kettle: Indirect—Medium—Preheat 6-8 minutes
Covered gas grill: Indirect—Medium—Preheat 6-8 minutes
Cooking time: 45-50 minutes
Serves: 6-8

3 slices white bread, buttered

2 tbsp sultanas (golden raisins)

cinnamon sugar

4 eggs

¼ cup (60 g/2 oz) sugar

pinch salt

3 cups (750 ml/24 fl oz) milk

1 tbsp brandy

1 tsp vanilla essence

grated nutmeg for topping

Halve buttered bread diagonally and arrange in base of 6-cup deep pie dish or oven dish. Place buttered side up, and overlap bread slices slightly. Sprinkle with sultanas and a light dusting of cinnamon sugar. In a large bowl beat eggs, sugar and salt, add milk, brandy and vanilla and stir until sugar is dissolved. Strain into pie dish, dust top lightly with nutmeg and place dish in a roasting pan. Add hot water to come halfway up sides of dish.

Place roasting pan with custard on barbecue grill and cook indirect, hood down, for 40-50 minutes until custard is set. Test with a knife—it should come out clean. Rotate custard during cooking if not browning evenly. Serve warm with cream.

Conventional oven: Preheat and bake at 180-190°C (350-375°F/Gas 4) for 40-45 minutes.

UPSIDE-DOWN CAKE

Charcoal kettle: Indirect—Medium—Preheat 6-8 minutes
Gas kettle: Indirect—Medium—Preheat 6-8 minutes
Covered gas grill: Indirect—Medium—Preheat 6-8 minutes
Cooking time: 35-40 minutes
Serves: 8

¼ cup (60 g/2 oz) butter or margarine

3 tbsp brown sugar, packed

14-16 canned apricot halves, drained

10-12 pitted prunes

2-3 tbsp walnut pieces

Cake Batter

¼ cup (60 g/2 oz) butter or margarine, melted

½ cup (125 g/4 oz) caster (superfine) sugar

1 tsp vanilla essence

1 egg

1¼ cups (150 g/5 oz) self-raising flour

½ cup (125 ml/4 fl oz) milk

Grease a 20 cm (8 in) square or 23 cm (9 in) round cake pan, about 5-6 cm (2-2½ in) deep. Cream butter with brown sugar and spread in the base of cake pan. Arrange apricot halves towards edge, rounded side down, and arrange pitted prunes towards centre. Fill in gaps with walnut pieces. Set aside.

To make cake, place melted butter in a mixing bowl, add sugar and vanilla and mix with a wooden spoon. Add egg and beat well with spoon for 2 minutes to dissolve sugar. Stir in flour alternately with milk. Pour batter over fruit in cake pan. Cake may be set aside for up to 1 hour before baking.

STRAWBERRY SHORTCAKE

> **Charcoal kettle:** Indirect—Medium—Preheat 10-12 minutes
> **Gas kettle:** Indirect—Hot—Preheat 10-12 minutes
> **Covered gas grill:** Indirect—Hot—Preheat 10-12 minutes
> **Cooking time:** 20-25 minutes
> **Serves:** 6-8

2 cups (250 g/8 oz) self-raising flour

1 tsp baking powder

pinch salt

2 tbsp caster (superfine) sugar

1/3 cup (90 g/3 oz) firm butter

1 egg

½ cup (125 ml/4 fl oz) milk

1/3 cup (90 ml/3 fl oz) cream

2 tsp melted butter

1 punnet (250 g/8 oz) strawberries

1 tbsp caster (superfine) sugar, extra

1½ cups (375 ml/12 fl oz) cream, whipped

Sift flour, baking powder and salt into a bowl and stir in the sugar. Cut butter into small pieces and rub or cut into flour until mixture resembles coarse crumbs. Beat egg with milk and cream and add almost all of this to the flour mixture, reserving about 2 teaspoons of the liquid. Mix with a round-bladed knife to a soft dough. Turn out onto a lightly floured board and knead lightly for 5 strokes only, to smooth the dough a little. Divide into two portions, one slightly larger than the other. Shape each portion into rounds 2 cm (¾ in) thick. Place larger round on a greased baking tray, brush top with melted butter and place smaller round on top. Glaze top with reserved egg-milk mixture. Shortcake can be set aside for about 20 minutes before baking if necessary.

Gently wash strawberries, drain well and hull them. Halve if large. Place in a bowl and sprinkle with the extra sugar. Whip cream lightly. Take out to barbecue with the shortcake.

Place shortcake on barbecue grill and cook indirect, hood down, for 20-25 minutes, until golden brown and cooked. Knock base of tray with knuckle—it will sound hollow when cooked. Let stand for about 10 minutes. Lift warm shortcake onto serving plate and with the aid of a knife, loosen and remove top layer. Spread a quarter of the cream on the base and cover with most of the strawberries and their juice. Place top in position and decorate with cream and strawberries. Serve warm with remaining whipped cream.

Conventional oven: Preheat and bake at 220-230°C (425-450°F/Gas 7) for 15-20 minutes.

DATE AND BANANA SLICE

> **Charcoal kettle:** Indirect—Medium—Preheat 6-8 minutes
> **Gas kettle:** Indirect—Medium—Preheat 6-8 minutes
> **Covered gas grill:** Indirect—Medium—Preheat 6-8 minutes
> **Cooking time:** 35-40 minutes
> **Serves:** 6-8

¼ cup (60 g/2 oz) butter or margarine, melted

½ cup (125 g/4 oz) caster (superfine) sugar

1 tsp vanilla essence

1 egg

1¼ cups (150 g/5 oz) self-raising flour

½ cup (125 ml/4 fl oz) milk

2 bananas

8 pitted dates

1 tsp cinnamon sugar

Grease a 20 cm (8 in) square cake pan or casserole dish about 5-6 cm (2-2½ in) deep. Place melted butter in a mixing bowl, add sugar and vanilla and mix with a wooden spoon. Add egg and beat well with spoon for 2 minutes to dissolve sugar. Stir in flour alternately with milk. Spread batter in prepared pan or dish. Peel and cut bananas diagonally in 1 cm (½ in) slices. Halve dates lengthwise. Arrange dates and bananas over batter and sprinkle with cinnamon sugar. If making dessert in advance, prepare only to stage before adding fruit and set aside for up to 45 minutes. Prepare and add fruit topping just before baking.

To cook, place on barbecue grill and bake indirect, hood down, for 35-40 minutes until cooked when tested. Let stand for 10 minutes and serve, cut in squares, with whipped cream or pouring custard.

Conventional oven: Preheat and bake at 180-190°C (350-375°F/Gas 4) for 30-35 minutes.

Strawberry shortcake

PEAR AND ALMOND CRUMBLE

Charcoal kettle: Indirect—Medium—Preheat 6-8 minutes
Gas kettle: Indirect—Medium—Preheat 6-8 minutes
Covered gas grill: Indirect—Medium—Preheat 6-8 minutes
Cooking time: 40-45 minutes
Serves: 6-8

¼ cup (60 g/2 oz) butter or margarine, melted

½ cup (125 g/4 oz) caster (superfine) sugar

1 egg

½ tsp vanilla essence

¼ tsp almond essence

1 cup (125 g/4 oz) plain (all-purpose) flour

2½ tsp baking powder

¼ cup (60 ml/2 fl oz) milk

½ cup (60 g/2 oz) ground almonds

6 canned pear halves, drained

Crumble Topping

¼ cup (30 g/1 oz) plain (all-purpose) flour

½ cup (60 g/2 oz) ground almonds

2 tbsp caster (superfine) sugar

½ tsp cinnamon

45 g (1½ oz) firm butter or margarine

Put melted butter into a mixing bowl and stir in sugar. Add egg and flavouring essences and beat with wooden spoon for 2 minutes to dissolve sugar. Sift flour and baking powder and fold into butter mixture alternately with milk. Stir in almonds and beat 1 minute. Turn into a greased and floured 20 cm (8 in) spring-form pan and spread evenly. Place pears in cartwheel fashion, cut side up, on top of batter. Sprinkle Crumble Topping over batter and pears. Dessert may be left for up to 45 minutes before baking if necessary.

Place pan on barbecue grill and cook, hood down, for 40-45 minutes until top is golden and cake has shrunk slightly from side of pan. Stand for 10 minutes before removing from pan. Serve warm with whipped cream or ice-cream.

Left: Citrus coconut impossible pie; right: Pear and almond crumble

Crumble Topping: Mix flour, almonds, sugar and cinnamon in a bowl, and rub in butter to form a crumbly mixture.

Conventional oven: Preheat and bake at 180-190°C (350-375°F/Gas 4) for 30-35 minutes.

CITRUS COCONUT IMPOSSIBLE PIE

Charcoal kettle: Indirect—Medium—Preheat 6-8 minutes
Gas kettle: Indirect—Medium-low—Preheat 6-8 minutes
Covered gas grill: Indirect—Medium-low—Preheat 6-8 minutes
Cooking time: 50-60 minutes
Serves: 6-8

¼ cup (60 g/2 oz) butter or margarine

½ cup (60 g/2 oz) self-raising flour

¾ cup (185 g/6 oz) caster (superfine) sugar

¾ cup (60 g/2 oz) desiccated (unsweetened) coconut

grated rind of 1 lime

grated rind of 1 lemon

½ cup (125 ml/4 fl oz) lime and lemon juice combined

4 eggs

1½ cups (375 ml/12 fl oz) milk

Butter should be very soft, but not melted. Place in bowl with all ingredients except milk and beat until smooth. Add the milk and beat for 1 minute. Pour into greased 25 cm (10 in) pie plate. Pudding may be set aside for up to 30 minutes before baking if necessary.

Place pie on an upturned layer-cake pan placed on barbecue grill during preheating. Shield sides with foil if necessary during cooking. Cook indirect, hood down, for 50-60 minutes until a knife inserted in centre comes out clean. Stand for 10 minutes before slicing and serve warm with cream or ice-cream.

Note: Other flavours may be used in place of the lemon and lime rind and juice. Replace these with: grated rind of 1 orange and ½ cup (125 ml/4 fl oz) orange juice; or grated rind of 1 lemon and ½ cup (125 ml/4 fl oz) passionfruit pulp; or grated rind of 1 lemon and ½ cup (125 ml/4 fl oz) crushed, undrained canned pineapple.

Conventional oven: Preheat and bake at 180-190°C (350-375°F/Gas 4) for 50-60 minutes.

CINNAMON PLUM CRUMBLE

Charcoal kettle: Indirect—Medium—Preheat not necessary
Gas kettle: Indirect—Medium—Preheat 6-8 minutes
Covered gas grill: Indirect—Medium—Preheat 6-8 minutes
Cooking time: 25-30 minutes
Serves:6

825 g (29 oz) can dark plums

2 tbsp brown sugar, packed

1 tsp cornflour (cornstarch)

½ tsp cinnamon

Crumble Topping

1 cup (90 g/3 oz) quick-cooking rolled oats

2 tbsp plain (all-purpose) flour

2 tbsp brown sugar, packed

½ tsp cinnamon

¼ cup (60 g/2 oz) butter or margarine

Drain plums well, remove seeds and place fruit in a 6-cup ovenproof dish. Mix brown sugar with cornflour and cinnamon and sprinkle over plums. Set aside.

To prepare topping, mix rolled oats with flour, sugar and cinnamon. Melt butter and mix in until combined. Sprinkle over plums just before cooking.

Place crumble on barbecue grill and cook indirect, hood down, for 25-30 minutes until top is golden brown. If top is not showing signs of browning in 15 minutes, elevate on an upturned layer-cake pan or place on warming rack if fitted in barbecue. Serve warm with lightly whipped cream.

Conventional oven: Preheat and bake at 180-190°C (350-375°F/Gas 4) for 20-25 minutes.

PECAN PIE

Charcoal kettle: Indirect—Medium—Preheat 6-8 minutes
Gas kettle: Indirect—Medium—Preheat 6-8 minutes
Covered gas grill: Indirect—Medium—Preheat 6-8 minutes
Cooking time: 45-50 minutes
Serves: 6-8

Pecan pie

1 unbaked 23 cm (9 in) Rich Shortcrust Pastry pie crust (page 38)

1½ cups (185 g/6 oz) pecan halves

3 medium-sized eggs

½ cup (125 g/4 oz) sugar

1 tsp vanilla essence

¾ cup (185 ml/6 fl oz) dark corn syrup or golden syrup

2 tbsp plain (all-purpose) flour

¼ cup (60 g/2 oz) butter, melted

1 tbsp whisky or bourbon

Make pie crust according to directions for Rich Shortcrust Pastry, page 38, freezing half of the pastry for later use. Roll out other half of pastry a little larger than pie plate and place in lightly greased plate. Fold the overhanging pastry under to build up the rim, press firmly and crimp with a fork or with fingers. Chill for 20-30 minutes. Arrange pecan halves, rounded side up, in the base of the pie crust.

In a mixing bowl, beat eggs with sugar, vanilla and syrup until frothy, then beat in flour, butter and whisky. Pour carefully over pecans. If there is to be a delay in baking the pie, do not pour in the egg mixture until just before baking—beat again before pouring onto the pecans.

Place pie on barbecue grill and bake indirect, hood down, for 45-50 minutes, rotating pie when necessary to brown crust evenly. Shield with foil if necessary. To test if cooked, insert the point of a knife halfway between centre of pie and crust—it should come out clean when cooked. Serve warm with whipped cream.

Conventional oven: Preheat and bake at 180-190°C (350-375°F/Gas 4) for 35-40 minutes. Test if cooked as above.

BREADS AND CAKES

reparation for a barbecue meal often begins a day or so in advance, with all those extras such as quick breads, cakes and muffins being baked in the kitchen oven. Not so with a barbecue kettle or covered gas grill! In the following recipes, kitchen preparation is mostly quick and easy and the baking is done outdoors; there's nothing quite like quick breads and muffins fresh from the 'oven'. Other recipes, such as the Boiled Apricot Fruit Loaf or Date and Pecan Roll, might benefit from the 'day or two before' cooking, and are just the types of baked goodies you can cook outside when you want to get out of the heat of the kitchen!

As many of the recipes are quick to put together, you might want to prepare them more often; for this reason directions are also given for conventional oven cooking.

FLAT BREADS

With the increasing Middle Eastern and Indian influences on the Western kitchen, one hardly needs to go through the lengthy process of making such breads from scratch. Rounds or rectangles, large or small, white or wholemeal (whole wheat), puffed or flat—whatever the shape, size or colour, they are readily available from supermarkets and delicatessens. They can be heated quickly over direct heat, about 20 seconds each side, and wrapped in a cloth to keep them warm and soft, or use one of the following ideas for something different. While purists might not agree, wholemeal flat breads are a good substitute for the chapatis so favoured for serving with Indian curries.

As the breads are best served warm, they should be heated as close to serving time as possible—before the main meal is cooked if used as a snack or nibble, or after the main meal if used to accompany it. Cooking directions assume the barbecue is already heated.

PESTO BREADS

Cooking time: 8-10 minutes

8 small, soft white pita breads

½ cup (15 g/½ oz) fresh basil leaves, loosely packed
2 tbsp chopped fresh parsley
2 small cloves garlic, chopped
60 g (2 oz) packaged cream cheese
¼ cup (30 g/1 oz) grated Parmesan cheese
¼ cup (45 g/1½ oz) pinenuts (pignolias)
2 tbsp olive oil
freshly ground pepper
extra pinenuts and Parmesan cheese for topping

The thicker white pita breads are best for this recipe; medium-sized breads are suitable, and 6 of these would be adequate.

Place basil, parsley and garlic in food processor bowl or blender jar and process to a coarse purée. Add cheeses, pinenuts, oil and pepper and process to a smooth, thick paste.

Place breads on baking trays and spread about 1 tablespoon of the pesto on top of each bread. Sprinkle about ½ teaspoon each of the extra pinenuts and Parmesan cheese on top.

Place in preheated hot barbecue, elevating trays as directed on page 14, so that breads can be heated quickly to allow topping to brown lightly. Cook 1 tray at a time if necessary, and cook indirect, hood down, for 8-10 minutes. Serve immediately in a cloth-lined basket as an accompaniment to barbecue meals, or cut in wedges and serve as finger food.

Conventional oven: Bake in preheated 190–200°C (375–400°F/Gas 5) for 6-8 minutes.

PIZZA BREADS

Cooking time: 5-8 minutes

6 medium-sized pita breads
1–2 tbsp olive oil
½ cup (125 g/4 oz) tomato paste
1 tsp sugar
freshly ground pepper
1 tbsp dried onion flakes (instant minced onion)
1 tsp dried garlic granules (flakes)
2 tsp dried basil leaves
1 tsp dried oregano leaves
1½ cups (210 g/7 oz) shredded mozzarella cheese

Choose the soft, pale-coloured pita breads if possible, or use wholemeal (whole wheat) pita breads if preferred. Brush tops with oil.

Mix tomato paste with sugar, pepper, onion and garlic flakes and spread about 3-4 teaspoons of the mixture on oiled side of each bread. Mix dried herbs with the cheese and sprinkle on top; breads should not be completely covered with the cheese. Place on the grill in preheated medium barbecue and cook indirect, hood down, for 5-8 minutes until cheese melts. Serve hot, piled in a cloth-lined basket, as an accompaniment to barbecued meals, or cut breads into wedges for serving as a finger food.

Conventional oven: Bake in preheated 190–200°C (375–400°F/Gas 5) for 6-8 minutes.

Sesame lavash; Pizza breads; Pesto breads; Feta and olive bread braid

FETA AND OLIVE BREAD BRAID

> **Charcoal kettle**: *Indirect—Medium—Preheat 5-6 minutes*
> **Gas kettle**: *Indirect—Medium—Preheat 5-6 minutes*
> **Covered gas grill**: *Indirect—Medium—Preheat 5-6 minutes*
> **Cooking time**: *15-20 minutes*
> **Serves**: *8-10*

1 small onion, thinly sliced

3 tsp olive oil

¾ cup (100 g/3½ oz) crumbled feta cheese (goat's milk feta for preference)

½ cup (90 g/3 oz) chopped, pitted black olives

1 tbsp chopped parsley

1 large braided loaf of white bread

2-3 tsp olive oil, additional

In a small pan, cook onion gently in olive oil until transparent. Tip into a bowl, add feta cheese, olives and parsley, and mix well. With fingers and the aid of a small paring knife, lift top braids on the bread individually to make a series of slits across the top of the loaf. Using a teaspoon, insert feta mixture into slits. Brush loaf with additional olive oil and place on a baking tray or piece of foil.

Place on barbecue grill and bake indirect in preheated barbecue, hood down, for 15-20 minutes until bread is heated through and crust is crisp. Serve hot or warm as an accompaniment to barbecue meals.

Conventional oven: Preheat and bake at 180-190°C (350-375°F/Gas 4) for 15-20 minutes.

SESAME LAVASH

> **Cooking time**: *8-10 minutes*

6 lavash or 3 large pocket breads

¼ cup (60 g/ 2 oz) ghee (clarified butter), melted

2 tbsp toasted sesame seeds

paprika

Lavash are thin, rectangular breads made from white flour; they are soft and bubbly in texture. Use these as they are. If using large pocket breads, choose either white or wholemeal and split each horizontally to make 2 rounds. Brush one side of lavash or smooth side of pocket breads with melted clarified butter or ghee, sprinkle with sesame seeds and dust lightly with paprika. Place on baking trays and bake indirect in preheated medium barbecue, hood down, for 8-10 minutes until golden brown and crisp; for gas kettle, elevate tray on upturned layer cake pan. Break into largish pieces and pile in a bread basket as a crisp nibble during a barbecue meal, served in the same way as the Italian grissini (which can also be added to the basket).

Conventional oven: Bake in preheated 190-200°C (375-400°F/Gas 5) for 6-8 minutes until crisp and lightly coloured.

111

BREAD BASKET

Charcoal kettle: Indirect—Medium—Preheat 5-6 minutes
Gas kettle: Indirect—Medium—Preheat 5-6 minutes
Covered gas grill: Indirect—Medium—Preheat 5-6 minutes
Cooking time: 10-12 minutes
Serves: 6

1 round cottage loaf or Italian bread, about 23 cm (9 in) diameter

¹/₃ cup (90 g/3 oz) butter or margarine

2 cloves garlic, crushed

1 tbsp chopped fresh herbs (parsley, chives, thyme)

Cut the top off the loaf to form a lid for the finished basket. Pull out the soft bread from base and top leaving the crust with a thin wall of soft bread (store soft bread in freezer for breadcrumbs).

Melt butter in a small pan, add garlic, and when hot but not browned, remove from heat. Stand 5 minutes, stir in herbs. Brush mixture on inside of bread case and lid. Just before required, place upright on barbecue grill with lid alongside, crust down, and bake indirect in preheated barbecue, hood down, for 10-12 minutes until crust is crisp—inside will still be moist. Use as a basket for presenting foods such as chicken legs and wings, small barbecued sausages or as directed in recipes.

Conventional oven: Preheat and bake at 180-190°C (350-375°F/Gas 4) for 10-12 minutes.

DAMPER (SODA BREAD)

Damper is regarded as one of Australia's national dishes, so named because the First Fleeters baked their unleavened dough in the embers of the cooking fire, damped with sand to keep the embers live. When the Irish introduced soda bread, Australian cooks added baking soda and an acidic ingredient to improve the texture and digestibility of their damper. While damper is now widely made with self-raising flour, a little butter and milk or water, this version with buttermilk has an excellent flavour and is just as moist next day as when first baked.

Charcoal kettle: Indirect—Medium—Preheat 8-10 minutes
Gas kettle: Indirect—Medium—Preheat 8-10 minutes
Covered gas grill: Indirect—Medium—Preheat 8-10 minutes
Cooking time: 25-35 minutes
Serves: 6

3 cups (375 g/12 oz) self-raising flour

1 tsp bicarbonate of soda (baking soda)

½ tsp salt

2 tsp caster (superfine) sugar

1¼ cups (310 ml/10 fl oz) buttermilk

2 tbsp oil

milk for glazing

Sift flour, soda and salt into a mixing bowl. Mix in sugar and make a well in the centre. Pour in buttermilk and oil and stir to a soft, sticky dough with a round-bladed knife. Turn onto a lightly floured board, dust top with flour and knead lightly with 3-4 strokes to smooth a little. Pat into a round and place in a greased 20 cm (8 in) layer cake pan or ovenproof casserole dish. The damper should be smaller than the base of the dish. Cut a cross on the top and glaze with milk. Leave aside for at least 45 minutes or up to 1 hour; damper will begin spreading and rising in this time and gives a better result when cooked.

Bake indirect in preheated barbecue, hood down, for 25-35 minutes until golden brown. Reduce heat to Medium-High if necessary after 20 minutes. Check if cooked by tapping the base of the pan—it should sound hollow. Serve hot or warm with butter as an accompaniment to barbecue meals. Also good served with butter and golden syrup, honey or fruit conserves.

Fruit Damper: Mix ½ cup (90 g/3 oz) mixed dried fruit and additional 1 tablespoon caster (superfine) sugar into sifted flour before adding buttermilk and oil. Finish and bake as above and serve warm with butter and honey.

Left: Damper; bottom: Scones; right: Boiled apricot fruit loaf; top: Date and pecan roll

Conventional oven: Preheat and bake at 190-200°C (375-400°F/Gas 5) for 25-30 minutes.

SCONES

> Charcoal kettle: Indirect—Medium—Preheat 8-10 minutes
> Gas kettle: Indirect—Hot—Preheat 10-12 minutes
> Covered gas grill: Indirect—Hot—Preheat 10-12 minutes
> Cooking time: 12-15 minutes
> Makes: 12-14

2 cups (250 g/8 oz) self-raising flour

1 tsp baking powder

½ tsp salt

30 g (1 oz) butter or margarine

¾ cup (185 ml/6 fl oz) milk

extra milk

Sift flour, baking powder and salt into a mixing bowl. Cut butter into small pieces and rub into flour with fingertips until mixture resembles fine breadcrumbs. Using a round-bladed knife, quickly mix in milk to make a soft, sticky dough; because moisture content of flour varies, it might be necessary to add an extra tablespoon of milk.

Turn out onto a floured board and lightly flour top. Knead lightly for 5-6 turns to smooth the dough. Pat out to 2 cm (¾ in) thickness and cut into 5 cm (2 in) rounds with a floured cutter. Place close together on a greased baking tray. Brush tops with milk. Scones may be held for up to 30 minutes before baking if necessary.

Elevate tray on barbecue grill (see page 14). Bake indirect in preheated barbecue, hood down, for 12-15 minutes until golden brown and well risen. Knock bottom of tray with knuckles—scones are cooked if it sounds hollow. Remove to a cloth-lined basket and serve immediately with butter or whipped cream and fruit conserves.

Sultana Scones: Before adding milk, stir in ½ cup (90 g/3 oz) sultanas (golden raisins).

Cheese Scones: Before adding milk, stir in ½ cup (60 g/2 oz) shredded natural Cheddar cheese. Glaze with milk, sprinkle lightly with grated Parmesan cheese and dust with paprika.

Conventional oven: Preheat and bake at 230-250°C (450-475°F/Gas 8) for 12-15 minutes.

BOILED APRICOT FRUIT LOAF

> Charcoal kettle: Indirect—Medium—Preheat 4-5 minutes
> Gas kettle: Indirect—Low—Preheat 6-8 minutes
> Covered gas grill: Indirect—Low—Preheat 6-8 minutes
> Cooking time: 1½-2 hours

3 cups (375 g/12 oz) mixed dried fruit

¾ cup (185 ml/6 fl oz) apricot nectar

¾ cup (125 g/4 oz) brown sugar, packed

½ cup (125 g/4 oz) butter or margarine

½ tsp mixed spice or ground allspice

½ tsp cinnamon

1 tsp bicarbonate of soda (baking soda)

1 tsp baking powder

½ cup (60 g/2 oz) chopped blanched almonds

2 medium-sized eggs, beaten

1 cup (125 g/4 oz) plain (all-purpose) flour

Place the mixed fruit in a large saucepan and add apricot nectar, brown sugar, butter and spices. Bring to the boil, stirring occasionally. Simmer for 3 minutes and remove from heat. Stir in soda and leave until cool. Line a 23 x 12 cm (9 x 4½ in) loaf pan with heavy-duty foil, extending it about 4 cm (1½ in) above sides. Grease the foil.

Stir baking powder into cooled fruit mixture with the almonds, eggs and flour. Mix well to combine and turn into prepared loaf pan. Cake may be held for up to 1 hour before baking.

Temperature of heated barbecue should be about 180°C (350°F) when cake is placed in for cooking, so preheat for the time required to reach this temperature. Place on the grill and bake indirect, setting gas barbecue onto low when hood is closed so that baking temperature will reduce to 150-160°C (300-325°F); half-close top vent on charcoal kettle. Bake for 1½-2 hours until cooked when tested. Leave in pan and wrap in a thick cloth so that cake cools slowly. Store in a sealed container and use after 3 days for best flavour.

Conventional oven: Preheat and bake at 150-160°C (300-325°F/Gas 2) for 1½-2 hours.

DATE AND PECAN ROLL

Excellent for cooking in the covered barbecue alongside other items, as the nut roll tin takes up little space on the grill.

> Charcoal kettle: Indirect—Medium—Preheat 5-6 minutes
> Gas kettle: Indirect—Medium—Preheat 5-6 minutes
> Covered gas grill: Indirect—Medium—Preheat 5-6 minutes
> Cooking time: 35-40 minutes

¾ cup (125 g/4 oz) chopped dates

¼ cup (60 g/2 oz) caster (superfine) sugar

¼ cup (60 g/2 oz) butter or margarine

½ cup (125 ml/4 fl oz) boiling water

½ tsp bicarbonate of soda (baking soda)

1 cup (125 g/4 oz) self-raising flour

¼ tsp cinnamon

¼ cup (30 g/1 oz) chopped pecans

1 small egg, beaten

Grease a nut roll tin with melted butter, line base with a round of baking paper or foil and grease also. Chill, then dust with flour, shaking out excess. A juice can, 18 cm (7 in) high, with 8 cm (3¼ in) diameter, may be used if nut roll tin is not available. Remove top cleanly, leave base intact.

Place dates and sugar in a mixing bowl with the butter and pour on boiling water. Stir in soda and leave until cool. Mix in flour, cinnamon and pecans, then stir in beaten egg. Spoon into prepared tin. Cover with greased lid or a greased piece of foil if using juice can, pleating foil on the top and moulding it securely down the side. Roll may stand for up to 30 minutes before baking if necessary.

Bake indirect in preheated barbecue, hood down, for 35-40 minutes or until cooked—test with a fine skewer. Remove lid or foil and stand for 5-6 minutes before removing roll from container. Roll should come away freely, otherwise remove base of tin or take off can base with can opener. Cool upright on rack. Serve warm or cold, sliced and spread with butter.

Conventional oven: Preheat and bake at 180-190°C (350-375°F/Gas 4) for 35-40 minutes.

MOZZARELLA AND PEPPER BREAD

Charcoal kettle: Indirect—Medium— Preheat 5-6 minutes
Gas kettle: Indirect—Medium—Preheat 5-6 minutes
Covered gas grill: Indirect—Medium— Preheat 5-6 minutes
Cooking time: 12-15 minutes
Serves: 8-10

1 large loaf French or Italian bread (oval-shaped)

3 tbsp melted butter

3 tsp green peppercorns

1 small red (bell) pepper, finely chopped

1 tbsp chopped fresh oregano

3 tsp dried onion flakes (instant minced onion)

14-16 slices mozzarella cheese (about 310 g/10 oz)

2-3 tsp olive oil

Cut diagonal slits in the bread halfway through the loaf, spacing slits about 2 cm (¾ in) apart. Brush melted butter inside each slit.

Rinse the peppercorns, drain well and place on a flat plate. Mash lightly with a fork and mix in chopped red pepper, oregano and onion flakes. Use a 500 g (1 lb) knob of mozzarella cheese for preference and cut slices about 5 mm (¼ in) thick. Press one side of each slice into the pepper mixture. Insert slices into slits—slices should not be completely inserted. Brush all over with olive oil and place on a baking tray or piece of foil.

Place on barbecue grill and bake indirect in preheated barbecue, hood down, for 12-15 minutes until bread is heated through and crust is crisp, with cheese melted and bubbly. Serve hot or warm as an accompaniment to barbecue meals. Slice bread straight across the loaf so that each slice contains strips of the cheese filling.

Conventional oven: Preheat and bake at 180-190°C (350-375°F/Gas 4) for 12-15 minutes.

CHEESE AND ONION DAMPER

Charcoal kettle: Indirect—Medium— Preheat 8-10 minutes
Gas kettle: Indirect—Hot—Preheat 8-10 minutes
Covered gas grill: Indirect—Hot— Preheat 8-10 minutes
Cooking time: 25-30 minutes
Serves: 6

1 quantity Damper (page 112)

½ cup (60 g/2 oz) shredded natural Cheddar cheese

⅛ tsp cayenne pepper

2 tsp dried onion flakes (instant minced onion)

4 spring onions (scallions), chopped

¾ cup (90 g/3 oz) shredded mozzarella cheese

2 tbsp grated Parmesan cheese

2 tbsp chopped parsley

When making damper, add shredded Cheddar, cayenne, onion flakes and half the chopped spring onions to sifted flour. Stir in, add buttermilk and oil. Finish, shape, glaze and slash top in a cross as for damper; leave for 45 minutes to rise—the slash opens up in the process. Fill this with a mixture of the mozzarella and Parmesan cheeses, parsley and remainder of chopped spring onions.

Place pan on barbecue grill and bake indirect in preheated barbecue, hood

Cheese and onion damper

Left: Spiced apple turnovers; right: Wholemeal date scones

SPICED APPLE TURNOVERS

> *Charcoal kettle: Indirect—Medium—Preheat 8-10 minutes*
> *Gas kettle: Indirect—Hot—Preheat 10-12 minutes*
> *Covered gas grill: Indirect—Hot—Preheat 10-12 minutes*
> *Cooking time: 15-18 minutes*
> *Makes: 12*

2 cups (250 g/8 oz) self-raising flour

1 tbsp caster (superfine) sugar

1 large egg

½ cup (125 ml/4 fl oz) milk

⅓ cup (90 g/3 oz) butter or margarine, melted

extra milk for glazing

2 tbsp raw (demerara/turbinado) sugar

½ tsp cinnamon

Spiced Apple Filling

⅓ cup (90 g/3 oz) cooked, unsweetened apple

3 tsp brown sugar

¼ tsp cinnamon

Mix flour and sugar in a bowl and make a well in the centre. Beat egg into milk and pour into flour with the melted butter. Mix to a soft dough with a round-bladed knife. Turn onto a lightly-floured board and knead lightly to smooth. Roll out to 1 cm (½ in) thickness and cut into 8 cm (3 in) rounds.

Prepare filling and place a heaped teaspoonful towards centre of each round. Moisten edge with milk, fold over and press lightly to seal. Place on greased baking tray, glaze with milk and sprinkle with combined raw sugar and cinnamon. Turnovers may be held for up to 45 minutes before baking.

Elevate tray over barbecue grill (see page 14). Bake indirect in preheated barbecue, hood down, for 15-18 minutes until golden brown. Check if cooked by tapping the base of a turnover—it should sound hollow. Serve warm.

Spiced Apple Filling: Drain excess moisture from apples if necessary. Mix with sugar and cinnamon, mashing with a fork.

Conventional oven: Preheat and bake at 220-230°C (425-450°F/Gas 7) for 12-15 minutes.

---

down, for 25-30 minutes until cheese is bubbly and lightly browned. Check if cooked by tapping the base of the pan—it should sound hollow. Serve hot or warm as an accompaniment to barbecue meals.

Conventional oven: Preheat and bake at 190-200°C (375-400°F/Gas 5) for 25-30 minutes.

WHOLEMEAL DATE SCONES

> *Charcoal kettle: Indirect—Medium—Preheat 8-10 minutes*
> *Gas kettle: Indirect—Hot—Preheat 10-12 minutes*
> *Covered gas grill: Indirect—Hot—Preheat 10-12 minutes*
> *Cooking time: 14-16 minutes*
> *Makes: about 14*

1 cup (125 g/4 oz) self-raising flour

1 cup (125 g/4 oz) wholemeal (whole wheat) self-raising flour

1 tsp baking powder

¼ tsp salt

1 tsp ground cinnamon

1 tbsp caster (superfine) sugar

½ cup (90 g/3 oz) chopped dates

1 large egg

½ cup (125 ml/4 fl oz) milk

¼ cup (60 g/2 oz) butter or margarine, melted

extra milk

Sift flours and baking powder with salt and cinnamon into a mixing bowl, returning husks from sieve to flour in bowl. Stir in the sugar and dates. Beat the egg and add to flours with the milk and cooled melted butter. Stir with a round-bladed knife to a soft dough, adding a little more milk if necessary.

Turn onto a board lightly floured with wholemeal flour and knead lightly to smooth the dough. Pat out to 2 cm (¾ in) thickness and cut into rounds with a 5 cm (2 in) floured cutter. Place slightly apart on a greased baking tray and brush tops with milk to glaze. Scones may be left for up to 1 hour before baking.

Elevate tray over barbecue grill (see page 14). Bake indirect in preheated barbecue, hood down, for 14-16 minutes until golden brown. Check if cooked by tapping the base of a scone—it should sound hollow. Serve warm with butter and honey.

Conventional oven: Preheat and bake at 230-250°C (450-475°F/Gas 8) for 12-15 minutes.

HONEY AND GINGER LOAF

> **Charcoal kettle**: *Indirect—Medium—Preheat 5-6 minutes*
> **Gas kettle**: *Indirect—Medium—Preheat 5-6 minutes*
> **Covered gas grill**: *Indirect—Medium—Preheat 5-6 minutes*
> **Cooking time**: *50-55 minutes*

1½ cups (185 g/6 oz) self-raising flour

1 cup (125 g/4 oz) wholemeal (whole wheat) flour

1 tsp mixed spice or ground allspice

¼ cup (45 g/1½ oz) brown sugar, packed

½ cup (90 g/3 oz) sultanas (golden raisins)

1 tbsp chopped mixed peel (candied citrus peel)

2 tbsp chopped crystallised ginger

½ cup (125 g/4 oz) butter or margarine

⅔ cup (200 g/7 oz) honey

1 tsp bicarbonate of soda (baking soda)

½ cup (125 ml/4 fl oz) dry ginger ale

1 tbsp lemon juice

1 egg, beaten

Line the base of a greased 23 x 12 cm (9 x 4½ in) loaf pan with foil or baking paper and grease the lining. Sift flours with spice into a mixing bowl and stir in brown sugar, sultanas, peel and ginger. Make a well in the centre.

Melt the butter and stir honey into hot butter until melted. Stir soda into ginger ale to dissolve. Pour both these mixtures into the flours and add lemon juice and beaten egg. Stir to combine and beat briefly with a wooden spoon until thoroughly mixed. Pour into prepared loaf pan. Loaf may be held for up to 40 minutes before baking if necessary.

Place on grill in preheated barbecue and bake indirect, hood down, for 50-55 minutes until cooked when tested. Stand for 5-6 minutes before turning out. Serve warm or cold with butter; very good spread with honey as well.

Conventional oven: Preheat and bake at 160-180°C (325-350°F/Gas 3) for 55-60 minutes.

Honey and ginger loaf

QUICK MIX BUTTER CAKE

> **Charcoal kettle**: *Indirect—Medium—Preheat 6-8 minutes*
> **Gas kettle**: *Indirect—Medium—Preheat 6-8 minutes*
> **Covered gas grill**: *Indirect—Medium—Preheat 6-8 minutes*
> **Cooking time**: *1-1¼ hours*

1½ cups (185 g/6 oz) self-raising flour

¼ cup (30 g/1 oz) cornflour (cornstarch)

1 cup (250 g/8 oz) caster (superfine) sugar

¾ cup (185 g/6 oz) soft butter or margarine

3 eggs

½ cup (125 ml/4 fl oz) milk

1½ tsp vanilla essence

Place all ingredients into large bowl of electric mixer. Mix on low speed to blend ingredients, then beat on high speed for 6-7 minutes, scraping down sides of bowl occasionally. Cake may be mixed by hand, in which case beat with a wooden spoon for 10 minutes. Turn into a greased and floured 23 cm (9 in) round cake pan or 20 cm (8 in) square cake pan; cake pans should be at least 6 cm (2½ in) deep.

Place on grill in heated barbecue and bake indirect, hood down, for 1-1¼ hours until cooked when tested. Check after 40 minutes and if browning too quickly, reduce gas barbecue heat to medium-low; partly close top vent on charcoal kettle. Stand for 5 minutes before turning out. Leave until cool.

Crumble-top Butter Cake: Mix 4 tablespoons quick-cooking rolled oats with 1 tablespoon desiccated (unsweetened) coconut and 1 tablespoon packed brown sugar. Stir in 1 tablespoon melted butter. After cake has cooked for 50 minutes (it should feel fairly firm on top), sprinkle on crumble mixture and press lightly with a spatula. Continue baking, hood down, until cake is cooked. Stand 5 minutes, then turn out onto a wire rack covered with a square of greaseproof paper or foil. Invert cake upright onto another rack to cool.

Conventional oven: Preheat and bake at 160-180°C (325-350°F/Gas 3) for 55-65 minutes; if using crumble topping, put on the cake after 45 minutes.

SPICED PUMPKIN CAKE

> *Charcoal kettle: Indirect—Medium—Preheat 5-6 minutes*
> *Gas kettle: Indirect—Medium—Preheat 5-6 minutes*
> *Covered gas grill: Indirect—Medium—Preheat 5-6 minutes*
> *Cooking time: 55-65 minutes*

1½ cups (350 g/12 oz) cooked, puréed pumpkin

¼ cup (90 g/3 oz) honey

¾ cup (125 g/4 oz) brown sugar, packed

¼ cup (60 ml/2 fl oz) oil

½ cup (125 ml/4 fl oz) melted butter or margarine

2 tsp baking powder

½ tsp bicarbonate of soda (baking soda)

1 tsp ground allspice

½ tsp ground ginger

½ cup (60 g/2 oz) chopped walnuts

½ cup (90 g/3 oz) chopped raisins

1 cup (125 g/4 oz) plain (all-purpose) flour

1 cup (125 g/4 oz) wholemeal (whole wheat) flour

2 eggs, beaten

walnut halves to decorate (optional)

You will need to cook about 400 g (14 oz) peeled pumpkin. Drain well and dry out a little before puréeing.

In a large mixing bowl mix the pumpkin with honey, brown sugar, oil and melted butter. Stir in baking powder, soda, spices, chopped walnuts and raisins. Sift or mix flours together and fold into pumpkin mixture. Lastly, stir in beaten eggs. Beat briefly with a wooden spoon to combine thoroughly. Turn into a greased and lined 23 x 12 cm (9 x 4½ in) loaf pan and decorate top with walnut halves if desired. Cake may be left for up to 40 minutes before baking.

Place on grill in preheated barbecue and bake indirect, hood down, for 55-65 minutes until cooked when tested. Stand for 10 minutes before turning out. Serve warm or cold. Butter or packaged cream cheese may be spread on the slices if desired.

Conventional oven: Preheat and bake at 160°-180°C (325-350°F/Gas 3) for 55-60 minutes.

APRICOT SOUR CREAM CAKE

> *Charcoal kettle: Indirect—Medium—Preheat 5-6 minutes*
> *Gas kettle: Indirect—Medium—Preheat 5-6 minutes*
> *Covered gas grill: Indirect—Medium—Preheat 5-6 minutes*
> *Cooking time: 50-60 minutes*

¼ cup (60 g/2 oz) butter or margarine, melted

1 cup (250 g/8 oz) caster (superfine) sugar

2 eggs

1 tsp grated lemon rind

1 tbsp lemon juice

¾ cup (125 g/4 oz) chopped dried apricots

1½ cups (185 g/6 oz) plain (all-purpose) flour

1½ tsp baking powder

½ tsp bicarbonate of soda (baking soda)

½ cup (125 ml/4 fl oz) sour cream

Put melted butter in a mixing bowl and stir in sugar with a wooden spoon. Add eggs and lemon rind and beat with spoon for 2 minutes to dissolve sugar. Stir in lemon juice and apricots. Sift flour with baking powder and soda and fold in alternately with sour cream. Turn into a greased and lined 20 x 9 cm (8 x 3½ in) loaf pan. Cake may be held for up to 40 minutes before baking.

Place on grill in heated barbecue and bake indirect, hood down, for 50-60 minutes until cooked when tested. Check after 40 minutes and if browning too quickly, reduce gas barbecue heat to medium-low; partly close top vent on charcoal kettle. Stand for 5 minutes before turning out. Cool completely before slicing to serve.

Conventional oven: Preheat and bake at 180-190°C (350-375°F/Gas 4) for 50-60 minutes.

Left: Quick mix butter cake; top: Spiced pumpkin cake; right: Apricot sour cream cake

BLUEBERRY MUFFINS

Charcoal kettle: Indirect—Medium—Preheat 6-8 minutes
Gas kettle: Indirect—Hot—Preheat 6-8 minutes
Covered gas grill: Indirect—Hot—Preheat 6-8 minutes
Cooking time: 20-25 minutes
Makes: 12

2 cups (250 g/8 oz) self-raising flour

½ cup (125 g/4 oz) caster (superfine) sugar

¼ tsp salt

1 egg

1 cup (250 ml/8 fl oz) milk

¼ cup (60 g/2 oz) butter or margarine, melted

¾ cup (90 g/3 oz) fresh or frozen blueberries

Put flour in a bowl and mix in sugar and salt with a fork. In another bowl, beat egg and stir in milk and melted butter. Add to dry ingredients with the blueberries; mix lightly and quickly only until dry ingredients are moistened. Do not overbeat. Spoon into 12 greased 8 cm (3 in) muffin pans to two-thirds fill.

If using a gas kettle, place a foil baffle on each side of the muffin pan tray (see page 13). Bake indirect in preheated barbecue, hood down, for 20-25 minutes until golden brown and cooked when tested with a fine skewer. Serve hot or warm as they are or with butter for breakfast, brunch or a snack. Also good when cold.

Conventional oven: Preheat and bake at 190-200°C (375-400°F/Gas 5) for 20-25 minutes.

CORN AND BACON MUFFINS

Charcoal kettle: Indirect—Medium—Preheat 6-8 minutes
Gas kettle: Indirect—Hot—Preheat 6-8 minutes
Covered gas grill: Indirect—Hot—Preheat 6-8 minutes
Cooking time: 20-25 minutes
Makes: 10

90 g (3 oz) streaky bacon slices

1 tbsp butter

1 cup (125 g/4 oz) self-raising flour

½ tsp bicarbonate of soda (baking soda)

½ tsp salt

1 tbsp caster (superfine) sugar

1 cup (185 g/6 oz) yellow cornmeal (polenta)

1 egg

1 cup (250 ml/8 fl oz) buttermilk

Heat a frying pan on the stove, add bacon and cook, stirring occasionally, until crisp. Remove bacon to a plate with a slotted spoon, add butter to pan and melt to combine with the bacon drippings.

Sift flour into a mixing bowl with soda and salt. Mix in sugar and cornmeal. In another bowl, beat egg, stir in buttermilk and combined bacon drippings and butter. Pour into the dry ingredients, add three-quarters of the bacon pieces and mix lightly and quickly until dry ingredients are moistened.

Spoon into 10 greased 8 cm (3 in) muffin pans to two-thirds full. Sprinkle a few bits of the remaining bacon on top of each muffin. Muffins should be baked soon after mixing, but they may stand for up to 30 minutes before baking.

If using gas kettle, place a foil baffle on each side of the muffin pan tray (see page 13). Bake indirect in preheated barbecue, hood down, for 20-25 minutes until lightly coloured and cooked when tested with a fine skewer. Serve hot or warm as an accompaniment to Chilli

Left: Blueberry muffins; right: Corn and bacon muffins

Con Carne, or with butter for breakfast or brunch.

Conventional oven: Preheat and bake at 200-220°C (400-425°F/Gas 6) for 20-25 minutes.

CHEESY FRUIT SCROLLS

Charcoal kettle: Indirect—Medium-hot—Preheat 8-10 minutes
Gas kettle: Indirect—Medium-hot—Preheat 6-8 minutes
Covered gas grill: Indirect—Medium-hot—Preheat 6-8 minutes
Cooking time: 18-20 minutes
Makes: 20-24

2 cups (250 g/8 oz) self-raising flour

½ cup (60 g/2 oz) plain (all-purpose) flour

½ cup (125 g/4 oz) packaged cream cheese, chopped

⅓ cup (90 g/3 oz) firm butter or margarine, chopped

1 large egg

⅓ cup (90 ml/3 fl oz) milk

¼ cup (60 g/2 oz) caster (superfine) sugar

1 tsp vanilla essence

2 tbsp melted butter or margarine

extra milk or egg wash for glazing

Fruit Filling

½ cup (90 g/3 oz) sultanas (golden raisins)

¼ cup (45 g/1½ oz) currants

2 tbsp chopped, blanched almonds

1 tbsp chopped peel (mixed candied citrus peel)

Put flours into food processor bowl with cream cheese and butter and process to fine-crumb consistency. Add egg, milk, sugar and vanilla and process to a dough. If processor labours under the load, tip mixture into a bowl and finish kneading by hand. Turn onto a floured board and knead lightly until smooth; add more flour if dough is sticky.

Roll out to a 40 x 30 cm (16 x 12 in) rectangle and brush with melted butter. Mix filling ingredients and sprinkle over dough. Roll up firmly from longer side. Cut into 2 cm (¾ in) slices and gently reshape into rounds. Place 2.5 cm (1 in) apart on 2 greased baking trays. Glaze

Cheesy fruit scrolls

with milk or egg wash. Scrolls may stand for up to 30 minutes before baking.

Bake indirect in preheated barbecue, hood down, for 18-20 minutes until golden brown. Serve hot or warm as they are or with butter, for breakfast, brunch or a snack.

Conventional oven: Preheat and bake at 200-220°C (400-425°F/Gas 6) for 15-18 minutes.

FRUIT AND NUT MUFFINS

Charcoal kettle: Indirect—Medium—Preheat 6-8 minutes
Gas kettle: Indirect—Medium—Preheat 5-6 minutes
Covered gas grill: Indirect—Medium—Preheat 5-6 minutes
Cooking time: 18-20 minutes
Makes: 18-20

½ cup (60 g/2 oz) chopped salted peanuts

1¼ cups (155 g/5 oz) self-raising flour

½ tsp bicarbonate of soda (baking soda)

¼ cup (60 g/2 oz) caster (superfine) sugar

½ cup (90 g/3 oz) chopped dates

1 egg

½ tsp grated orange rind

½ cup (125 ml/4 fl oz) orange juice

¼ cup (60 g/2 oz) butter or margarine, melted

Tip peanuts into a sieve and shake to remove excess salt, then chop. Sift flour and soda into a mixing bowl and stir in sugar, peanuts and dates with a fork, taking care to separate date pieces. In another bowl, beat egg and stir in orange rind, juice and cooled melted butter. Pour into dry ingredients and mix lightly and quickly until dry ingredients are moistened. Do not overmix. Spoon into 18-20 greased 5 cm (2 in) muffin pans (deep patty pans) to almost fill.

Cook the two trays of muffins together if space permits, or one after the other; muffins can be held for up to 30 minutes before baking. Bake indirect in preheated medium barbecue, hood down, for 18-20 minutes until golden brown and cooked when tested with a fine skewer. Serve hot or warm as they are or with butter, for breakfast, brunch or a snack. Also good when cold.

Conventional oven: Preheat and bake at 190-200°C (375-400°F/Gas 5) for 15-18 minutes.

INDEX